THE BIRDS
OF FIFE

To Chris

THE BIRDS
OF FIFE

An Outline of their Status and Distribution

ANNE-MARIE SMOUT

Illustrations by
DAVID MITCHELL

JOHN DONALD PUBLISHERS LTD
EDINBURGH

ISBN 0 85976 155 X

Exclusive distribution in the United States of America and Canada by Humanities Press Inc., Atlantic Highlands, NJ07716, USA.

Phototypeset by Key Phototypes, Edinburgh.
Printed in Great Britain by Bell & Bain Ltd., Glasgow.

Contents

Introduction

This book concerns mainland Fife only, as delineated by the Boundary Commissioners in 1891. Although the whole idea of *The Birds of Fife* sprang from the publication of the *Fife and Kinross Bird Report,* which has appeared yearly since 1980, I decided very early on that Kinross, with Loch Leven, was worthy of a book all of its own, and also that the islands in the Firth of Forth, especially the Isle of May, had already been dealt with far more competently than I would ever be able to: firstly with W J Eggeling's book *The Isle of May* (1960), with a second edition published by Lorian Press in 1985, and secondly with the annual reports in *Scottish Birds* (as well as a special supplement in 1974, also by Eggeling), thus keeping the information well up to date.

The task, as I saw it, was to establish how many species had been recorded on mainland Fife, when and where they occurred, and in what kind of numbers. Rarities, of course, have a glamour all of their own, and Fife is undoubtedly well up in the league table in this respect with a total of 282 species in all, discounting the May. As work on this book progressed, however, it became increasingly clear to me that the greatest interest lies not with the rarity, about which all that can be said is that it has occurred so and so many times, but with the more regular and the common species, where it soon becomes of absorbing interest to trace what the available data show us about their distribution. I have attempted for every species mentioned to put down where is the best place in Fife to see it, the maximum numbers ever recorded; for the residents how summer habitat may vary from wintering grounds, and for the summer and winter migrants also first and last dates of occurrence. All this has been set against a background of the historical material I have been able to gather, so that any long-term changes may be established.

In spite of its size (513 square miles or 130,708 hectares or just over 13 ten-kilometre squares), the scenery of Fife is tremendously varied and offers a surprisingly wide variety of habitats for the birdwatcher to enjoy (see accompanying table). The county is shaped like a parallelogram, and is very sharply defined on three sides, being bounded to the north by the Tay, to the east by the North Sea, and to the south by the Firth of Forth, which must be one of the prime places for sea watching in the British Isles. Fife is fully covered by Ordnance Survey Maps 1:50,000 Nos. 58, 59, 65 and 66.

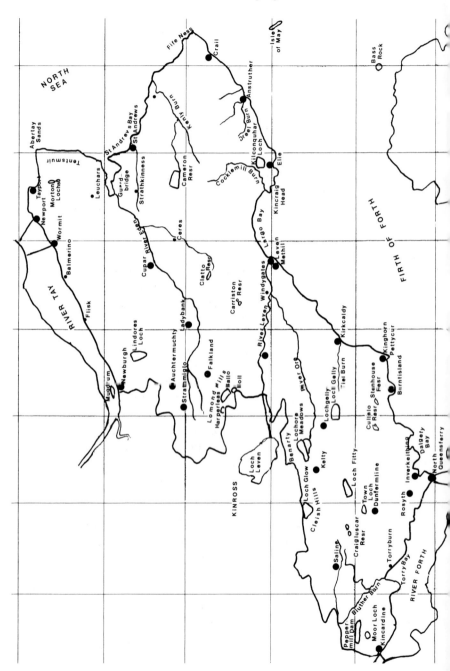

Table: Official Land Area Breakdown.

	ha	%
Fife Region	130,708	100.0
Urbanised land	11,300	8.6
Agricultural land	96,000	73.4
Woodland	15,000	11.5
Derelict land	1,300	1.0
Other	6,498	5.8
Coastline length		185 kilometre

From *Fife in Figures* (Extract and Abstract of Statistics), Fife Regional Council Department of Physical Planning, Fife House, Glenrothes (1982).

If we start in the north-west corner, the reed beds along the southern shore of the Tay, as it flows down from Perth, have come to an end before we reach Newburgh, which lies just east of the boundary with Perthshire. Here the southern banks of the Tay are formed by a continuation of the Ochils, and periodically the Old Red Sandstone is exposed along this shore right down to Tayport, making the coast of North Fife fairly steep in places. Where deposits of the river have formed low-lying fields, such as the partly flooded area east of Newburgh, some excellent places are to be found for geese in winter, with both Pinkfeet and Greylag foraging here during the day. In cold weather numbers of geese here seem to rise, which could be due to visitors from Perthshire seeking milder climates. The southern banks of the Tay are mostly clothed with deciduous woodland, notably at Flisk and Balmerino, but there are fewer waders along this shore than one would expect from the extent of mudbanks exposed at low tide. Shelduck, however, breed along the shore in small numbers, and several species of duck are also frequently found on the river, especially around Mugdrum island, where good numbers of Teal and Mallard have been reported. Harvie-Brown (1906) considered Mugdrum a favourite haunt of migratory birds, and 'the haunt of innumerable Starlings, Tits, Rails, Rose-coloured Pastors and other species', and called it 'a paradise of Wild-fowl and migrants' (FT:xliv), but lack of recent reports suggests that this is no longer the case. I have been told by a local farmer that Mugdrum deteriorated as a habitat when the reeds were no longer cut for commercial use, but left to grow anyhow. It was just below Newburgh, however, that a very fine Bittern was obtained last century, but sadly there have been no records of Bitterns in Fife since 1925. Good numbers of Goldeneye have been seen around Newburgh on the Tay, and on this river too, though further down, are to be seen Goosander and Merganser, occasionally in considerable numbers.

The wader population increases very markedly along the Tay below Newport. Millais said about this area in 1901 that between Tayport and Tentsmuir Point were the best flats for waders in Scotland, and here he had obtained many of his rarest specimens. This area is now considered of national importance (i.e. holds more than 1% of the national total) for Oystercatcher, Sanderling, Bar-tailed Godwit and Redshank (EstB:246). Many rarer waders, such as Greenshank, Ruff and Curlew Sandpipers are also frequent visitors here, and off Abertay Sands are vast numbers of wintering Eider, which yearly reach international importance, and this has been the case at least since 1939 (WGB:198). Good numbers of many other species of duck may also be seen here such as Common and Velvet Scoter and Long-tailed Duck, but it is a difficult area to watch. Scaup used to be very numerous here in Millais days, but they have long since left for other haunts.

At the north-east corner of Fife lies Tentsmuir, which is perhaps one of this century's ecological tragedies, but more of that later. The shores around this once very wild place used to support great numbers of breeding terns, ducks and waders, but now, due to disturbance and predation by both man and beast, the shore breeding birds are reduced to practically nil. Nevertheless there are many splendid things to be seen along this stretch of sandy coast: divers, grebes, seaduck, skuas and passing flocks of terns and waders as well as many other migrants, with Snow Buntings and Twite in winter. Tentsmuir Point was designated a National Nature Reserve in 1956, and access to the coast is either by foot past Morton Lochs and Fetterdale, or at Kinshaldy, where the Forestry Commission has laid out a very pleasant parking area.

No doubt the constantly changing shoreline, moulded by the currents of the sea, also has a good deal to do with the changing fortune of Tentsmuir for breeding birds. Thus along the east coast the tall sand dunes are continually being worn away and the sand shifted up towards Tentsmuir Point and Abertay Sands. How much of this has been going on even since the Second World War is evident from the now quite bizarre position of the large concrete anti-tank blocks, put there in 1940 to foil a German invasion. Henry Boase thought that these and other wartime measures, as well as the afforestation of the area, had a great deal to do with the rapidly altering shoreline and the disappearance of some good nesting areas (BNF:130). Leuchars

Airfield to the south has also expanded greatly since the war, although most birds seem to get used to the noise in time.

The estuary of the River Eden, which flows out just south of Leuchars and the part of Tentsmuir called Earlshall, is partly mud, partly sand. This comparatively small area, from Guardbridge to the sandhills of Earlshall, with Shelly Point and East Shore to the north, and the West Sands of St Andrews to the south, is the jewel in the crown of the county for wildfowl and waders. It attracts large numbers of migrants, and in bad weather it also provides shelter for seaduck. On the salt marshes along the south bank, large flocks of Wigeon and Teal can be seen in winter, and in migration time it is this estuary where the rarer migrants turn up, such as Spotted Redshank, Little Stint, Curlew Sandpiper (80 in September 1985). The estuary is of national importance for seven species of wintering waders (Oystercatcher, Ringed Plover, Grey Plover, Black-tailed Godwit, Bar-tailed Godwit, Redshank and Dunlin) and of international importance for wintering Shelduck. The Black-tailed Godwit flock is of special interest, as it is the most northernly in Britain and Europe. The estuary has been a Local Nature Reserve since 1984, and is now wardened by a Fife Ranger. A small number of species also attempt to breed here. The estuary can be overlooked from the disused railway line running between the high water mark and the A91, and there is a car park at Guardbridge (on the St Andrews road), which may be used to advantage with a telescope.

Beyond the sandbank, which is also the home of the Royal and Ancient Golf Club, lies St Andrews Bay, a veritable eldorado for all sorts of sea birds: huge numbers of Scoter, both Common and Velvet, are here for much of the year, as well as the rare Surf Scoter in the last few winters, grebes of all species, auks, divers—maximum numbers of both Red-throated and Black-throated in the last thirty years have been reported here—and in addition: one of the last flocks of wintering Scaup, occasional small flocks of Pintail etc, etc. One just has to look at the Wildfowl counts to see what immense variety is here to be enjoyed.

The sedimentary rocks of the Castle Cliff under the town of St Andrews itself provide nesting places for the biggest colony of Fulmars in Fife, and Sand Martins used to nest by the harbour until necessary repair work entailed clothing the remaining sandy cliffs with nets, thus making it a no go area for burrowing creatures. From Castle Cliff, however, a number of interesting migrants have been observed, and it was from here that the Little Swift was seen in spring 1985. It is also a good place from which to overlook the bay and the waders of the rocky coast.

The pillbox, Fife Ness.

The coast from now on all around the East Neuk consists of rocky outcrops, and it is of this area that Sir Archibald Geikie said, 'If I were asked to select a region in the British Isles where geology could best be practically taught by constant appeals to evidence in the field, I would with little hesitation recommend the east of Fife as peculiarly adapted for such a purpose', and he went on to describe its volcanic necks, raised beaches, fossils and kames. There is a most spectacular coastal walk from St Andrews to Boarhills and beyond, where Eider and other seaduck may be seen off shore, and many small birds inhabit the thick vegetation, which covers the slopes and dens on the way; whereas along the rocky shores different waders such as Purple Sandpiper, Turnstone, Redshank and Oystercatcher find a living. The best places on this coastline are usually at the points where the small rivers and burns reach the sea, such as the Kenly Burn at Boarhills, and further south the Dreel at Anstruther and the Cocklemill Burn at Shell Bay.

Fife Ness is the most easterly point of Fife, and as such a tremendously good place in migration time. Whatever signals birds receive from land when they migrate, and especially when they become lost or seek land in bad weather, this promontory is the place above all which attracts them, certainly on mainland Fife. The mystery of migration still remains largely unsolved, in spite of much recent research, but the fact remains that on good days (by which is meant foggy or beastly rainy days with miserable easterly winds if not gales) Fife Ness can become the most exciting place for birdwatching, and at least as good as if not better than any other promontory on the east coast of Scotland. For example in spring 1985 on one day could be seen 15 Bluethroats, and all of the following: Black and Common Redstart, Wheatear, Pied Flycatcher, Whinchat, Ring Ouzel, Red-backed Shrike, Lesser Whitethroat, Chiffchaff, Willow Warbler and a Hobby, and within a week of this an Ortolan Bunting, a Scarlet Rosefinch, a Radde's Warbler and a Siberian Stonechat had also been recorded here.

The point itself is specially good for sea-watching, including such species as divers, petrels, shearwaters, geese, duck, skuas, terns and auks; in fact anything might turn up here. It is very strange that there is no sense of these dramatic migrant falls in any of the earlier writers, even Baxter and Rintoul, although these ladies were extremely interested in migration and did much pioneering work in this field on the Isle of May. Did it never occur to them to look? It is difficult to say who 'discovered' Fife Ness, but it happened sometime in the late 1960s and early 1970s, and observers such as J Cobb, D W Oliver and R W Byrne played a large part. Dr James Cobb deserves especial credit, because in the early 1970s he leased the rough patch near the point (which up till then was grazed by cattle and burnt regularly), and started planting shrubs and trees by the hundreds. In ornithological terms, his labour of love has paid off many times over, and now Fife Ness is in danger of totally monopolising birdwatchers' attention, when much useful work could be done elsewhere in migration time. Two small areas have very recently (1985) been made Scottish Wildlife Trust reserves: one is 'Jim Cobb's Patch', the other a three-quarter mile stretch, south-west of the point, along the coast towards Crail.

The shore continues as rocky sandstone interspersed with limestone and volcanic rock to Shell Bay, allowing for one or two beaches, notably at Elie. As mentioned above, the places where rivers and burns run into the sea are especially attractive to birds, both waders and duck. Thus Anstruther, where the Dreel Burn runs into the Firth of Forth, can be a very surprising place: there is the usual population of rocky shore waders, such as Turnstone, Curlew, Ringed Plover, Redshank, Purple Sandpiper and Oystercatcher, but on passage we are often graced with the company of Whimbrel, Ruff, godwits, plovers, sandpipers and Knot, which frequent the small expanses of sand and mud exposed as the tide drops. It must also be admitted that old fashioned sewage pipes are still in operation here, and that this has undoubtedly a lot to do with the richness of the birdlife. In the three years we have lived in our present house we have seen no less than 125 species from our windows, including a Caspian Tern in autumn 1985, which also, of course, goes to show the truth of Gilbert White's dictum, 'That district produces the greatest variety which is the most examined'.

The coastal path which runs along all the way from St Andrews, via

Fife Ness and Crail continues past Elie, Kincraig, Largo Bay, Kirkcaldy and right up to North Queensferry, allowing access to the sea practically all the way. Largo Bay, of course, was the principal haunt of 'the good ladies' Miss Baxter and Miss Rintoul, who lived near here all their lives, and it is excellent birdwatching country. It is again worth examining the outfalls of the rivers for waders, and Leven sands is one of the best places in Fife to see Sanderling, whereas off shore the duck are often thick on the water: here is the last remaining principal site for wintering Scaup in the country, and here too are great flocks of Goldeneye, Eider, Common as well as Velvet Scoter, Merganser and grebes of all kinds. Leven is also good for white gulls, as is Kirkcaldy.

From Leven onwards, towards the west, the coalmeasures dominate the geology of the county, and West Fife is much more industrial than any other part of the county, with mine workings and associated industries. The coastline is a series of beaches interrupted from time to time by rocky, volcanic outcrops such as at Kinghorn, Burntisland, Inverkeithing and North Queensferry. Here can be seen Long-tailed Duck and Red-throated Divers. There are no rivers, however, between the Tiel Burn at Kirkcaldy and the Bluther Burn which runs out at Torry Bay. The stretch west of Kirkcaldy holds waders as well as parties of terns in late summer, many of which are juveniles, no doubt brought here by their parents from nesting places on the islands in the Forth. Pettycur sands especially, but also Dalgety Bay, support large numbers of gulls and waders, as well as terns in summer, while the area west of the Forth Road Bridge, which is mud and sands for long stretches, has produced many interesting records in the past. In the 1950s the area from Cultness to Rosyth was reclaimed, and amazing numbers of waders were then recorded here, including the first Wilson's Phalarope for Scotland. The Rosyth sewage farm area is still quite good for Ruff. For many years a King Eider was about off Crombie Point, and further west around Torry Bay, where the Bluther Burn runs out, another land reclamation scheme has been in operation with an attendant rise in the numbers of waders. Many records came from here, especially in the 1950s. Large parties of Mute Swan also winter here, but the area is probably under-recorded today.

Leaving the coast behind us, Fife is also very rich in inland waters, and there are several lochs of outstanding interest to the birdwatcher: in the north is Lindores Loch, a natural loch which, according to the *New Statistical Account,* was once the haunt of the Osprey. Not so long ago it was a noted breeding place for Pochard and several other species of duck, but it is now very heavily fished, and the birdlife under considerable stress. The reed beds however, still afford some protection to numbers of Great Crested Grebe and other birds, and it is worth watching. Further east are Morton Lochs, a group of artificial ponds in Tentsmuir forest and a National Nature Reserve since 1954. There is one public hide here, and two hides for members only. A fixed number of keys are available by subscription from the Nature Conservancy Council (12, Hope Terrace, Edinburgh 9). These lochs were once stocked with carp, which also brought in the Swan mussel *Anadonta cygnea,* so delectable to many duck that even Goosander and Common Scoter used to feed here, but these have long disappeared. Nevertheless a number of interesting birds are still around Morton Lochs at various times of the year: duck such as Teal and Shoveler are common, and on passage Greenshank, Spotted Redshank, Green Sandpiper and other rarities call in for a quick snack. It is also here that Fife's only two Spoonbills have been seen (in 1984 and in 1969).

Cameron reservoir south of St Andrews now also has a hide, and keys are available to members of the Scottish Ornithologists' Club (SOC) and the Scottish Wildlife Trust (SWT) by subscription from the local SOC Branch. This loch quite regularly gets Smew in winter, and Whooper Swan, and it is the best place in Fife to see geese come into roost. To be present here in the late gloaming on a clear November evening when the geese come in is an unparalleled experience. Distant honking will herald the arrival for some time, and then suddenly the moment comes when they appear over the horizon, gradually flooding the sky like the incoming tide. Skein after skein moves on in great battalions, and when the flanks are overhead, the excitement reaches its peak, and the entire air is set singing with goose noise and the vibration of flight feathers, as they break formation and drop, almost untidily, onto the water to be greeted by the forerunners. 5,000-6,000 are by no means unusual, most of these being Pinkfeet.

Another loch of equal interest, is Kilconquhar in the East Neuk of Fife. This loch has long been regarded as natural, but recent research by Geoffrey Whittington at St Andrews University shows that it owes its present form to flooded peat diggings, similar to the Norfolk Broads. Here Little Gulls come in to feed and roost on autumn evenings, Goldeneyes gather in hundreds before they leave the country in spring, and up to 1,000 Swallows may be seen on a September evening. The loch provides breeding grounds for several species of duck, and Little and Great-crested Grebe. It is also a good place for uncommon migrants. Access to the loch is round the churchyard.

In West Fife there are a number of excellent lochs and reservoirs:
Lochore Meadows, which at one time was drained and cultivated, but
then reflooded due to subsidence, has been extended and designated a
Countryside Park with part of the area a Regional Nature Reserve. This
combination has been a tremendous success, and is a model of what
can be achieved. A hide on the south-west side of the reserve is now
open to the public and accessible from the B996 near Kelty. The area is
carefully wardened by rangers, and a yearly report of all the many
interesting birds seen around here is also available from Fife Ranger
Service. Lochore Meadows, as well as the Lomond Hills reservoirs to
the north-east, are especially good for breeding duck, and hold good
numbers of wintering duck and swans of all species. Ballo reservoir, in
particular, is good for Whooper and Bewick's Swans, as well as the
occasional Goosander. Other lochs and reservoirs in West and Central
Fife are Peppermill Dam, Tulliallan, Townloch Dunfermline, Cullaloe,
Carriston reservoir, Loch Fitty and Loch Gelly. These last two have
Whooper Swans in winter, and a number of breeding duck. It was also
in the extensive reedbeds of upper Loch Gelly that the Corncrake was
heard in 1985, but the fortune of these waters, as well as that of many
other smaller lochs, is precarious. Recent changes in legislation
regarding the maintenance of reservoir dams is a potential threat to
most of the smaller artificial waters, and they are always under a certain
amount of threat anyway from boating, fishing and other leisure
activities.

River Eden, looking upstream from Guardbridge.

Fife only has two rivers of any importance: the Eden which springs
from beyond Strathmiglo, runs via Ladybank and Cupar, to empty out
beyond Guardbridge, and the Leven, which drains Loch Leven, picks
up the River Ore above Windygates before reaching the Firth of Forth
at Leven. Especially the Ore is fairly heavily polluted due to

surrounding industries. Dippers, though, may still be seen on the Leven at Glenrothes and on several smaller burns, such as the Kenly at Boarhills. Kingfishers are present but are much rarer. Many of the rivers and streams also flow through delightfully wooded dens which provide ideal habitats for many smaller birds, as for example Dura Den and Dunino Den.

The only landfast boundary of Fife is the westerly one, which is shared with Stirling, Kinross, and Perthshire, and it is here that Fife can boast its uplands. The boundary runs along the top of the Cleish Hills, includes Benarty south of Loch Leven, and continues across the most westerly end of the Lomond Hills, before undulating gently down towards Newburgh in the north. The range of the Lomond Hills divides the county into a northerly and southerly part, and a ridge continuing towards the east is aptly named 'The Rigging of Fife'. The Lomond Hills also provide the only remaining substantial area of heather, which moorland supports a number of Red Grouse, as well as Cuckoo (which are mostly parasitic on Meadow Pipits), Snipe, Whinchat, Wheatear and many other species of birds, The highest point in Fife is the West Lomond at 1731 feet. A couple of hours' amble from the Craigmead car park either to that or to the slightly lower peak of the East Lomond (also reached from a more easterly car park) will reward the energetic with incredible views: a wide circle that on clear days will take in all of Fife and much of Central Scotland, up north as far as the Angus glens and down south towards the Borders. This area is in the process of being designated a Regional Park which, if it goes through, will include Benarty, right across to Lochore Meadows, and will thus have created a huge and wonderful wildlife and recreational area in Central Fife. A yearly 'Bird Report' is available from Fife Ranger Service both for Lochore and the Lomonds.

Dr Johnson's much quoted remark in 1774, that there were no trees of any size or age in Fife, though scarcely true at that time, is today sadly applicable to much of the East Neuk. There are, however, exceptions, mostly on private grounds. Much of the accessible deciduous woodland is in Central Fife, around Falkland, where the rare Wood Warbler has bred in recent years, and Blackcaps and Garden Warblers are not unusual. Further east the woods around Kemback and Dura Den hold Long-tailed Tit, and Magus Muir, by Strathkinness, has Redpoll, Whitethroat and other warblers. Further north, there are the woods between Balmerino and Flisk, where a public footpath runs near the shore. There are also small areas of alder and birch in

Tentsmuir, much frequented by Redpoll and Sisken, although most of this forest is now covered by the Forestry Commission's plantations of poor-quality pine.

Tentsmuir was up till the First World War a most remarkably wild place, kept more or less as a bird sanctuary by interested parties. The area was roughly divided up into three parts: Scotscraig in the north, Kinshaldy in the middle, and Earlshall to the south. William Berry of Tayfield, who leased the shooting rights of the northerly part, wrote a most excellent description of what it used to be like in *The Annals of Scottish Naturalist History* (1894), which I will quote at some length: 'The Tents Muir is a large tract of barren moorland, flat as the sea which borders it along its entire length. . . . The elevation above sea-level of the whole of this area is quite inconsiderable—perhaps eight or ten feet, or even less; but it is broken up and partially sheltered from the sweep of the winds by lines or chains of sandhills, which rise to the height of thirty or forty feet, and trend, speaking generally, in the direction from east to west; a similar chain forms a continuous rampart along the seashore. The soil, if such it can be called, is simply blown sand, only anchored in its pesent position by the vegetation which has somehow established itself upon the surface. . . .'

Red Grouse was successfully introduced here, and it was especially to this wild area that the Sand Grouse was drawn, during the remarkable irruption in the latter half of the nineteenth century.

In 1894 the Act for the preservation of birds was adopted for the area by the County Council of Fife, due almost entirely to the efforts of W Berry. This not only provided a safe breeding place for many kinds of wildfowl, but almost the whole 7,000 acres of low-lying heath and dune were managed specifically for wildlife purposes, with water levels carefully controlled to provide pools and marshes. It is stated in *Wildfowl in Great Britain* (1963) that Tentsmuir was at that time one of the finest resorts for Teal in the country, and was used by ducks of a dozen different species (WGB:200). After the First World War the area was sold first to the City of Dundee, and subsequently in 1924 to the Forestry Commission to be planted with timber. Planting began almost at once, and species which might harm young trees, such as Black Grouse, were extirpated. Wire-netting to keep out rabbits was put up, and as a result many baby Shelduck and baby Eider perished, because they could not get through to reach the sea. As Henry Boase said in *Birds of North Fife:* 'It is a sorry tale, the wrecking of a unique, primitive area with its own peculiar associations of plant and animal—a loss which can never be replaced, for the afforestation has destroyed utterly a balanced community' (BNF:129).

There have thus been many losses, but also some gains: the maturer plantations provide habitat for Tawny Owl, Woodcock, Jay and both the Great Spotted and the Green Woodpecker, while small birds nest in the trees, such as Spotted Flycatcher, warblers, tits, finches and Goldcrest, and there are flocks of Sisken in winter.

There are small havens of deciduous or mixed woodland in West Fife, such as the wood lining Dalgety Bay, but coniferous plantations make up by far the greatest area of woodland in Fife. Devilla forest near Kincardine presents the richest habitat of its kind outside Tentsmuir. It is a favourite haunt of the Green and the Great Spotted Woodpecker; Tree Pipits breed here, as do many warblers, for example Blackcap and Garden Warbler (10 pairs in 1984); Redpoll and possibly Sisken, as well as many other species. There are also extensive plantations on the slopes of the Lomond Hills, frequented by Crossbill and Redpoll among other things.

And finally we come to the cultivated and arable land of which Fife has a good measure, rich, high yielding soil, especially in the north and to the east of Kirkcaldy. Farmland provides the habitat for so many of our common species, and although many farmers are not necessarily against birds as such, more of these could perhaps be persuaded: not to drain all mirey places, not to tear up so many hedgerows or cut down copses, but to leave a measure of rough land for the smaller birds to nest in and feed on. Another proposal is to leave a couple of yards around each field unsprayed. This has been tried elsewhere with much success for the birdlife and little inconvenience or expense to the farmer. It is also of the utmost importance that poison should not be spilt, or half-empty canisters thrown out to rust in ditches or clearings. Apart from being unsightly, these also constitute a real danger to both beast and bird. The reader just has to turn to the entry for House Martin to discover what kind of disaster may follow accidental spillage of, for example, fungicide. Nobody could wish that kind of agony on any living creature. Domestic gardens also come under 'cultivated' land, and much can be done in a small way to encourage a rich birdlife by growing the sort of plants that birds like, while a carefully tended bird table has provided a lifeline for more than one wintering Blackcap in recent years. There are several books on the market:

The Garden Bird Book ed. by David Glue (Macmillan).
Birds in Your Garden by Nigel Wood (Hamlyn).
The Back Garden Wildlife Sanctuary Book by Ron Wilson (Penguin).
The Wildlife Garden by Chris Baines (Elm Tree Books).

Stonechat.

In my study of the birds of Fife I have been drawn to and inspired by a number of older accounts. The earliest records I have been able to find come from the Household Accounts of James V, 1525-1533 *(Excerpta E Libris Domicilii Domini Jacobi Quinti Regis Scotorum,* published in Edinburgh in 1834). Here are given amongst other things, the various species of fowl which were either donated by local lairds or purchased locally for the King's table when he was in residence at Falkland Palace during this period. The list is most interesting: Teal, Snipe, Grouse, Plover (Lapwing?), Gannet, Crane, Swan, Partridge, Skylark, Wild Goose and Wild Duck. Several other species were also mentioned such as Heron, Bittern and Redshank, but not, alas, for Fife.

The first real collector of information on the wildlife of Fife was, however, Sir Robert Sibbald who included a list of 20 'aquatic birds' in his *History Ancient and Modern of the Sheriffdoms of Fife and Kinross* (1710). Sibbald was born in Edinburgh in 1641 and, after studying medicine abroad, became Natural Historian, Geographer and Physician to Charles II. He was the chief founder of the Royal College of Physicians in Edinburgh, and had previously published in 1684, at the King's request, the work *Scotia Illustrata, sive Prodromus Historiæ Naturalis, etc.* comprising 113 pages of botany, 12 of mammals and 9 of birds. Although a pioneer in the science of natural history, it is clear that

Sibbald was not a practical worker in the field, but rather an avid compiler of data. This, however, should not be taken as a damning criticism of his work, for the genuine naturalist in the field did not emerge for about another 150 years. The editor of the second edition of the *History of Fife and Kinross* (1803) included a number of interesting and useful comments on Sibbald's list as footnotes.

The next useful information on Fife's birds is to be found in the *Statistical Account of Scotland* (1791-1799), also called the 'First' or 'Old' Statistical Account. This mammoth work was conceived, collected and published by Sir John Sinclair of Ulbster (1745-1835), and a facsimile of the whole work was republished with an index and an introduction to each volume by EP Publishers from 1970 to 1983. We know from the surviving questionnaire sent out to all the clergy of the Church of Scotland in 1790 that question 39 asked: 'What quadrupeds and birds are there in the parish? What migratory birds, and at what times do they appear and disappear?' Only five ministers in Fife (Anstruther, St Monance, Carnbee, Kilconquhar and Carnock), made any attempt to answer the question, and the details are to be found here under the appropriate species.

The *Old Statistical Account* was followed by the *New Statistical Account* (1834-45), which gave rather more extensive zoological information from a larger number of parishes in Fife.

Some Fife records can also be gleaned from such general works as MacGillivray's *A History of British Birds* (1837) and Yarrell's *History of British Birds* (1843), while the publication in 1871 of the first issue of the *Scottish Naturalist* heralded a whole new era for local coverage of all aspects of the zoological and biological sciences. Robert Walker FGSE, of St Andrews University, published many short articles, including a very interesting list of 'Rare Birds in East Fife' *(Scot. Nat.* 1871:81-87). Another list, of the birds of Culross and Tulliallan, was drawn up by John J. Dalgleish, Member of the British Ornithologists' Union, and published in D. Beveridge's *Culross and Tulliallan* (1885).

But the first really informative book to deal with any part of Fife in depth came with the publication of Harvie-Brown's *Fauna of the Tay Basin and Strathmore* in 1906. John A Harvie-Brown of Dunipace (1844-1916) was a man of enormous energy, a keen sportsman himself and surely the most prolific writer on Scottish wildlife there has ever been. From 1892 he co-edited (with Prof. J W H Trail and W Eagle Clarke) the *Annals of Scottish Natural History,* a quarterly magazine which incorporated *The Scottish Naturalist* mentioned above (it continued right up to 1964, reverting after 1911 to the original title). He also conceived the idea of covering the whole of Scotland's wildlife in depth with a series of 'Vertebrate Faunas', and was aided in this venture by T E Buckley, the Rev. H A Macpherson and A H Evans, the first volume to appear being *A Vertebrate Fauna of the Sutherland, Caithness and West Cromarty* in 1887. Although the series was never to be completed, a further 8 volumes were published in Harvie-Brown's own lifetime, the volume on the Tay Basin being the only one edited entirely by himself. The ruling idea behind the division of the country into areas was based on natural rather than political boundaries, with watersheds playing a central function: thus *The Tay Fauna* covered the entire area drained by the River Tay, including all of North Fife, the Eden estuary and as far south as the 'Rigging of Fife' mentioned earlier and Fife Ness. As Harvie-Brown was the first to acknowledge in his preface, he had received much invaluable help from people with local knowledge. He made extensive use of the lists of W Berwick of Pathcondie, Monimail, for earlier records, as well as many game books, and he mentioned in particular William Evans of Edinburgh (who was collecting material for a Forth Fauna at the time), W Berry, J G Millais and George Bruce.

It was William Berry of Tayfield (1865-1954) who had secured the application of the Birds Protection Act to Tentsmuir in 1894. He was also a keen sportsman naturalist, who had helped Dr Eagle Clarke, the keeper of the Royal Scottish Museum in Edinburgh, to build up a complete new collection of skins which were properly dated and labelled, and thus many examples in this fine collection originate in Fife. He also compiled a 'List of the Birds of Tayfield, Tentsmuir and Neighbourhood 1872-1947' which has kindly been put at my disposal by his son Dr John Berry.

The Land Birds about St Andrews by George Bruce was published in 1895. George Bruce, said by Harvie-Brown to be a 'wellknown local genius', was a poet, dramatist, actor and bandmaster. He was also a keen birdwatcher, egg collector and bird stuffer, and his book on the birds of St Andrews is marvellously entertaining with anecdote after anecdote. Although there is no reason to doubt much of what he wrote, Bruce was unfortunately not always as sound a naturalist as one could have wished, and Baxter and Rintoul decided that nothing he said could be trusted. I have rather followed Harvie-Brown's lead, who exercised his own judgement as to Bruce's accuracy: I have only quoted records where these have been corroborated by other evidence.

John Guille Millais (1865-1931) was a sportsman naturalist *par excellence*, as were of course most of the nineteenth-century naturalists, when identification was not proved till the bird was in the hand—dead. Millais was never happier than in the company of his gun and his dog, and *The Wildfowler in Scotland*, which he published in 1901, is a beautifully atmospheric book, showing the writer's deep understanding and love for natural things, and the chapters on his adventures with a punt gun in the Tay and the Eden estuaries should not be missed. Nor were his seemingly bloodthirsty expeditions without a more serious purpose, and I can do no better than quote his own words: '. . . I wanted to obtain, not only a complete series of the various ducks which inhabited the British Islands but enough specimens to illustrate the periodical changes of plumage in a duck's life. To do this means, of course, considerable slaughter, one may have to kill hundreds of the same species to secure a good example of each period of change, but *pace* the Humanitarians, ducks must die that aldermen may dine, and surely it is a more noble fate to perish in the cause of science than in that of the dinner-table. The vast majority of the slain do find their way there—one could do nothing else with them; but the one treasure (possibly only one in fifty) is safely packed away in cotton-wool, skinned and preserved for the collection' (p. 74).

Millais was also an excellent artist, being not for nothing the son of John Everett Millais, the Pre-Raphaelite painter, and his two major works, *British Surface-Feeding Ducks* (1902) and *British Diving Ducks* (1913), contain not only plate after plate of skins in his collection, but also many superb illustrations in colour of the various ducks. It is definitely time Millais was rediscovered.

When William Evans died without having completed the Fauna of Forth, Dr Eagle Clarke persuaded Miss Rintoul and Miss Baxter to take on the task, and *A Vertebrate Fauna of Forth* was duly published in 1935, thus completing from our point of view the detailed study of Fife, with their careful and scholarly account of the birdlife of the southern part, a country which nobody knew better than they. Leonora Jeffrey Rintoul (1878-1953), born at Lahill House, Largo, and Evelyn Vida Baxter (1879-1959), born at Gilston, Largoward, grew up firm friends and birdwatchers. Through Dr Eagle Clarke they became very involved in the study of migration, and spent many days and weeks on remote islands including the Isle of May. This led to their celebrated paper on drift migration in *Ibis* (1918), and they also published a *Geographical Distribution and Status of Birds in Scotland* (1928). They took over the editing of the 'Reports on Scottish Ornithology' in the *Scottish Naturalist* in 1911, carrying this on for 20 years, and their greatest work, *The Birds of Scotland,* in 2 volumes, completed in 1953 just before Miss Rintoul's death, was a monumental work of the greatest importance for Scottish ornithology as a whole. They were both founder members of the SOC in 1936, and the demi-centenary in 1986 will be celebrated by, among other things, the publication of *Birds in Scotland,* their work brought up to date so to speak by another great ornithological lady, Miss Valerie Thom.

Before the *Scottish Naturalist* finally ceased publication, the *Edinburgh Bird Bulletin* had appeared on the scene in 1950, and included many observations and records for Fife. This was succeeded by the SOC's *Scottish Birds* in 1958, and especially in the early days, up to about 1976, the report in the quarterly issues carried much full information about Fife, but as more areas became involved in sending in records, the individual coverage naturally became less detailed, and the need for a locally orientated publication was felt. This gap has been filled with the *Fife and Kinross Bird Report,* published yearly since 1980.

Mention must also be made of Boase's *Birds of North Fife.* Henry Boase, who died in 1974 at the age of 82, spent much of his spare time studying especially waterfowl in the Tay and produced a number of papers on the subject. After retiring from the Dundee jute industry in 1958, he was able to write up his life's observations in *Birds of North and East Perthshire* (1961), *Birds of Angus* (1962), *Birds of North Fife* (1964), and *Bird records of the Tay Area* (1970). None of these was ever published, but copies of his typescripts are held in the SOC library in Edinburgh, and in some other libraries (see SB8:86). I have made extensive use of these carefully compiled notes, as well as of J Grierson's *Check-list of the Birds of Tentsmuir,* which was published as a special supplement to *Scottish Birds* (1962). Jack Grierson was Secretary of the Dundee branch of the SOC for a number of years, and he did much valuable work in the 1950s, at a time when only a few birdwatchers were very active in this area. His list has been an invaluable source of information, as have been his many articles on the Eden estuary in the *Edinburgh Bird Bulletin.*

Last, but by no means least, I should like to mention Dr John Berry, whose *Status and Distribution of Wild Geese and Wild Duck in Scotland* (1939) has been extremely useful, and who as Director of Nature Conservation in Scotland (1949-1967) worked so hard for Scottish Wildlife, and was instrumental in Morton Lochs and Tentsmuir Point being made into National Nature Reserves; he made his wonderful library available to me, and from his deep love and knowledge of the birds of Fife I have learned much.

In compiling *The Birds of Fife* a number of difficulties have emerged, chiefly to do with the inadequacies of available records. Comparison with early records is made difficult, as these often do not mention any numbers, but only 'huge flocks' or 'large assemblies', and such terms are of course very relative (see, for example, Herring Gull). Today some areas appear definitely to be under-recorded, and it is also surprising how often Wildfowl Trust counts, or counts for BTO surveys, do not find their way to the local recorder, thus making the picture drawn by our local bird report unnecessarily incomplete. I would therefore urge all birdwatchers to remember to send in their records, including those made for specific surveys to the local recorder, whose name and address may be had from the SOC.

Another problem is more difficult to solve, as it is to do with the nature and mobility of birds. However carefully counts are made, they may not always present the full picture, which can be illustrated by the following example: two separate counts exist for Teal on the Eden estuary on 13 February 1972. One observer reported to *Scottish Birds* that there were 1000 Teal there that day, whereas the Wildfowl Trust (WT) count, by a different observer, was recorded as only 80. Obviously something had disturbed the duck in between, they were in a different place, or the tide had changed. Maybe the Wildfowl Trust counts recorded them elsewhere, we do not know.

In the number game, it is also possible that the same flocks of birds are counted at the same time in two different squares, thus in effect playing a double game. There is a danger of this, for example in Largo Bay where, in the *Winter Atlas,* the same birds could have been counted twice.

I should like to thank the British Trust for Ornithology (BTO) for allowing me to reproduce the maps of the *Atlas of Breeding Birds in Britain and Ireland,* which were based on a five-year survey carried out under the auspices of the BTO from 1968 to 1972. The maps may give a rather inflated impression of how common or widespread certain breeding species are, because five years is a long time, and many changes can happen. Nevertheless, a shorter time could hardly allow for full national coverage, and it is a most valuable publication. As these

data are now fifteen years old, they provide interesting comparison with
the 1980s. A new *Breeding Atlas* is planned for 1988-1992.

I am also very grateful to the BTO for allowing me to use the data for
the *Winter Atlas* (to be published as a companion volume to the *Breeding
Atlas* in 1986). As the *Breeding Atlas,* this survey is based on the
10-kilometre squares in the National Grid, and the purpose of the
survey is to show where birds winter and in what numbers. The figures
arrived at are based on birds counted in a 'standard day' of
birdwatching (six hours) for each square, and methods have been
devised to compute figures where watches have been less than the full
six hours. Supplementary records of rarer species or exceptional
numbers seen outside the six hours have also been included. The
survey ran for three winters (mid-November to end of February
1981-84), and I am extremely obliged to our local BTO representative,
Wendy Mattingley, for giving me her time in helping with the figures
and working out a system of appropriate symbols. It must be stressed
that our maps could in the end differ considerably from the—at the
time of writing—unpublished *Winter Atlas,* especially as we have
attempted to use Fife records only, where squares are divided between
more than one county. For one or two squares, such as NO10, and
NS99 in Central and West Fife respectively, we had in many cases
insufficient data to include any symbols at all, as these squares cover
only very little of Fife.

In the maps under each species, the *Breeding Atlas* has consistently
been placed to the left on the page, and the maps of the *Winter Atlas* on
the right-hand side. The symbols used are: round dots always for the
Breeding Atlas and squares for the *Winter Atlas,* as follows:

Winter Atlas
- ▪ 1-5
- ◼ 5-15
- ■ 16-99
- ■ 100-1000
- ■ 1000+

The symbols for the *Winter Atlas* are not those employed by the
BTO. It must also be stressed that birds move about, and the picture
which emerges may be inflated. It must also be kept in mind that the
survey ran over three winters.

Breeding Atlas:
- Possibly breeding
- Probably breeding
- ⬤ Confirmed breeding

Details of the applications of these symbols are set out on p.17 in the *Atlas of Breeding Birds in Britain and Ireland* (1976). There is no indication of numbers.

That Fife is excellent birdwatching country can be seen from the table published in *The Birdwatchers Yearbook 1986*, where Fife comes out third equal in the 'County Birdwatch Tallies' with 120 species seen in 24 hours by a team of four. There is no doubt, however, that the growing number of birdwatchers creates its own pressure on the countryside. It is therefore of the greatest importance that birdwatchers take enormous care not to spoil things for others and therefore, ultimately, for themselves. The following general points should be observed anywhere:

1. Do not trespass without asking permission.
2. Do not point binoculars at close quarters at the windows of occupied houses.
3. Do not beat down vegetation, but keep as much as possible to the paths.
4. Keep disturbance to birds and their habitat to a minimum.
5. Do not harass rare migrants.
6. Be considerate, and mindful at all times that not everybody watches birds, and that there are other outdoor activities too.

The Birds of Fife can be kept up to date with the yearly *Fife and Kinross Bird Report* (see Bibliography).

Abbreviations used in the Systematic List are explained in the Bibliography.

Finally I should like to acknowledge my great debt to a number of people who have helped with their advice and detailed knowledge in the preparation of this book: first of all, my thanks go to Christopher Smout, who suggested the book in the first place, and without whose encouragement and expert advice there would have been no book at all; and also to Valerie Thom and Frank Hamilton for helping to solve some tricky problems; to Frank Spragge, Wendy Mattingley, Ian Strachan and Dougie Dickson for lending many detailed records; to Jim Cobb for details of migrant and ringing records; to David Salmon for letting me have all the Wildfowl Trust counts, Allan and Lyndsay Brown for additional Mute Swan data, Mick Marquiss for Heron data; Bill Glower, Pete Kinnear, Dick Byrne, Ian Cumming, Brian Combes, Julian Branscombe, Bill Harper, Dougal Andrews and Brian Boag for records and other information; to David Mitchell for doing such lovely drawings, and to all the birdwatchers whose records I have used, without whom this book would have been impossible.

The Russell Trust and the Scottish Ornithologists Club made generous contributions towards the costs of manuscript preparation, and I thank them profoundly.

Heron.

Systematic List

The systematic order follows that proposed by Professor Voous. Species which are presumed escapes and uncertain records are placed within square brackets.

Red-throated Diver   *Gavia stellata*

Common winter visitor and passage migrant

The Red-throated Diver is the commonest diver off the coast of Fife, recorded every month of the year, though seldom in June. It can be seen almost anywhere in the coastal waters from Tayport to Torry Bay, with the largest concentration recorded from St Andrews Bay (eg. 70 on 23 January 1952 and 50 on 15 February 1982); Tayport (32 on 9 February 1983 and 30+ on February 1984); Largo Bay and Fife Ness.

There is a strongly marked spring passage off the East Neuk from late March to early May, and a return that peaks in September and October. Observers from Fife Ness have recorded as many as 30 passing in an hour on good days. The sea off Tentsmuir is another good place for autumn birds (20 on 27 August 1978).

The Red-throated Diver is occasionally reported from inland lochs, eg. Townhill Loch, Dunfermline, where one was seen on 18 December 1983, Kilconquhar Loch, Lochore and Morton Lochs. Here a young bird spent a month in May and June 1980—it had a fish hook attached, and flew to the Tay to feed.

There is no evidence of change in status or numbers in the last 20 years, but Baxter and Rintoul considered that it had markedly decreased since the 1920s. They spoke of 'great numbers' in Largo Bay 1909-10 and 'crowds all the way from the Eden to the mouth of the Kenly' in November 1920 (B of S:516).

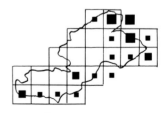

Black-throated Diver *Gavia arctica*

Regular winter visitor and passage migrant

This diver is usually seen only in small numbers, though some good numbers have been recorded on spring passage such as 59 in St Andrews Bay on 16 March 1980, and 16 in Largo Bay on 3 June 1981. All available records of this species since 1980 fall within a period between 20 August and 21 June, when it has been seen all along the coast of Fife from Tayport to Torry Bay, though Baxter and Rintoul recorded that 'the largest numbers we have seen together was when crossing in a ferry from Newport to Dundee on 21 January 1933, when we saw quite 50 divers, mostly Black-throated, though a few were Red-throated' (B of S:509). They considered that the Black-throated Diver was becoming more common (1953), but this hardly seems the case now.

The best places to watch for this diver, apart from the above-mentioned areas, are Tentsmuir and Fife Ness, here especially on passage: eg. 12 on 16 April 1982.

Black-throated Divers are very occasionally seen inland: thus one was on Kilconquhar Loch on 20 February 1965; and there are other records from Morton Lochs (December 1954) and Ballo Lochs (6 June 1930).

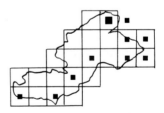

Great Northern Diver *Gavia immer*

Scarce winter visitor

Much rarer than the two previous species, but occurs in similar localities. All recent records fall between September and late May, but largest numbers are usually in winter rather than on passage (6 at Fife Ness on 4 February 1968; 5 at Tentsmuir on 18 December 1968). Baxter and Rintoul saw a bird in Largo Bay 'as late as 30 June', but there is no indication of any alteration in numbers over the past century.

It has only once been recorded inland in Fife: at Cullaloe reservoir on 8 January 1955 (EBB5:60).

This is the only species of diver recorded by Sibbald in *The History of Fife and Kinross* (1710).

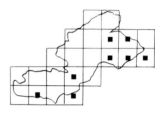

White-billed Diver   *Gavia adamsii*

Very rare winter visitor

There are three records only of this diver: one in the Tay estuary, 'present for some weeks' during February and March 1954 (EBB4:49); one, found dead, at Earlsferry on 1 January 1965 (SB8:217); and one in the Tay estuary—'probably Fife'—oiled, 9 or 10 March 1968 (SB5:194 & 308).

Little Grebe   *Tachybaptus ruficollis*

Resident

This grebe is generally distributed, and breeds throughout the region wherever there is water of suitable extent. The area is largely deserted in winter, though birds may occasionally be seen on salt water in severe weather, such as at St Andrews, Methil and Inverkeithing. Most breeding birds are back in mid-February or March, and may flock on arrival (23 at Cameron reservoir on 21 February 1983; 24 at Kilconquhar on 19 March 1984). Parties are more common, however, in the autumn (38 on Cameron on 13 September 1981; 36 on the Lomond Hills reservoirs on 16 October 1983; 24 on Loch Fitty on 16 September 1984; and 18 at Carriston reservoir on 8 September 1978).

Reedy waters, such as Kilconquhar Loch, are particularly favoured in summer.

Baxter and Rintoul considered the Little Grebe to have increased greatly 'within recent times' (1935), but there is no evidence of any change in status the last twenty years.

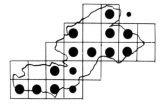
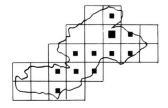

Great Crested Grebe   *Podiceps cristatus*

Breeds, and winters in substantial numbers locally

The first breeding record of the Great Crested Grebe in Fife is mentioned by Baxter and Rintoul as being on Lindores Loch as recently as 1880. Since then it has become so numerous that there is hardly a suitable loch or reservoir in the area which does not have at least one pair. Their breeding success, however, varies considerably: during the late 1960s and 1970s breeding was constantly being reported as 'poor', with few or no chicks (see also 'Great Crested Grebe enquiry 1973', SB8:151-159), but fortunately this trend has recently been reversed, so that in 1980, 7 pairs on Kilconquhar were counted with 15 young, 1 pair on Morton Lochs with 4 young, and 14 pairs with young on Lindores Loch the same year; in 1982, 10 pairs on Lindores had more than 20 young in the water on 28 August, and 9 pairs there in 1983 fledged 16 young. During 1983, 28 breeding pairs were counted in Fife.

Very occasionally the Great Crested Grebe is seen on the open sea in summer at St Andrews Bay and Largo Bay.

The Great Crested Grebe leaves the lochs in winter for the open sea, where it often flocks in favourite places such as St Andrews Bay (101 on 12 March 1980, 183 in February 1982, 80 there on 23 November 1983), and also at Methil with 66 on 26 October 1980, and 42 at Torry Bay on 5 January 1982; while Baxter and Rintoul recorded 'on 3 February 1934 a very large assemblage of Great Crested Grebes in the Forth off Culross—at least 500 birds' (VFF:327).

In spring there is some evidence that they gather inland in flocks before returning to their proper breeding grounds: there were 46 at Kilconquhar on 12 April 1981, and 24 birds at Morton Lochs on 30 March 1969, when only 5 pairs bred there.

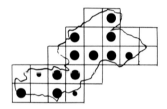 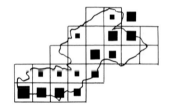

Red-necked Grebe   *Podiceps grisegena*

Scarce winter visitor

There are records of this bird from every month of the year, but most records fall between September and early May. It may be seen on the sea most frequently between Tayport and Inverkeithing, usually as singles or in pairs: 5 in Largo Bay on 15 September 1984 is the biggest number together reported in recent years, but 4 were counted at Inverkeithing on 27 December 1984; 4 at Lundin Links on 7 March 1971; 4 were in summer plumage in Largo Bay on 15 April 1982; and 2 pairs were displaying in Shell Bay on 9 May 1981.

Occasionally it occurs inland, even in summer. Lochs, where it has been seen, are Carriston, Kilconquhar, Lindores and Morton Lochs.

There is no evidence of any change in status this century. Baxter and Rintoul recorded it as in 'some years being far from uncommon . . . on 19 December 1933, after a long period of winds from northerly and easterly quarters we saw at least a dozen when walking from Aberdour to Burntisland' (VFF:328). In 1984 there were about 20 sightings compared with 8 in 1983, and 11 in 1982.

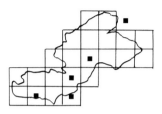

Slavonian Grebe *Podiceps auritus*

Regular winter visitor in small numbers

The best places to see this grebe are St Andrews Bay, where a remarkable count of 62 was made on 8 April 1983—'in small parties . . . many were displaying' (F&K 1983)—and at Tentsmuir, where there were 10 off Kinshaldy on 10 March 1982, and 7 on 27 February 1972. There were also 7 in Largo Bay on 24 March 1972, and it appears that the larger numbers are always in the spring.

Inland it has been recorded from Cameron reservoir, Kilconquhar Loch, Loch Fitty, Loch Gelly and Morton Lochs from August onwards.

There is no apparent change in status in the last 30 years, though Harvie-Brown (1906) only regarded it as 'uncertain and occasional' in the Tay area, and a young male shot on the Tay river in early January 1862 was considered rare enough to be exhibited at a meeting of the Royal Physical Society (FT:353). Henry Boase, on the other hand, thought it had become more frequent in North Fife in the years leading up to 1964 (BNF:12).

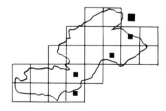

Black-necked Grebe　　　　　　　　　　*Podiceps nigricollis*

Scarce winter visitor, has bred

This grebe is less common off the coast of Fife than the previous species.
It has been reported most frequently from St Andrews Bay, but also
from the Eden estuary, Largo Bay, Burntisland and Inverkeithing.
Most records are from October to the end of January, and are all of
single birds: eg. in St Andrews Bay on 4 October 1983, on 17 November
1982, and on 8 November 1975; in the Eden estuary on 22 October 1979
and on 25 October 1978; at Tentsmuir on 21 December 1971; and at
Limekilns on 20 February 1977.

The Black-necked Grebe is mentioned by Thom in *Birds in Scotland*
(1986) as breeding locally in the Central Lowlands, and Fife is
mentioned in the list of counties where it has bred.

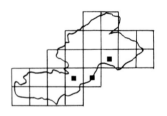

Black-browed Albatross　　　　　　　　　　*Diomedea melanophris*

Very rare

Only two sightings: one at Elie Ness on 23 August 1969, and one at Fife
Ness on 8 August 1972 (SB7:308). This was without doubt the same
bird which returned to the Bass Rock for several years. This species is
normally found in the Antarctic Ocean.

Fulmar   *Fulmarus glacialis*

Resident

The status of this bird has changed radically in the last hundred years. In 1878 the only breeding record in Scotland was from St Kilda, and as late as 1935 Baxter and Rintoul could report no definite breeding record in Fife, but were 'hopeful to do so soon', as they had seen birds 'prospecting' at Elie and Caiplie the year before (VFF:322). Now there are several colonies around Fife of varying sizes. The largest is without doubt that at St Andrews on the Castle Cliffs. It was not till 1943 that birds began to frequent the ledges here, and breeding was not proved till 1946, with 9 pairs in 1948. In 1976 120-150 pairs bred here.

Other breeding colonies along the coast are known from Randerston, Crail, Kincraig, Dysart, and on 'most suitable sites' (Ballantyne, 1982) between Buckhaven and Aberdour. Fulmars have nested irregularly at Caiplie and Pittenweem. There are two inland colonies, one at Benarty Crags, where there were 6 pairs in 1982, and the other at Lucklaw Quarry, where 12 birds had returned by 27 February 1983.

Most Fulmars leave the area in the late autumn, only to return to the main breeding colonies as early as January and February: 250 reported at St Andrews on 13 December 1982 indicates an exceptionally early return that year. Birds seem to come earlier and stay later at the main colonies, whereas singles or small parties may be seen flying up and down the south coast of Fife mainly between April and September. Occasionally birds are reported 'prospecting' inland, eg. at Kingskettle on 1 June 1983; and at Lochore Meadows on 24 May and 31 June 1984.

Big movements of Fulmars in spring and autumn are indicated by the records: thus 700 per hour flew north at Fife Ness on 20 April 1978, and 1500 per hour for two hours were going north on 29 August 1976.

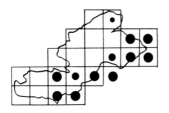 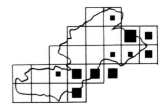

Cory's Shearwater   *Calonectris diomedea*

Rare vagrant

This Mediterranean/South Atlantic species has been recorded on three days in the last seven years, all at Fife Ness:

2 at Fife Ness on 26.8.1984
1 at Fife Ness on 29.8.1979
2 going north at Fife Ness on 15.4.1978

There are two earlier records of single birds being seen by Miss E. V. Baxter travelling on a boat, on both occasions, between mainland Fife and the Isle of May. The first was on 20 September 1957, and the second on 3 November the same year (SB1:8-10).

Great Shearwater   *Puffinus gravis*

Rare vagrant

There have been four recent records, all from Fife Ness. They are: 2 on 24 August 1984, and singles on 28 and 29 August 1976. Before that the only record was one given by Harvie-Brown of 'the sternum of a bird of this species picked up on the sands at St Andrews on 9 September 1881' (FT:345).

The Great Shearwater is normally found in the South Atlantic Ocean.

Sooty Shearwater *Puffinus griseus*

Regular visitor on autumn passage

This shearwater occurs in the Firth of Forth in varying numbers from
the end of July to November, with the vast majority of records falling
between August and September. Only two spring records have been
reported: one bird was seen at Fife Ness on 15 May 1976, and another
there in March 1985.

The most advantageous place to watch for Sooty Shearwaters is
undoubtedly Fife Ness, where exceptional numbers have been
recorded, such as 202 on 11 September 1976, 65 flying north in two
hours on 13 August 1983, 59 in two hours on 1 October 1976, and 54 on
29 August 1976.

Other places, where it has been recorded, are St Andrews,
Anstruther, Largo Bay and Kirkcaldy.

This species seems to be on the increase. Baxter and Rintoul
described it in *A Vertebrate Fauna of Forth* (1935) as 'never occuring in
great numbers', indicating that as many as a dozen together was rare
(VFF:319).

Manx Shearwater *Puffinus puffinus*

Regular on passage

Manx Shearwaters can be seen regularly on passage around the coast
of Fife from Tentsmuir to Culross. They occur in smaller numbers in
the spring, building up during the summer to become common in the
autumn.

The biggest spring passages have been recorded from the south
coast of Fife, where 200 per hour were passing Elie Ness on 2 May 1964;
240 per hour were flying north at Fife Ness on 16 June 1975; and 300
were at Kirkcaldy on 23 June 1980. It has been recorded as far up as
Culross, where there were 8 on 22 June 1974.

In the autumn very big numbers have been recorded from
Kirkcaldy (1,550 on 15 August 1984), and from St Andrews Bay (1000
on 27 July 1983). Big numbers have also been seen at Fife Ness and
Inverkeithing, and passage was noted off Tentsmuir Point on 11
September and 18 September 1976.

Occasionally birds are seen in winter. Thus one was recorded off Kirkcaldy on 7 November 1982; and another at Fife Ness, flying north, on 28 December 1954.

It appears that shearwaters have become much more common. Baxter and Rintoul reported in 1935 that the Manx Shearwater was, 'In the middle of last century, only known as a rare visitor', and that 'It has steadily increased in numbers and is prolonging the time of its stay in the Firth [of Forth]' (VFF:319). That this happy trend has continued seems to be confirmed by the records received in recent years.

The Balearic Shearwater or west Mediterranean race *P.p. mauretannicus* has been recorded in Fife on several occasions:

1984—single birds off North Queensferry on 23.8; off Anstruther on 26.8; and off Fife Ness on 16.9.
1981—one off Fife Ness on 3.10.
1977—one going north at Fife Ness on 23.9
1969—one S at Fife Ness on 19.8, and one N on 19.8

Only one previous record exists of a bird of this race shot in the Firth of Forth on 19 August 1874 (Scot. Nat. 1916:249).

Storm Petrel   *Hydrobates pelagicus*

Uncertain, but probably regular in small numbers

There are only relatively few records of the Storm Petrel from the coast of Fife. There is, however, some reason to suppose that it is the petrel's nocturnal habits, which make the records so few and far between, because, with the use of tape lure at night, a number of Storm Petrels have recently been observed at Fife Ness: eg. c. 10 on two occasions in August 1985, and 4 there (1 trapped) on 15 September 1984, thus proving that they are about, at least during these months. Two were also mist-netted at East Shore (Eden estuary) on the night of 23 August 1985.

Almost all other recent records are from the Forth area and from autumn and winter: singles at Fife Ness in September 1979 (again mist-netted with tape lure) and on 12 September 1970; one was picked up at Pittenweem on 8 November 1956—after a SE gale (it died); one found oiled at St Monance in November 1973; one seen—again in strong SE wind at Elie Ness on 5 April 1966 (the only spring record); and one at Burntisland on 28 November 1975.

Further back, one was seen in the Tay estuary on 16 October 1946 (BNF:14); and Baxter and Rintoul recorded it as 'not uncommon in autumn and winter . . . especially after a gale', and mentioned watching 4 in Largo Bay on 23 January 1904 'flitting low over the waves there' (VFF:317). (This was the same year that the lighthouse keeper of the Bass Rock 8 miles south of Anstruther found a petrel of this species with an egg.) It was also mentioned by them as having occurred at Burntisland after stormy weather, and Dr Harvie-Brown had seen great numbers in the upper Forth area on occasions, and had shot 3 at Kincardine on 13 November 1867. Sibbald included it in his list in the *History of Fife and Kinross* (1710).

Recent records suggest that the Storm Petrel occurs regularly in the Firth of Forth in late summer, but it is difficult to estimate in what numbers. It does, however, appear to be seen less often in daytime than used to be the case.

Leach's Petrel   *Oceanodromo leucorhoa*

Rare vagrant

Drummond Hay mentioned a record of a bird shot in St Andrews Bay on 29 April 1868 (Scot.Nat.1871:81), and it is listed in Baxter and Rintoul's *Geographical Distribution and Status of Birds in Scotland* (1928) as an occasional visitor to both North and South Fife, but no details are given. The only recent record, however, is a bird seen off Fife Ness on 29 September 1983, though 12 petrels seen from Anstruther on 8 October 1983 may have been of this species.

Gannet   *Sula bassana*

Common

The Gannet may be observed, between February and October, anywhere along the coast of Fife from Tayport to Kincardine Bridge, but especially in the Firth of Forth area. One of the Gannet's main breeding colonies in Britain is on the Bass Rock—from which it gets its Latin name—only 8 miles south of Anstruther, and it can be seen at about any time travelling between that and the feeding grounds, singly or in files of varying sizes. Occasionally large gatherings occur around fishing boats, as eg. at Pittenweem, where 200 or more have been seen soaring and diving, resembling at a distance snowflakes in a child's 'snow storm' toy.

The main body of Gannets leaves the area before the middle of September: 543 were counted going north at Fife Ness in an hour on 12 August 1984, and there was a westerly passage of immatures at Kincardine Bridge on 24 August 1983. Recent peak counts past Anstruther have been 500 on 14 September 1982, 200 on 11 September 1983, and 200 on 12 September 1984.

Most Gannets have left the area by the middle of November, but a few individuals stay on during winter; thus 7 birds were counted off Anstruther on 22 December 1981, and 2 off Fife Ness five days later. Baxter and Rintoul (1953) mentioned certain years, when 'hundreds remain at the Bass . . . carrying nesting material in Christmas week' (B of S:468).

The time of return varies: 100 were seen around a fishing boat at Anstruther on 9 January 1985, and *Scottish Birds* (3:85) reported 'sudden return with good numbers up past Elie Ness' on 12 January 1964, 'where none were seen the day before'.

As one might expect, ringing records show that the Gannet may travel a very long way: thus a bird which was ringed on 17 July 1981 at Skarvklakken (Nordland), Norway, was found dead at Kinghorn in October 1983 (1735 km), and birds ringed on the Bass Rock have been found as far away as Gambia and Senegal. Very occasionally the Gannet is found inland: eg. a juvenile turned up at Falkland on 19 September 1982.

The earliest record we have of this species is of 6 'Solan Geese' purchased for King James V's table at Falkland Palace in August 1529 (ExDJV), and Sibbald mentioned the Gannet in the *History of Fife and Kinross* (1710). The Gannet appears always to have been plentiful, and there is no evidence of any change in numbers. It has never nested in Fife.

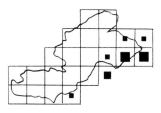

Cormorant   *Phalacrocorax carbo*

Locally common on coast and inland throughout the year

Small groups may be seen at any time of the year along the coast from Newburgh to Kincardine, but all peak counts in the last 15 years have occurred between September and January, and have been in the north at Tentsmuir (760 on 29 December 1973); over 400 fishing by the Tay Bridge on 11 January 1982; with 360 a little further east on 19 December the same year. Unlike the Shag it is quite common in the River Tay right up to Newburgh and beyond. Off the south coast at Kirkcaldy there were flocks of 450 on 17 January 1982, with 160 there on 25 September 1983; and at Culross about 100 on 1 January 1977. There is some evidence that these big flocks move about in search of food: eg. up to 300 per hour were recorded at Fife Ness 'some days in December' 1969.

The Cormorant also occurs inland in small numbers, more usually in spring: 40 were at Cameron reservoir in February 1972.

Sibbald mentions the Cormorant in the *History of Fife and Kinross* (1710). The Cormorant does not breed on the mainland of Fife, and there is no evidence of any change in status in recent years. At the time of writing a BTO survey is being carried out (winter 1985/86), and the results will no doubt be published in the usual journals.

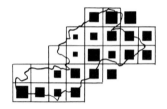

Shag   *Phalacrocorax aristotelis*

Common locally throughout the year

The Shag is especially common around the coast of East Fife, where enormous numbers may be seen moving about in the autumn: 3,000 were passing west off Anstruther on 17 November 1982, 2,000 there on 17 November 1983, and 1,700 on 12 October 1981. Other large numbers have been recorded off Kingsbarns, Fife Ness and Elie. Unlike the Cormorant, the Shag becomes less common the further up the estuaries of the Tay and Forth one goes, though 165 were counted on 18 December 1983 as far up as Dysart, where it has been increasing lately.

For the north, Grierson mentioned in his 'Check-list of the Birds of Tentsmuir' (1962) that the Shag was not common off that area, which still holds true, though it has certainly increased there too in recent years. In 1964 Boase gave it as 'occasional' up to Newport (BNF:16).

The Shag is seldom seen inland. One at Morton Lochs on 2 February 1982 was unusual.

The status of the Shag is very interesting. It was mentioned by Sibbald in the *History of Fife and Kinross* (1710), and also by the minister of Anstruther Wester in the *Old Statistical Account* (1793), and it has obviously been around for a long time in some numbers. The last couple of decades, however, have seen an increase that is little short of an explosion. Baxter and Rintoul wrote in 1935 about the Shag and the Cormorant that 'In winter at the East Neuk of Fife the numbers are, generally speaking, about equal' (VFF:201). Recent records, however, suggest that the Shag is now vastly more common than the Cormorant. This is no doubt due to the huge increase in breeding numbers in the Firth of Forth: in 1936 only 10 pairs were breeding on the Isle of May, whereas now more than 1000 pairs nest there, and on some of the other islands too (see also SB8 (supplement) on the breeding birds of the May).

With the increase of breeding in the Forth, the movements of the Shag also appear to have changed. Baxter and Rintoul (1953) found their 'huge assemblages in April, possibly birds on the way to their breeding grounds. Eg. on 28 April 1936 we saw hundreds and hundreds at Balcomie . . . ', whereas all the maximum counts in recent years have been in the autumn.

That the Shags around our coasts often travel quite a long way is shown by several ringing records from the Isle of May: eg. one ringed there on 11 August 1977 was recovered off Utsira (Rogaland), Norway on 2 December the same year, and another ringed on 21 June 1981 was recovered on 26 December 1981 at Ijmuiden, Netherlands (619km).

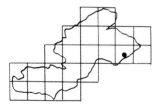 

Bittern *Botaurus stellaris*

Very rare visitor

There are no recent records of this bird in Fife, and only a few older records with dates given. W. Berry recorded that a Bittern was 'obtained' at Tayport on 2 December 1925; whereas another was shot at Morton Lochs on 6 April 1917 and the skin sent to the Royal Scottish Museum (SB2:132); before that Henry Boase mentions a male shot near Cupar on 11 January 1910 (BNF:19). Baxter and Rintoul had a record of a Bittern got near Kinneddar, five miles from Dunfermline, in the winter of 1906-07 (VFF:248), and Harvie-Brown said a 'very fine example' was shot immediately below Mugdrum House in the spring of 1863 or 1864, which might have been part of a large flight of Bitterns, which apparently reached our shores that winter (FT:219).

Sibbald in the *History of Fife and Kinross* (1710) said it was rare in Fife, but that it haunted Loch Leven (in Kinross) and that it might have been commoner at one time.

Little Bittern *Ixobrychus minutus*

Rare visitor

There are two records in the last 15 years: a male was at Morton Lochs on 23 May 1979, and another male was at Gillingshill reservoir on 10 June 1970.

Baxter and Rintoul (1953) mentioned that it was recorded from Fife but gave no details; Henry Boase thought they referred to a Little Bittern shot on the River Eden at the Hill of Tarvit on 17 May 1912 (BNF:20).

[Night Heron *Nycticorax nycticorax*

Only one record: of a bird seen at Dunfermline on 16 July 1957 (EBB7:79 & SB1:31). This was, however, considered to be a wanderer from Edinburgh Zoo.]

Grey Heron   *Ardea cinerea*

Common resident

The Grey Heron is a common sight throughout the year wherever there is a suitable habitat of rivers, burns, lochs, rock pools and sandy estuaries. Probably the best place is the Eden estuary, where several individuals are usually present at any time, and where large numbers have been recorded in the autumn, such as 20 by Guardbridge on 8 August 1984, and 19 at Shelly Point on 11 September the same year. Another favourite place in the autumn is Morton Lochs, where 53 were present on 30 September 1979.

The breeding success of the Heron has recently been very good. In an article in the *Fife and Kinross Bird Report* (1981) Mick Marquiss stated that in 1980 there were then 10 known colonies in Fife of varying size (from 1 or 2 nests to 25 pairs), with 108 pairs in all. Later figures show that this rose to 116 in 1981; was 105 in 1982; 97 in 1983; 108 pairs in 1984, but only 96 in 1985 (M. Marquiss and others). An average brood of 2.3 was recorded in 1981 and 1982, falling to 2.0 in 1983.

The population of Herons has evidently varied throughout the last fifty years or so. Baxter and Rintoul (1953) listed a number of heronries, many of these as being extinct at the time (VFF:246), and in the *Birds of Scotland* (1953) they said that although 'there are a good many small colonies, Fife has now no large heronry' (B of S:342). This is still the case.

Ringing has shown that young birds in particular may travel a very long way. Thus one ringed as a chick at Tentsmuir on 30 May 1975 was recovered at Kasba Tadla, Morocco on 12 January 1976, and others

ringed near St Andrews have been found in Spain, Belgium, North
Yorkshire and Donegal.

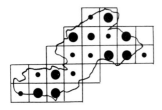   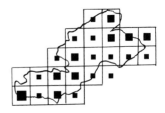

White Stork   *Ciconia ciconia*

Rare visitor

There are only two records from Fife, both recent: one was seen by Dr
and Mrs Berry at the old meteorological station at Tayport on 1 June
1985; and another was at Cameron reservoir on 23 April 1977.

Glossy Ibis   *Plegadis falcinellus*

Very rare visitor

Only one very old record of a bird shot at Kilconquhar Loch in
September 1842 (Yarrell's *British Birds,* vol 4, 1843).

Spoonbill   *Platalea leucorodia*

Very rare visitor

Two records only, both from Morton Lochs: one adult on 11 and 12
August 1984, and another on 2 April 1969.

[Flamingo   *Phoenicopterus*

None of the birds seen in Fife are regarded as truly wild. The Greater
Flamingo, *Phoenicopterus ruber,* as well as the Chilean race occur, and
favourite haunts are Tayport (near the meteorological station), and
Eden estuary. There were, eg., several sightings in May 1985.]

Mute Swan *Cygnus olor*

Common resident

The Mute Swan breeds on a number of lochs and reservoirs in the area, and also on some rivers. In 1983 BTO organised a National Mute Swan Census (see SB13:140-148), and it was found that the Fife population (in April and May) was 61 birds, out of which 29 were non-breeders, 12 held territories, but only 10 pairs attempted to breed. A later update on the breeding success of these 10 pairs (which was not part of the survey) reads like a tale of woe: only 2 pairs did eventually produce any cygnets at all, and even most of these were dead by the end of the year. This was, however, a particularly bad year, as it is reckoned that each pair should raise 2-3 cygnets yearly to maintain the *status quo,* for on the face of it there appears to have been little or no reduction in numbers since 1955-56, when the first survey took place. But it is not as simple as that, as Fife was probably then under-recorded and, as it is also pointed out by the organisers, it is extremely difficult to compare the two surveys, as they were conducted at different times of the year. Another survey in 1961 produced 23 breeding sites in Fife and 10 territorial sites, which was well up on the 1955-56 figures, and the *Breeding Atlas* found the Mute Swan breeding in 17 out of 22 squares in Fife over the five-year period 1968-72, but of course did not give any numbers.

After breeding, the Mute Swan leaves to moult, and ringing results show that many of our birds move to the Montrose Basin in Angus during this time.

In autumn Mute Swans are often seen in flocks: there were 40 at Torry Bay on 18 August 1984, and 30 at Lochore Meadows on 3 October 1983. In winter, maximum numbers have been recorded at Torry Bay (60 on 7 January 1982), but the Mute Swan is also sometimes seen then in unusual places such as Anstruther and Elie harbours.

The Mute Swan has always been a common sight in Fife. The earliest record of swans here comes from James V's household accounts, when 2 *cigni* were donated to the King during his stay at Falkland in October 1532 (ExDJV,Apx:36), whereas in the *Old Statistical Account* of Kilconquhar (1793) it was reported that 'Between 60 and 70 swans used greatly to enliven and adorn this loch; but they deserted it about 20 years ago. There are 9 at present'. Harvie-Brown (1906) pointed out that in many cases the Mute Swan was just to be regarded as only half wild, and that in the past it was often 'domestic'.

Comparison with earlier centuries is therefore misleading, but earlier this century Dr John Berry saw 70 Mute Swans near Mugdrum Island in late April 1931 (BNF:42), where only a few are seen today, and the records of the Wildfowl Trust also show that many little lochs and reservoirs, which during the 1960s and early 1970s could boast 10 or 20 Mute Swans in winter, now only have 2 or 4 birds. So it appears that the Mute Swan has decreased overall in the last fifty years or so, with a marked upswing in the 1960s and early 1970s. On a national level the Mute Swan was estimated in 1983 to have dropped by 3.8% in Scotland from the levels of the 1955-56 census.

The lead poisoning which has accounted for such massive deathtolls elsewhere seem fortunately to be little in evidence in Fife.

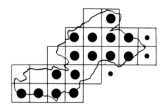
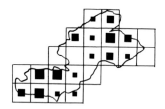

Bewick's Swan   *Cygnus columbianus*

Regular winter visitor in small numbers

Up till the last few years Bewick's Swan was regarded as a scarce winter visitor only, but a notable flock has been building up in Central Fife, especially on the Lomond Hills reservoirs, where they peaked at 28 on 25 November 1984 at Ballo, compared with maximum numbers there of 13 between 13 November and 18 December 1983, and 8 there on 7 December 1981.

Elsewhere recent records have come from Lochore Meadows, Loch Gelly, Carriston reservoir, and in East Fife from Cameron reservoir, Kilconquhar Loch and the Eden estuary, all between late October and the end of January.

Baxter and Rintoul wrote in 1953 that 'In all our years of work in Fife we have only seen Bewick's Swan twice' (B of S:364); and H. Boase (1964) has only 2 records from North Fife: 2 on Morton Lochs in

January 1947, and one on Cameron reservoir in 1954 (BNF:44). One can only hope that this lovely little swan will continue to grace our lochs in increasing numbers.

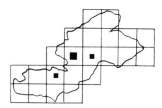

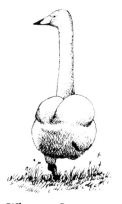

Whooper Swan *Cygnus cygnus*

Common winter visitor

The earliest autumn record in the last 30 years is of 3 walking ashore at Crombie Point from very rough seas on 16 September 1962, and there are September and early October records also from Kilconquhar, Balcomie golf course, and Tayport, as well as an unusual record of 5 at Dairsie on 4 October 1968. The first autumn sighting on the Lomond Hills reservoirs in 1983 was on 17 October with 2 birds on Ballo. Peak numbers are all from Central Fife, and have been recorded at Leslie (310 on 18 November 1971), Kingskettle (280 on 27 November 1971) and Ballo reservoir (216 on 28 October 1973), with good numbers too on Lochore Meadows, Loch Fitty and Loch Gelly. In fact most lochs and reservoirs in Central and West Fife have had records of Whooper Swans in the last fifteen years. Numbers have also been seen at

Cameron reservoir, the Eden estuary, Cambo and Randerston in East Fife.

Sometimes the Whooper Swan may be seen on salt water, eg. between Kinghorn and Kirkcaldy, and in Largo Bay, especially where streams flow into the sea, and in the Tay estuary.

Most birds have left by the end of March to fly to the breeding grounds (2 Whooper Swans seen in Fife with neckbands, one in 1981 and another in 1984, had both been marked in Iceland), but occasionally a few linger on. Thus one was at Lochore Meadows through the summer of 1984; 2 were seen in Largo Bay on 20 May 1984, and one stayed on at Culross as late as 10 July 1976.

Harvie-Brown (1906) regarded the Whooper Swan as a common winter visitor and said it was occasionally abundant, as eg. in early 1879, when several were shot at Newburgh and one at Edenmouth. Baxter and Rintoul (1935) also said it was a regular winter visitor in varying numbers, and mentioned that it was not uncommon on Kilconquhar Loch, from where they had an old record of 20 in very rough weather in 1823.

Numbers have obviously long varied, and there is not enough information available to indicate any real change in status. It is clear, however, that numbers were generally very high in the 1970s, and also that wintering numbers on the Lomond Hills reservoirs have increased markedly in the last 20 years at least. It is interesting that *Wildfowl in Great Britain* (1963) mentioned many inland waters in Central and West Fife, but not Ballo reservoir at all for Whoopers.

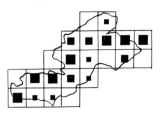

Bean Goose   *Anser fabalis*

Scarce winter visitor

There are not many records of Bean Geese in recent years from Fife: 23 at Kilconquhar on 26 December 1971 is the biggest flock seen in the last 15 years, but 10 flew west over Fife Ness on 14 October 1984, calling.

Further back there were 4 near Cameron reservoir with Pinkfeet and Greylag on 2 April 1967; and 2 at Kilconquhar on 27 February 1970.

Interestingly enough, it was the Bean Goose which was the common goose earlier last century. Robert Gray in *The Birds of the West of Scotland* (1871) quoted Harvie-Brown as saying that 'It is our commonest goose on the east coast, punishing the farmers' newly sown beans in early spring . . . ', and Gray added that, 'When travelling through that county (i.e. Fife) in the winter time, I never fail to observe small flocks coming from the higher grounds in the afternoon, and steering for the mouth of the Eden . . . '(p.344). But about 1870 a change set in. Dalgleish found both the Bean and the Pink-footed Goose common about Kincardine in 1885, but by the beginning of this century both Harvie-Brown and Millais regarded the Bean Goose as uncommon in North Fife. Dr John Berry has stated that between 1920 and 1940 a flock of Bean Geese roosted on Cameron reservoir and fed on certain hill pastures south of Drumcarrow during the day (WG+WDS:31 and pers.com.), and *Wildfowl of Great Britain* (1963), in connection with Cameron reservoir, said that as recently as 1953 there were accounts of several hundred Bean Geese here, but after 1954 the numbers dropped and (by 1963) had ceased altogether, 'representing a loss of perhaps a quarter of the British population' (WGB:199).

Dr Berry also mentions another flock which colonised the Lomond Hills reservoirs, especially Harperleas, the island in Ballo, and Holl reservoir, which increased to some hundreds, but that too disappeared some time back, probably due to loss of nesting grounds in North Sweden through industrial development.

The race which frequented Fife was the Western Bean Goose *(A.f.fabalis)*.

Pink-footed Goose   *Anser brachyrhynchus*

Common winter visitor

There are few more exciting events in the year than to hear the first arrival of geese and to see their splendid V-formations move across the sky. The Pink-footed Goose arrives from the north two or three weeks earlier than the Greylag Goose, and first arrivals are generally reported around the middle of September, though occasionally they come earlier: thus on 27 August 1963 there were c. 1,600 on the Tay estuary, they were heard over St Andrews that morning at 6.30 a.m., and three hours later over Lundin Links (SB2:486). The main arrival, however, is not usually till October, when vast flocks may fly over Fife, some to stay, some to pass on south. Such a great arrival was observed, with an estimated 10,000 Pinkfeet, during the afternoon and evening on 11 October 1961, 'Flying southward and settling at Tentsmuir . . . There was a strong SW wind and the geese migrating over the sea kept very low over the water . . . they were clearly making as much use as possible of the "boundary layer" of air . . . Later from Broughty Ferry, Tentsmuir Point could be seen black with newly arrived geese . . . ' (SB2:324). The very big influx in the Lothians during the next three days were thought to be the same birds.

Peak numbers are reached in Fife about the first half of November, when huge flocks may be seen at dusk coming into roost, or leaving it at dawn. The Pink-footed Goose's favourite roosting place in Fife is undoubtedly Cameron reservoir, where November numbers in recent years have varied between 4,000 (1984) and 8,000 (1983 and 1971), though big roosts have also been noted on the Tay at Newburgh, and at Tentsmuir Point (WGB:200), with smaller numbers at Peppermill Dam and Tulliallan in West Fife, and the Lomond Hills reservoirs in Central Fife.

During the day they feed in smaller parties around Fife, mostly on barley stubble, and good places to see them are Newburgh and eastwards along the Tay to Wormit; around Cameron reservoir; and in the general area west of the Peat Inn.

As frost sets in and food runs out, many geese leave the area for the south or west, but some Pinkfeet are usually about till the end of April: there were eg. 2,000 at Newburgh on 26 April 1984.

The Pink-footed Goose has long been regarded as having replaced the Bean Goose, which was the commonest goose in the area last century. Dr John Berry mentioned that his grandfather first noticed a specimen of the Pink-footed Goose in 1872 among the considerable bags of geese shot by him in East Fife (WG+WDS:39), and by 1953 Baxter and Rintoul could say that they saw in Fife 'Big flocks every winter, and in some years incredible numbers . . . ' (B of S:375).

In an article on 'Recent change in Scottish barley acreages and the possible effect on wild geese' by Janet Kear (SB3:288), it is suggested that there is a direct correlation between the greatly increased barley acreage in modern farming and the increase in Pinkfeet during the last century.

The Fife population seems to have reached its maximum sometime in the 1960s and appears stable. Pinkfeet may fly as far as 25 miles between feeding places and their roost. No other goose flies as far (WGB:257), and this may account for the large concentration at comparatively few sites in the area.

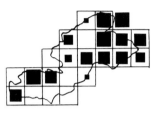

White-fronted Goose *Anser albifrons*

Scarce winter visitor

Both the Greenland *(A.a.flavirostris)* and the European *(A.a.albifrons)* race visit Fife from time to time. Records are mostly from Kilconquhar, where the biggest number in the last 15 years have been 23 (Greenland) on 23 November 1970, with other records from here in spring, and from Morton Lochs, eg. 2 (Gr) on 17 March 1984, 1 (European) on 21 February 1984, and 3 (Gr) on 17 February 1980.

Other recent records have come from Randerston, Cameron reservoir, Vicarsford near Leuchars, and Newburgh. Further back there were 9 on the sands between Culross and Kincardine on 3 February 1952. Contrary to Baxter and Rintoul's statement (1953) that Greenland White-fronts were becoming commoner in the Tay area, it appears that the White-fronts which frequented the flooded land between Tayport and the Eden estuary during the earlier part of this century were all of the European race (Dr Berry pers.com.). Any increase that may have occurred before the middle of the century has sadly not been sustained, and both the White-fronted races are now very scarce.

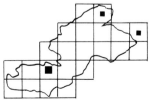

Greylag Goose   *Anser anser*

Common winter visitor

The Greylag arrives in the autumn about the end of September or early October: eg. 3,000 flew south in 11 skeins over St Andrews at 7 p.m. on 1 October 1983, with 24 at Kilconquhar on 17 September 1967 being the earliest arrival in the last 30 years. Maximum numbers are reached in November, with eg. 1,877 roosting on Ballo reservoir on 13 November 1983, and 1,250 on Cameron reservoir on 14 November the same year.

Since 1951 and up till the last few years there was a substantial flock of Greylag roosting on Kilconquhar Loch (1,856 on 13 December 1970, 1,896 on 7 November 1971, 1,900 on 12 March 1972, and 1,500 there on 12 February 1978), but after the hard winter of 1981-82, when a flock of 2,000 was seen at St Monance on 9 January 1982—almost too weak to fly—they have not been back to Kilconquhar with any regularity, though 350 were seen there on 26 December 1984. Greylags apparently used to roost here before the Second World War, were driven away by wartime disturbances, but returned again in the 1950s (WGB:197).

In Central Fife the biggest roost is undoubtedly Carriston reservoir, which has had large numbers of Greylag in the last 20 years or so (eg. 1,500 on 18 March 1984); and another place with good numbers is Glenrothes (1,230 on 14 March 1984). Numbers up to 800 have also been reported from Loch Fitty, and Tank Dykes/Star Moss in the 1980s (WT counts), and records from other areas are 1,400 feeding with Pinkfeet at Newburgh on 26 January 1985; 1,120 at Guardbridge on 24 January 1984; and 820 at the Eden estuary on 2 February 1985. There were 3,476 on Lindores Loch in December 1977 (WT counts) but this appears to have been unusual, and only very small numbers have been reported from here since.

The Greylag population in Great Britain was 21,000 in 1959; 65,000 in 1970—all but 1,400 of these in Scotland; and in 1983 the total population was 82,000 (WWC, 1983-84), but the numbers wintering in Fife do not seem to have increased in the same proportion, the area no doubt having reached its maximum density.

Most Greylags have left the area by the middle of April, but a few stay on during the summer months, eg. one was on the Eden estuary during the summer of 1985, and 4 were there in August 1970 and 1972; and there are also summer records from Morton Lochs. The few pairs that have tried to breed in Fife in recent years have probably been feral, although Dr John Berry says that genuine wild birds certainly bred at Morton Lochs, and probably also at Tentsmuir around 1930. He has a photo of a 'genuine' Greylag on her nest taken on 5 April 1931, but adds that it could have been a wounded bird with a devoted mate staying behind.

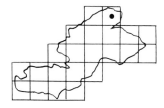 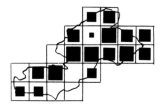

[**Snow Goose**   *Anser caerulescens*

Very rare winter visitor

Whereas the Snow Goose in its wild state is found as far away as in Arctic America and NW Greenland, it is also a favourite wildfowl collection bird, and often kept in captivity. This means that it is difficult to say how many of the birds we see are escapes, and how many are true vagrants, but most of them are likely to be the former. It is suggested in the *Shell Guide to Birds of Britain and Ireland* (Ferguson-Lees, Willis and Sharrock, 1983) that wild birds are often in company with Greenland White-fronts, and there is one record of a bird with Greenland White-fronts on Morton Lochs on 16 April 1968, but as that year several escaped birds were also seen in the area, it is likeliest that this bird was also an escape.

The most recent records from Fife are 3 at Crail on 8 June 1979, and one (blue) at Kilconquhar on 5 November 1978. Other records have come from Morton Lochs, Tentsmuir, Tayport, Cameron, Carnbee, Auchtermuchty, Burntisland and Inverkeithing.

In 1966 there were reports of one (blue) Lesser Snow Goose *(A.a.caerulescens)* having been seen at Morton near Tayport on 26 February, and presumably the same bird near Morton Lochs on 3, 19 and 27 December that year. Also 2 Ross's Geese *(Anser rossii)* with Pinkfeet were seen at Dunbog in December 1963.]

Canada Goose   *Branta canadensis*

Scarce passage migrant

There are records of the Canada Goose from every month of the year except December, in the last 20 years. It has been reported slightly more often from East Fife than from West or Central Fife, but never in any great numbers. Their favourite localities seem to be Kilconquhar Loch (31 on 4 September 1983, 14 on 4 September 1982); Lochore Meadows (11 on 31 May 1983); along the Tay estuary, at Newburgh (38 on 6 November 1970), Newport and Tayport; and they have also been seen several times over Anstruther (eg. 35 on 9 June 1985), at Fife Ness (32 flying north on 3 June 1984), and at Elie Ness on migration. Most birds are seen on their way to and from the moulting area on the Beauly Firth in Inverness-shire, and ringing returns there indicate that many originate in Yorkshire and Sussex. In the very cold winter of 1981-82, 18 flew over Cellardyke on 10 January 1982, which was unusual.

From the Wildfowl Trust counts it appears that 2 were regularly seen on Carriston reservoir from September 1970 to March 1974, but there is no information as to whether they stayed on during the summer or attempted to breed. A pair, which nested on Morton Lochs in 1966, were hybrids, as was the pair which bred here successfully in 1985.

The Canada Goose was introduced into Britain in the seventeenth century. The *Handbook of British Birds* (1943) states that 'it has decreased in Scotland, but is still well established in several parts of the

Tay and Forth area' (HBB III:217). Since then there has been a further decline, as this is no longer the case.

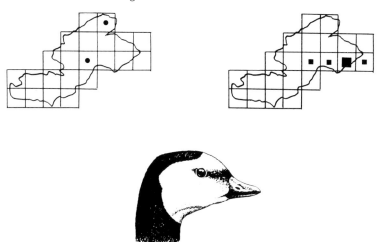

Barnacle Goose *Branta leucopsis*

Passage migrant and regular winter visitor in small numbers

This lovely little goose has, according to the old reports, never been common on the east side of Scotland. It can be seen in North and East Fife, usually—but perhaps less often than was formerly the case—in ones or twos in company with Pinkfeet during the winter months. In 1962 up to 5 were seen at Newburgh in January, and there were reports of a flock of 30 in the area; similar numbers were said to have wintered in the same area in 1959-60 and 1960-61.

There has, however, been an increase in numbers at migration time in later years. In 1981 18 were passing Fife Ness on 3 May, and in 1983 a remarkable passage was noted, when between 200 and 300 were moving north at Fife Ness in several parties over several hours on 1 May, all birds flying very low over the water.

In autumn up to the 1980s there had only been reports of small numbers on migration: 19 at Shelly Point on 8 October 1949, 3 at Elie Ness on 3 September 1967, 38 passing Fife Ness on 25 September with 20 at Anstruther on 3 October 1976, 6 at Cameron on 16 October 1977 (WT counts), and 17 at the Eden estuary on 24 September 1978. But a dramatically big movement took place on the evening of 25 September

1982, when 335 Barnacle Geese were passing south in one hour at Fife Ness and 80 were at the Eden estuary the next day. A similar movement took place in 1983, with 107 flying over Anstruther on 2 October, and there were 32 at the Eden estuary on 1 October, as well as 26 at Fife Ness four days later on 5 October. In 1984, 200 flew west up the Eden estuary on 13 October and 60 south at Fife Ness the same day. That year there had also been 4 at Fife Ness on 14-17 September, and 6 there on 21 October.

All these records may point to a development—or simply to a discovery—of an alternative migration route for the Barnacle Goose, namely to approach Scotland from the north-east, and to cross over to the Solway Firth by way of the Firth of Forth and the comparatively short distance over land.

There is an interesting ringing record of a male ringed on 27 February 1970 at Snuk (Friesland), Netherlands, which was found dead at Guardbridge on 1 February 1979.

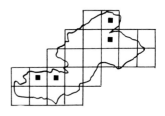

Brent Goose   *Branta bernicla*

Scarce winter visitor

Both the Dark-breasted *(B.b.bernicla)* and the Pale-breasted race *(B.b.hrota)* occur in Fife, but neither of them is now common. In January 1937 Dr Berry recorded a flock of 120 (Dark-breasted) at Guardbridge (WG+WDS:44), and Grierson in his 'Check-list of the Birds of Tentsmuir' (SB2:Special Supplement) stated that it was 'Once common in winter, over 100 being recorded on occasions, but [it] is now a rare visitor'. Today the Brent is usually recorded as singles or in small parties of 2-5 individuals, from a large variety of localities, mostly along the coast from Tayport in the north-east to Torryburn in the south-west. Its favourite place is undoubtedly the Eden estuary, where it has been seen most years since 1968, from January to April. There was a remarkable flock there early in 1985, which peaked at 26 on 8 March.

Other areas, where it has been recorded more than once in the last 20 years, are Tayport, St Andrews, Fife Ness (where 27 (Pale-breasted) flew south on 13 February 1966), and Largo Bay. Inland one (Pale-breasted) was seen on Cameron reservoir on 16 October 1983 (WT counts).

The earliest autumn record is 3 at Tentsmuir on 6 September 1981, and the latest spring record were 2 at the Eden on 14 June 1983. The numbers in 1985 were unusual, and it is too early to say if any change in status is on the way.

There is not enough information to indicate any recent area preference or overall trend in the occurrence of the Dark-breasted v. the Pale-breasted races. Dr Berry mentioned in *The Status and Distribution of Wild Geese and Wild Duck in Scotland* (1939) that only the Dark-breasted occurred in the Tay area. In 1970, however, most of the records from Tayport and the Eden were of the Pale-breasted race, albeit in very small numbers: 3 being the maximum count; and in 1982 5 out of 6 birds recorded in Fife were Pale-breasted, but the 26 in March 1985 were Dark-breasted.

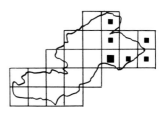

[Ruddy Shelduck   *Tadorna ferruginea*

There is only one record: one out of a pair was shot by W. Berry at Morton Lochs on 18 December 1934. The pair were probably escapes from breeding pens at Lindores Loch (SB2:136).]

Shelduck   *Tadorna tadorna*

Resident and winter visitor

This duck breeds locally in Fife, and especially at Tentsmuir and on the Eden estuary, where numbers, however, have dropped since 1954, when Grierson mentioned that nearly 200 pairs bred on Earlshall with others nesting at Tentsmuir and Shelly Point. In 1976 there were still 130 pairs at Tentsmuir, but since then numbers here have dropped much further. In the 1980s other breeding records have come from the Tay River (6 pairs between Balmerino and Flisk in 1985); and along the south coast of Fife, scattered pairs from Balcomie to Kincardine.

Most adults leave the area in the summer to moult, but a few remain, apparently to look after the juveniles on the Eden estuary in July and August. Here 320 juveniles were counted in August 1954, compared with 119 on 7 July 1978, and only 28 juveniles on 31 July 1984.

The adult birds return in October and November, joined by other migrant birds. By far the biggest concentration is on the Eden, where their numbers reach international importance (over 1% of the European population), but they may also be seen in some numbers elsewhere along the coast (293 at Torry Burn on 17 September 1984); and occasionally on inland waters as Kilconquhar Loch. Maximum wintering numbers in the Eden since 1980 have been 1,974 on 7 February 1982 and 1,670 on 18 December 1983, which compares favourably with previous years' records; and although the breeding population has certainly declined, it appears that the numbers of Shelduck in Fife in winter have increased substantially this century: Millais eg. related that he had once seen a flock of 500 at the mouth of the Eden (FT:230), whereas such a flock would not be very unusual today.

The Shelduck was mentioned in the *New Statistical Account* of Dunfermline (1844), and also under Inverkeithing, where the uncommon but 'large species of Anas with a red mark of a horseshoe form on the breast' must surely have been the Shelduck.

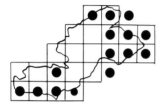 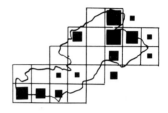

[Mandarin   *Aix galericulata*

Uncommon visitor

One recent record only of 3 at Newport on 11-12 November 1975. There is a feral colony at Perth. There is also an older record of a female at Kirktonbarns on 5 November 1924 (W Berry's unpublished notes).]

Wigeon   *Anas penelope*

Common winter visitor and breeds in very small numbers

The Wigeon was mentioned in the *New Statistical Account* of Inverkeithing, but Dalgleish (1885) considered it uncommon. Now, it winters in large numbers in the area and is especially numerous on the Eden estuary, where peak counts in the last fifteen years have been

2,500 on 13 February 1972, 1,742 on 16 January 1982, and 1,440 on 16 January 1981; but considerable numbers may also be seen elsewhere in Fife in winter, eg. there were 410 at Torry Bay on 14 January 1982, 390 at Lochore Meadows on 17 January 1981, and 249 there on 29 November 1983, 300 at Cameron reservoir on 13 November 1982, and 278 on Ballo reservoir on 27 November 1983. Smaller numbers many be seen on many other inland waters, as well as on the sea.

Most Wigeon leave the area in April, but a few remain to nest here. Harvie-Brown (1906) said that Wigeon bred in Perthshire well before 1880, but did not mention Fife. Baxter and Rintoul (1935), however, mentioned that they first discovered Wigeon breeding in Fife at Ballo reservoir in 1930, and that by 1934 it was 'much more numerous, quite a number of young and old being there' (VFF:221). At least 3 pairs bred at Ballo in 1983. One pair bred at Morton Lochs in 1953 and produced young, but there are no reports of breeding from here recently.

Henry Boase called the Wigeon mainly a winter visitor to North Fife and recorded that there were a great many on Lindores Loch in January 1916; and Dr John Berry said that the Wigeon was abundant about Tayport in the earlier parts of the century (WG+WDS). The account of the Eden estuary in *Wildlife in Great Britain* (1963) says that the Wigeon 'appears to have recovered at any rate locally, from the sharp decline that took place between 1920 and 1939' (WGB:198). Here are also given 'regular' as well as 'maximum' numbers for various localities in Fife during the 1950s: eg. the maximum for the Eden was 4,600—peaks which are never reached today. Nevertheless, the counts for the Wildfowl Trust since 1960 show that numbers generally stayed high through the 1960s and up to about 1976, when a marked decline took place. The trend in the 1980s so far, however, has been optimistic, though it is well behind the 1950s figures.

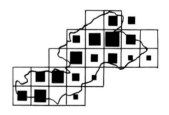

American Wigeon or Baldpate *Anas americana*

Very rare visitor

Only four records of this species:

1 on Eden estuary on 10.1.1971 (SB7:92)
1 on Morton Lochs on 12-13.10.1956 (SB2:133)
1 in North Fife on 29.11.1938
1 in St Andrews Bay on 24.11.1919 (B of S:403)
(1 on Eden estuary on 24.11.1919: no doubt the same bird as above)

All records have been of male birds: as with other species of duck, it is difficult to be sure that some or all of these are not escapes.

Gadwall *Anas strepera*

Winter visitor, breeds in small numbers

The status of the Gadwall is fairly complicated. Harvie-Brown (1906) mentioned a record of a male and a female obtained at Newburgh at the beginning of 1859, but considered it 'rare', whereas Millais thought it a regular autumn and winter visitor to Tay and Eden (FT:232). Baxter and Rintoul (1953) observed that the Gadwall was a recent addition to the list of birds breeding in the county, and suggested that it had been spreading from Loch Leven since 1923, in which year the Gadwall was first found breeding on Loch Gelly, and since then on Otterston, Kinghorn and Cullaloe lochs, all within 20 miles of Loch Leven. They had also seen Gadwall in May and June on Burntisland and Clatto reservoirs and Ballo Loch, and there were reports of it having bred on Lindores, Mugdrum Island and 'a small Loch near Newburgh'—no doubt Lochmill Loch—(B of S:393). Grierson, however, said that it had been found breeding in North Fife as early as 1918 at Morton Lochs (SB2:133).

Records since 1958 suggest that only 4-5 pairs nest fairly regularly in Fife, and also that the Gadwall is a very sporadic breeder. Favoured places are Cameron reservoir, Kilconquhar Loch, and Lochore Meadows, and it has also bred at Morton Lochs and possibly Carnbee reservoir. It may be present in summer in places where it does not necessarily breed: there were eg. 10 at Morton Lochs on 27 June 1976.

C

Wintering numbers also vary greatly but usually peak in September and October: 237 on Kilconquhar on 12 September 1971, 164 there on 15 October 1972, and 103 on 16 September 1974 are by far the largest counts in recent years. In 1984 the maximum count was 18 at Kilconquhar on 27 September, and there were only 2 at Cameron reservoir on 1 January that year compared with 21 there on 23 January 1972.

The Gadwall is rarely seen on salt water, although there was an exceptional party of 10 in Largo Bay on 26 March 1977. In the *Birds of Scotland* (1953) it was mentioned that 'Large numbers are sometimes recorded on arrival in autumn on the Firth of Tay . . .' (B of S:395), which no longer appears to be the case.

Only 22 individuals were reported in all of Fife in 1984, indicating a sad decline compared with the statement in *Wildfowl in Great Britain* (1963) that the Gadwall 'has increased markedly during this century, partly as the result of introductions and may still be doing so' (WGB:279). This increase apparently went on into the early 'seventies before a decline set in. The story is the same for many other species of duck: that the 1960s represented a tremendous upward swing in numbers, which was not sustained beyond the early 1970s. Even allowing for a levelling off of numbers, the Gadwall has declined drastically in recent years, but as it has always been fairly sporadic, it is to be hoped that numbers will soon rise again.

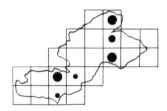 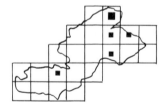

Teal   *Anas crecca*

Scarce breeder, but common winter visitor

The Teal winters in fairly large numbers in Fife, where it starts arriving in late August and September: 500+ recorded from Mugdrum Island on 25 August 1975 is the largest August flock in the last 20 years. It may, from this time onwards, be seen throughout the winter on many inland waters as well as on the sea, especially on the latter in cold weather, and peak numbers are recorded most frequently from Morton Lochs (1,600 on 25 November 1980, 1,400 on 10 October 1981, but only 300 there on 1 January 1984); and from the Eden estuary (1,000 on 13 February 1972, 627 on 15 February 1983, and 239 on 18 March 1984). Good numbers are also usual at Kilconquhar and in West and Central Fife on Lochore Meadows, Ballo reservoir and on the sea at Cult Ness. Boase (1964) said that Teal was definitely scarce along the south shore of the Tay, except at Mugdrum (BNF:20), and this appears still to be the case.

By March and April most of the winter visitors have left for the breeding grounds, but a few also nest here. The number of Teal which breed in Fife has dropped very considerably this century. In *Wildfowl in Great Britain* (1963) it is mentioned that 'Prior to the drainage and afforestation that took place between 1890 and 1920, Tentsmuir itself was an excellent centre for breeding and wintering duck . . . At that time it was one of the finest resorts for Teal in the country' (WGB:200). Now only a few breed here.

For South and West Fife, Baxter and Rintoul (1935) mentioned Teal as breeding at Tulliallan and a few pairs also 'about Burntisland, Kilconquhar Loch and the Ballo lochs' (VFF:200). It still breeds on Ballo (1 or 2 pairs in 1984). A pair bred at Falkland in 1982, and in 1981 a pair bred at Morton Lochs producing 6 young, while a nest with 3 eggs was reported from Wemyss on 11 April 1980. The *Breeding Atlas* showed the Teal as definitely breeding in 5 squares, with unsubstantiated records for another 4 squares (1968-72), and it is possible that the breeding of this species is under-recorded today.

The Teal has long been known in Fife. We know that it was present here as early as August 1528, when Teal was purchased for King James V at Falkland Palace (ExDJV:115), and Teal was also mentioned in the *New Statistical Account* of Inverkeithing (1836).

The Green-winged Teal *(A.c. carolinensis),* which is the American race, has been recorded in Fife, the most recent being a drake at the Eden estuary on 12 December 1978, which stayed till the end of the year. Another drake was here on 7 May 1974, and 2 drakes on Morton Lochs on 12 October 1968 were considered the first for the area (SB6:28).

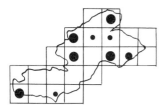
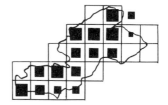

Mallard   *Anas platyrhynchos*

Common resident with numbers much increased in winter

The Mallard is a very common duck throughout the area, and in winter flocks can be seen both on the sea and on most inland waters from mid-October till February and March when they disperse. The largest flocks in the last 20 years have been recorded from the Eden estuary: 14,000 on 20 January 1965 was, however, exceptional. Grierson mentioned in his 'Check-list of Birds in Tentsmuir' that 2,000 were reached in 1950-51 on the Eden in November and again in February (SB2:132). At Methil there were 2,500 on 18 January 1968; and 2,000 in St Andrews Bay on 24 November 1968. All these are long-established places for wintering Mallards, as they are also mentioned by Baxter and Rintoul in the *Birds of Scotland* (1953): 'We have seen thousands in Largo Bay, and off the mouth of the Tay and Eden, while on 25 November 1911 we saw thousands in the sea off St Andrews—the biggest flocks we have seen of any duck anywhere . . .' (B of S:391).

Inland peak counts have been at Kilconquhar Loch (3,150 about the middle of November 1972, 2,650 on 23 January 1971), and sizeable flocks too at Morton Lochs, Ballo reservoir, Lochore Meadows, Cameron and Carriston reservoirs.

The Mallard was mentioned in the *New Statistical Account* of Kilconquhar (1836), and there is no evidence of any change in status.

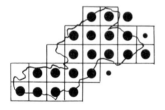
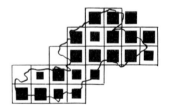

Pintail   *Anas acuta*

Regular winter visitor, has bred

The Pintail may be seen in winter on some of the estuaries, lochs and reservoirs in the area, but never in any great numbers. The biggest gathering recorded in the last 20 years were 77 on the Eden estuary on 16 January 1977, and there were 38 there on 3 March 1984; while Grierson thought flocks of 100 to 150 were usual in the 1950s (SB2:133), which is also supported by the *Wildfowl in Great Britain* (1963). Such numbers are not reached now on the Eden or elsewhere. Apart from the Eden, favourite places are Morton Lochs and Kilconquhar, and there are also records from Cameron, Carnbee and Ballo reservoirs, Lindores Loch, and Lochore Meadows. Occasionally the Pintail is found on the sea, such as in St Andrews Bay, where 50 were counted on 23 December 1984.

The Pintail started breeding in the county only this century. Baxter and Rintoul had records of proved breeding at Loch Gelly (1920), Cullaloe (1928), the Ballo lochs (1934), and at Kinghorn Loch (1935). They had also seen a Pintail with downy young at Clatto reservoir in 1926 (B of S:404). More recently a female and 4 ducklings were seen at Tentsmuir on 30 June 1972; and a female with 3 well-grown juveniles was on Cameron reservoir on 13 September 1981, but breeding was not proved. It did, however, breed at Tentsmuir in 1983.

Baxter and Rintoul (1935) observed that the Pintail had become commoner compared with earlier accounts: 'In 1858 an adult male Pintail shot in South Fife was considered a "sufficient rarity to be exhibited", but since then it has become more plentiful' (VFF:225); and Harvie-Brown thought it rare till about 1880, mentioning that examples had been shot on the tidal Tay and the Eden in 1873-74, and that it was considered 'quite a rarity' at the time. Millais said that it was 'A visitor in small numbers to the Tay and Eden estuaries where I have

shot it. In some seasons quite a number come about Mugdrum'
(FT:236).

Like most other duck, the Pintail had a peak period in the 1950s and
again in the early 1970s but is less plentiful today.

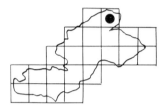

Garganey   *Anas querquedula*

Rare visitor

There are only a few records of this species, and nearly all are within the
last sixty years. The dated records are as follows:

Spring:
1 at Morton Lochs 5.6.81
1 at Kilconquhar 26-27.5.73
1 at Morton Lochs 29.3.64
1 male at Shelly Point 25.5.52
1 male and 1 female at Fife Ness 13.4.52
(with drake Teal. See EBB2:58)

Autumn:
1 at Eden estuary 16-17.8.85
1 at Peppermill Dam/Tulliallan 14.9.68 (WT counts)
1 at Morton Lochs 22.9.63
1 at Lochore 13.11.60 (the latest date)
6 at Morton Lochs 13.8.47 (SB2:133)
(These last 6 are the biggest number ever recorded together in Fife).

Dr John Berry said that Garganey had been recorded on several
occasions at Tayport and Newburgh between 1929 and 1939
(WG+WDS). The Garganey was not mentioned by Harvie-Brown for
North Fife, but there is a record in Gray's *Birds of Western Scotland* (1871)
of a bird shot on the Firth of Forth by a Mr Singer of Kincardine.
Though no details are given, it is a fair assumption that this bird was
shot in Fife. The Garganey did not start increasing in the south of
Britain till the first half of the twentieth century.

Shoveler

Anas clypeata

Breeds in small numbers: more present in autumn

The Shoveler is most commonly seen from April to November on lochs and reservoirs. Breeding reports recently have come from Kilconquhar Loch (20 pairs in 1970, but only 3 pairs there in 1983, and one pair in 1984), Morton Lochs, Ballo and Clatto reservoirs, Loch Gelly (where 18 ducklings were seen with one adult duck on 4 June 1985) and Lochore Meadows, but the Shoveler has undoubtedly declined drastically as a breeding bird in the area in recent years. Baxter and Rintoul (1953) wrote, 'In 1926 we noted that Shovelers were "now a common breeding duck in Fife"' (B of S:407), and even in 1962 Grierson could write that the Shoveler was 'invariably present at all seasons on Morton Lochs' (SB2:134). The increase had been noted as early as 1906, when Harvie-Brown observed that the Shoveler had become much commoner. He said that it used to be rare, at least up to 1880, and also that it first bred at Tentsmuir in 1900 (FT:233). The available records show that the Shoveler was still common in the early 1960s, when the Wildfowl counts reported it at several inland locations where it has not been seen in recent years. Numbers remained high well into the 1970s, eg. a maximum count of 348 was made at Kilconquhar Loch on 17 September 1972, and a few birds stayed around the whole winter during those years, but then a decline set in. There was a brief revival in 1981, when 127 were seen on Kilconquhar in November, but the maximum count in 1984 in Fife was down to 50 birds there on 4 November.

So the impressive increase which took place earlier this century is not being sustained.

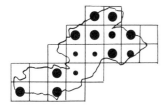
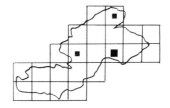

Red-crested Pochard   *Netta rufina*

Very rare visitor

There are only three records of this species: an immature male was seen on Kilconquhar Loch on 12 September 1979 and stayed till November; a male spent most of the winter of 1956-57 on Morton Lochs (BB52:44); and one 'beautiful' male was on Lindores Loch on 24 April 1947 (B of S:410).

Pochard   *Aythya ferina*

Resident, and in winter common locally

The Pochard is one of our regular breeding ducks in Fife, and in the last 20 years it has been recorded nesting at Kilconquhar Loch, Morton Lochs and Lochore Meadows. It used to breed at Lindores Loch, but has declined there due to disturbance since the 1960s.

Harvie-Brown (1906) said the Pochard was considered rare about 1813, and it was regarded only as a winter visitor till 1897, when 3-4 nests were found at Lindores Loch (FT:239). For the south, Baxter and Rintoul maintained that the Pochard—like a number of other species—had spread from Loch Leven in Kinross, with the first proved breeding record of Pochard at Kilconquhar in 1921. Other early records of breeding were mentioned at Loch Gelly (1920) and Cullaloe (1928) (VFF:227).

The biggest recent gatherings in summer have been at Kilconquhar Loch (50 on 25 June 1983) and at Ballo reservoir (up to 20 males in July and August 1983).

In winter the population is vastly increased by migrant birds, which come in October and peak in December and January, when they may be seen both on the sea and on inland waters. The biggest numbers have been recorded inland at Kilconquhar, where there were 2,100 on 16 January 1966—'about twice the normal'—and 1,800 on 13 December 1970, but only 200 on 9 October 1983; and at Lochore Meadows (700 on 22 October 1982, 466 on 26 October 1983), while there are other reports from nearly every fair-sized loch or reservoir.

Big sea counts are usual in December and January when the inland waters freeze over. Favourite areas are Largo Bay (1,800 at Methil on 2

January 1974, 700 in an aerial count there on 27 November 1981), and at Kirkcaldy (205 on 21 December 1980). Baxter and Rintoul (1935) also had records of large flocks at Kincardine (VFF:226).

Pochard was mentioned as 'abundant' in the *Old Statistical Account* of Kilconquhar (1793), where it is called the 'Herald duck', so this has plainly long been a good locality for the species. It also says that 'In the evening, they fly off in a body to the sea, as is supposed, and return through the night'. This habit of Pochard has also been noted elsewhere recently, eg. at Duddingston in the Lothians. In the *New Statistical Account* it is mentioned under Dunfermline as an occasional visitor.

Baxter and Rintoul drew attention to the extraordinary imbalance which appears to exist between the sexes of this species, where by far the greatest number seen are always male, certainly in winter and quite often in summer: 'On June 22 1936 we counted 55 drakes on Kilconquhar Loch, where only a few pairs bred. We have many records of similar gatherings . . . On Kinghorn Loch, which is a small sheet of water, on 31 January 1936 we counted 2,500 Pochard drakes' (B of S:412). Sadly no such gatherings are seen on Kinghorn Loch today, as it is much disturbed, but the excess of drake Pochards goes on: the 700 on Lochore Meadows in 1982 were all drakes.

As with most species of duck, the very big wintering numbers recorded in the 1960s and 1970s are no longer with us in the 1980s, and the breeding numbers may have fallen too. The national total, however, seems to have remained stable (WWC, 1980-84).

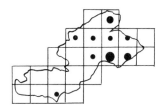 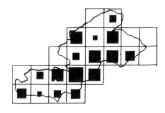

Tufted Duck   *Aythya fuligula*

Common breeder, resident

This duck is present and breeds on all suitable lochs and reservoirs in the area—that is, on waters extending above one or two acres. Breeding takes place comparatively late and ducklings are not usually seen till July. Biggest post-breeding numbers recently recorded are from Lochore Meadows, where there were 361 on 22 July 1984.

In winter the Tufted Duck flocks—possibly joined by migrant birds—and large numbers have been recorded on lochs as well as on salt water locally, when the inland waters freeze. Peaks at Kilconquhar Loch have been 1,134 on 14 December 1969, and 1,000 on 7 November 1971, but good numbers are also recently reported from Lochore Meadows, Lindores Loch, Morton Lochs, Ballo and Craigluscar reservoirs and Raith Loch. On the sea, maximum numbers were 600 at Largo Bay on 12 January 1982, and 500 at Methil on 22 January 1984.

This duck was mentioned in the *New Statistical Account* as an occasional visitor to Dunfermline parish. Baxter and Rintoul (1935) observed that the Tufted Duck has only been breeding in our area since the end of the nineteenth century, and as with several other species of duck, it was thought to have spread from Loch Leven, with the first firm breeding records from Loch Gelly (1883), where by 1935 there were 'enormous numbers'. For North Fife, Harvie-Brown said that it was first found breeding on Lindores Loch in 1896, after which it increased enormously (FT:241). The spread of the Tufted Duck through Fife was traced in detail by Baxter and Rintoul in the *Vertebrate Fauna of Forth* (1935), and other places where it bred before the turn of the century were Loch Fitty, Otterston, Cullaloe, Balhousie and Carlhurlie reservoirs. On Kilconquhar in 1905 it outnumbered all other duck put together, but 'now (1935) there are comparatively few' (VFF:230). Big numbers have, however, been back to Kilconquhar since, and though the peak numbers of the 1960s and early 1970s are not reached now, the population of Tufted Duck seems to be in a very healthy state.

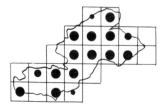 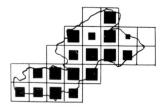

Scaup *Aythya marila*

Winter visitor

This duck winters locally in substantial numbers off the coast of Fife, but tremendous changes are taking place in its distribution, and there are only two places where it may be seen now in any numbers: Largo Bay and St Andrews Bay. Even here, it seems to be decreasing rapidly.

It is interesting to note how the Scaup has changed its points of concentration several times this century: Millais (1901) considered the Tay and Eden estuaries the best places in Britain for wintering Scaup, saying that those in the Tay were all adult birds, whereas the immatures gathered in the Eden estuary and further south. By 1939, however, Dr John Berry observed that a great reduction in numbers in these areas had taken place since 1924 (WG+WDS). The Scaup has now completely deserted the Tay for the Firth of Forth, but it may still be seen in St Andrews Bay (700 on 6 January 1979, and 130 on 30 January 1984, compared with 2,000 seen here on 8 January 1966), representing one of the last two major flocks in Fife. Baxter and Rintoul (1935) also stated that although the Scaup did not occur off Fife in such large numbers as along the south side of the Firth of Forth, it was nevertheless considered common in winter off Burntisland, and it also occurred off Aberdour, Torryburn and Culross, but that only occasionally were there flocks in Largo Bay: '... it is not by any means a regular winter visitor there' (VFF:228). In the 1960s it was Largo Bay that without doubt became the greatest concentration point for Scaup in Fife, and it has remained so since.

The Scaup feeds largely on small creatures which in turn feed on sewage, and it is believed that the general clean-up of our coastal sewage system has affected the Scaup's population drastically. Thus the entry for Scaup in the *Wildfowl and Wader Counts* (1979-80) mentions that although the vast numbers off Leith and Seafield—which peaked at 25,000 in the late 1960s—were reduced to less than a thousand in 1979, 'the numbers on the north side of the Firth of Forth at Largo Bay have increased only marginally during the period of decline on the south side'.

Maximum counts in Largo Bay off Leven and Methil have recently been 2,650 on 26 December 1981, 2,680 on 14 January 1982, but only 1,400 there on 19 January 1984 (WT Counts). Burntisland had a good concentration in the late 1960s and early 1970s but this has declined since. A small flock has been coming regularly to Anstruther these last few years (24 on December 1981, only 8 in 1982, but 29 on 28 February 1985), Scaup being present here from the middle of January till April.

Occasionally the Scaup is seen inland. It was apparently frequently on Morton Lochs in the early 1900s, when W. Berry saw 30 there on 18 October 1913 (BNF:24), but is not seen there now. Since the 1960s it has, however, been seen on Carriston and Cameron reservoirs, Kinghorn Loch (22 on 12 October 1980) and Kilconquhar Loch. Here there was an unusually large number of 250 on 17 March 1971. That year vast numbers had also been recorded on the sea at Methil in Largo Bay (3,000 on 23 January) and at Burntisland.

The Firth of Forth has been supporting the main population of Scaup in the British Isles as a whole for decades now, and before that the Tay and Eden estuaries, and it would be very sad if this fine duck disappeared altogether from the area.

Eider   *Somateria mollissima*

Resident and winters in large numbers

This duck occurs in greater numbers than any other species around the coast of Fife, and may be seen at any time from Tayport to Torryburn, though it gets rarer as one goes up the estuaries.

It breeds regularly in several places, and in an article on the 'Breeding Eiders in the Tay Region' (SB8:159-176) as many as

1,500-1,800 pairs were reckoned to nest during the early 1970s in the area of Tentsmuir-St Andrews, with a few more from Kinkell to Fife Ness. Since then the numbers have dropped again, and the breeding population of the 1980s is more like what it used to be earlier in the century: 80 pairs were believed to nest on Scotscraig in 1924, but stopped breeding there when the Forestry Commission took over, as the small-meshed rabbit fencing did not allow ducklings to get through to reach the beach. Grierson (1962), however, thought that 50 to 60 pairs were nesting annually on Earlshall Moor and others at Shelly Point. Other breeding areas used to be the links between Largo and Elie (VFF:235), but the Eider seems to have deserted that too for the Isle of May. Some birds probably still breed at Kincraig.

The Eider does not start breeding till it is several years old, and then only the female attends the nest and looks after the brood. Males and non-breeding birds may then flock at sea, eg. there were 6,000 off Tentsmuir on 5 June 1984, and a staggering 11,000 in Largo Bay on 24 May 1972, but this was a particularly good year for Eider with 1,000 ducklings counted off Tentsmuir on 25 June the same year.

In autumn and winter, truly vast flocks gather, especially at the mouth of the Tay: 15,000 Eider were seen here on 5 November 1983, and that was not unusual. Grierson (1962) gave a very good description of such a flock there '. . . which defies counting. In places it was nearly fifty birds deep and it stretched for a mile and a half, upwards of 20,000 birds must have been present' (SB2:135). Interested readers should also consult B. Pounders, 'Wintering Eiders in the Tay estuary' (SB6:407-419). Ringing records have shown that many of the Eiders, which spend the winter here, breed in the Netherlands: thus a chick ringed in July 1964 at Vlieland was recovered in March 1975 at Tayport, and another chick ringed at Terschelling was recovered on 23 December the same year at St Andrews (R&M).

The Eider is a thoroughly maritime duck and is very rarely seen on inland waters. It has occurred on Morton Lochs, when the Swan mussel *(Anodonta cygnea)* used to grow here, but it has not been back for many years.

Oiling has been a big problem in the past, as this species seems particulary hard hit, eg. in early March 1968 1,127 birds were collected, hit by Tay oil (SB5:189-196); and again in January 1970, when 2,112 were found dead or dying on the east-coast beaches, hit by North Sea oiling (SB6:235-250).

The Eider has obviously increased vastly since records were first written up. Sibbald in the *History of Fife and Kinross* (1710) mentioned that the 'Duntur haunts the May . . . I have not yet got a description of it'—so he could never have seen one, and it was probably uncommon, though Sibbald was undoubtedly more a collector of information than a naturalist working in the field himself. It is interesting that the Eider is still called the Duntur in Shetland.

It was not mentioned in any of the statistical accounts, and Harvie-Brown (1906) reported that since 'a share of special protection has been accorded to them—along with other species—there has been a distinct increase . . .' He was thinking especially of Tentsmuir, which on the excellent advice of W. Berry of Tayfield had been turned into an early nature reserve in 1896 by the then Secretary of State for Scotland (see also the Introduction).

Today, in spite of some apparent decrease in numbers breeding on mainland Fife, there is no doubt that the population of Eider is in a very healthy state.

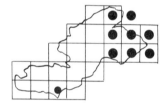 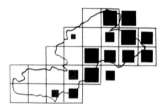

King Eider   *Somateria spectabilis*

Casual winter visitor

One male bird of this species spent several winters in the Firth of Forth off Culross from 1974 to 1977, where many observers had excellent views, but otherwise the King Eider appears to have become much rarer here. Robert Walker said that he had seen 6-7 in St Andrews Bay on 6 March 1872, which stayed around till April that year, and they had occurred in the Tay in the same month (Scot.Nat.1873:49). Harvie-Brown (1906) called it rare and an occasional visitor to the mouth of Tay, especially in severe winters, and that 'large numbers' were seen in 1879-80, when several were 'obtained'. They were seen most frequently on the Tay, off the Eden estuary and in St Andrews Bay (FT:247). Indeed Dr John Berry (1939) did not consider it as being very uncommon in the Tay estuary. In the period 1925-1935 he recorded the species on 5 occasions off Abertay Sands, and 5 were seen at Tentsmuir Point on 29 December 1927 alone (WD+WGS). There have been no records from this area in the last thirty years.

Long-tailed Duck *Clangula hyemalis*

Winter visitor in varying numbers

This duck usually arrives about the middle of September—but has been recorded as early as 16 August, when 2 were seen at Fife Ness in 1970—to flock around the coast of Fife from Tayport in the north-east to Pettycur in the south, and it has been seen as far west as Longannet. It leaves again in late April and May. Maximum numbers recently have been recorded from Kinshaldy (600 on 23 October 1982), and Leven (550 on 11 March 1984), but good numbers are also reported from St Andrews, Methil and Pettycur.

Millais (1913) found it common in the Tay estuary, and Dr John Berry (1939) considered it extremely abundant in winter (flocks of 2000). Baxter and Rintoul observed that the Long-tail was an 'abundant passage migrant' and could be seen in October passing southwards in flocks for 'hours at a stretch' at Fife Ness (B of S.423). Elsewhere they also mentioned that it occasionally occurred in Largo Bay in considerable numbers, 'but they are not regular winter visitors there' (VFF:232). Now Largo Bay, especially off Leven, is one of the best places to see large numbers of this duck in Fife.

Occasionally the Long-tailed Duck occurs inland, and there are several records from Kilconquhar Loch and Lindores Loch, where birds have stayed for several months at a stretch; and also from Morton Lochs, and from Carriston reservoir.

Published records suggest that the Long-tailed Duck has become much less common in the second half of this century.

Common Scoter *Melanitta nigra*

Winter visitor, and locally common throughout the year

This Scoter occurs around the coast of Fife from the mouth of the Tay right along to Kincardine, but only locally in large numbers, and though it is much more abundant in autumn, winter and spring, it also occurs in summer (a fact which was observed by Dr Berry as early as 1927); thus 350 were seen in St Andrews Bay on 17 June 1983. Maximum numbers in 1984 were reached in St Andrews Bay with 1,500 on 2 April and 2,270 on 23 November; whereas there were 1,700 at Tentsmuir on 18 December 1982, with 1,500 there on 27 August 1978. Other good places to see the Common Scoter are Methil (1,900 on 27 March 1983), and Shell Bay (600 on 12 December the same year).

Occasionally the Common Scoter is seen on inland lochs: there was a duck on Kilconquhar on 11 April 1964, and 2 drakes there on 2 February 1982.

Numbers of this duck seem to have levelled off at a rather lower plateau than the peaks reached in 1966 (c.6,000 in St Andrews Bay on 8 January that year), and they appear fairly stable.

Harvie-Brown (1906) said that it was 'Common in large flocks, especially in St Andrews Bay, the mouth of the Eden, and off the Tay . . .' (FT:248), and so it remains today.

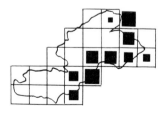

Surf Scoter   *Melanitta perspicillata*

Rare vagrant

The last few years have seen a remarkable number of this otherwise rare American species: only 11 birds have so far been reported for Fife, and 6 out of these have been seen in the last 5 years. The records are as follows:

1 female St Andrews Bay 16.2.85
1 (imm) male St Andrews Bay 9.12.84-31.1.85
1 pair St Andrews Bay 4.3.-5.4.84
1 male Largo Bay 25.4-2.5.81
1 male Pathhead 17-18.2.80
1 male St Andrews Bay 14-18.12.75
1 male off Tentsmuir 2.10.66
1 Eden estuary 30.5.55
1 male Largo Bay 17.1.46 (B of S:441)
1 off Edenmouth early Jan. 1928 (SB2:135)

The Surf Scoter was not mentioned by Harvie-Brown or any other of the earliest writers.

Velvet Scoter   *Melanitta fusca*

Winter visitor, locally common

As the names suggests, the Velvet Scoter is much less common than the Common Scoter, and numbers of wintering birds around the coast of Fife seem to vary from year to year, sometimes even from week to week—far more so than the Common Scoter. This may be due to the fact that the Velvet Scoter is even more maritime and often stays further out at sea—and thus out of sight—than its cousin. Peak counts are usually in St Andrews Bay (450 on 17 March and 12 December 1984); at Largo Bay (1,500 on 16 February 1972); and there were 450 in Shell Bay as late as 9 May 1981. Occasionally the Velvet Scoter is seen in the Firth of Forth as far up as Inverkeithing (30 October 1983) and Longannet (1961).

This duck has never been recorded inland in Fife, but a few individuals remain off the coast in summer: eg. 3 were seen off the East

Shore at Tentsmuir on 26 June 1966; and there were 6 in Shell Bay on 19 May 1985. There is also a mysterious record of 900 going north at Fife Ness on 16 August 1970. Could these possibly have been a very early return of migrants?

The Velvet Scoter was mentioned by Baxter and Rintoul (1935) as having been common in the Firth of Forth up to Kincardine in 1867 and 1885, though not as common as the 'Black' or Common Scoter. There was also an exceptional occurrence on 6 June 1906, when they saw 'enormous flocks of Velvet Scoter in Largo Bay, and others further out as far as the eye would reach up and down the Firth' (VFF:238). For North Fife, Harvie-Brown (1906) said that 'I have seen large flocks frequenting St Andrews Bay, and off the mouth of the Eden, and have heard of them often remaining there all summer . . .', and he quoted Millais as relating that 'During a westerly gale in February 1885 a large number of Velvet Scoters entered the Eden estuary for shelter. By building a shelter and trench of sand, I secured as many specimens as I wanted in an hour. They are very tough birds to kill' (FT:249).

Available records point to a decline in wintering numbers, certainly since the early 1970s.

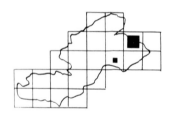

Goldeneye　　　　　　　　　　　　　　　　*Bucephala clangula*

Common in winter

The Goldeneye is widely dispersed and common in Fife in winter. It may be seen, usually in small parties, anywhere along the coast from Newburgh to Kincardine and on many lochs and reservoirs inland. This duck arrives fairly late—in the second half of October and November—while a few may come earlier: a female at Lochore Meadows on 9 September 1981 is the earliest date in recent years. It does not leave again till late April or May. An aerial count in 1981 reported 450 from the Tay to Kirkcaldy on 27 November, and there were 260 in St Andrews Bay alone on 14 November 1976, but big flocks on the sea do not usually build up till later in the season, when eg. 1,000 were seen at Methil on 9 March 1980, 800 at Pathhead on 11 January 1979, and 475 off Kirkcaldy on 9 February 1983. Ballantyne (1982) speaks of up to 2,000 off Pathhead without giving dates.

In spring large flocks are often recorded inland, where the Goldeneyes assemble before leaving for the nesting grounds. The favourite loch then is undoubtedly Kilconquhar, where there were 350 on 29 March 1984, but 1,030 on 9 April 1972. Other places which attract large numbers are Raith Loch (250 on 20 December 1979), and Loch Gelly.

By the middle of May most birds have left the area, but a few stay behind to spend the summer here. Baxter and Rintoul already mentioned this to be the case in 1935, and said they were hopeful that 'it will, ere long, be found nesting' (VFF:235). This was 50 years ago, and although there are summering records from almost every year in the last 30 years, no nesting has so far been proved in Fife.

Harvie-Brown (1906) considered the Goldeneye a common winter visitor then, and although the numbers of Goldeneye seem nationally to be declining (WWC 1983-84), the wintering population in Fife appears fairly stable, at least in the last fifteen years.

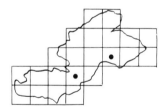 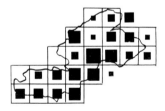

Smew   *Mergus albellus*

Fairly regular winter visitor in small numbers

This beautiful duck is not common in Fife, though there are records for most years. It may occur in any month between October and the middle of April, but most records fall between the middle of November and March. It has twice occurred in June: one was at Kilconquhar Loch on 26 June 1966, and another on Cameron reservoir from 15-18 June 1968, Red-heads in both cases. The biggest number ever recorded in the area was a sensational 20 on Kilconquhar Loch on 16 December 1961 (by Thomas Speed), where they had been building up since 19 November (WT counts). That year was apparently particularly good for Smew elsewhere in Britain. A pair was reported from Kirkcaldy 1-31 December 1973, with 3 there the next year on 19 March 1974, but most sightings are of single birds, with the most frequent records (10 or more) coming from Cameron reservoir and Kilconquhar Loch. Other inland waters, where it has occurred, are Morton Lochs, Lindores Loch, Stenhouse, Carriston and Holl reservoirs, Loch Fitty, Beveridge Pond (Kirkcaldy), and Peppermill Dam, though mostly only once. The sea records are almost as numerous: Tentsmuir (1 dead, March 1968), Eden estuary, St Andrews, Methil, Kirkcaldy, Pathhead, Cult Ness and Longannet, again mostly one record only for each locality.

Harvie-Brown (1906) put the Smew as an 'occasional winter visitor, usually only in very severe winters' (FT:256), and there is no apparent change of numbers in Fife in the last 20 years.

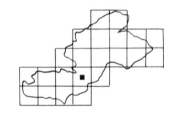

Red-breasted Merganser   *Mergus serrator*

Locally common throughout the year, but does not breed

The Red-breasted Merganser occurs anywhere along the coast of Fife—though it is scarce west of the Tay railway bridge—in singles, pairs or small parties, and it has been recorded in every month of the year. Big parties may also occur locally at any time: thus there were 250 off Tentsmuir as early as 3 July 1983, 510 on 18 August 1984, 560 there on 22 September 1983, and 1,000 on 11 October 1980. The numbers here generally drop somewhat in winter and early spring, when the Merganser possibly seeks more sheltered waters, and big parties may be seen elsewhere during this time, eg. 135 at Newport on 11 December 1983, and in the Firth of Forth at Largo Bay, Pettycur (159 on 8 April 1984), Burntisland and Aberdour. As late as 28 June 1934, Baxter and Rintoul saw a 'fair-sized party' off the Cockle Burn in Largo Bay (VFF:240).

The Merganser is very rarely seen inland. Grierson mentioned that it used to come to Morton Lochs when these were stocked with fish, and there were 2 here on 12 March 1977. The Wildfowl Trust counts also give records of the Merganser from Townloch (Dunfermline) and Loch Glow.

There is no sign of any change in status.

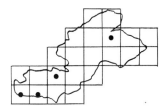 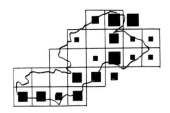

Goosander *Mergus merganser*

Winter visitor in small numbers

The Goosander occurs in the area on both salt and fresh water, but rarely in any great numbers. Unlike the Red-breasted Merganser it does not usually occur here in summer, the earliest date in recent years being one at Boarhills on 28 August 1985, and the latest 5 flying south over East Lomond on 1 May 1983.

One of the best places to see them is the Tay, up as far as Flisk, but especially at Newport, where there were 150 in early April 1970 and 50 on 23 January 1983. By far the greatest numbers reported in the last 30 years were an astonishing 1,000 at Tayport on 23 January 1973, with 800+ there on 5 December the same year, seen by two different observers (SB8:227), which, judging from the numbers in the *Wildfowl and Wader Counts,* would represent almost a third of the entire British population.

Inland, the Goosander seemed to favour Morton Lochs for six or seven years: 3 females were seen here on 27 November 1965, with numbers increasing yearly to 30 on 16 March 1969, peaking at 60 the following year about the same date, before falling to 41 on 17 February 1974, and they have stopped coming since 1976. Recent maximum numbers inland are from Ballo reservoir (20 on 29 February 1984), with reports also from Lindores Loch, Craigluscar and Cameron reservoirs.

The Goosander was mentioned by Sibbald in the *History of Fife and Kinross* (1710), and Harvie-Brown (1906) quoted Millais about the Tay River as saying that the Goosander was 'A variable visitor to the district in winter and spring. Sometimes the Tay and Loch Leven (Kinross) are full of Goosanders, and in another year not one is to be seen' (FT:254). For South Fife, Dalgleish (1885) reported it common in winter about Kincardine, and whereas the Goosander is no longer common in West Fife, there appears to be little or no recent change in status of this species.

Ruddy Duck   *Oxyura jamaicensis*

Occasional visitor

This American species was introduced in Somerset and the West Midlands earlier this century, and it has become very successful, continuing to increase and spread. There is now a small breeding population as far north as Angus.

The first record for Fife came from Kilconquhar Loch, where one was seen on 20 June 1965 which stayed to the end of July (SB3:422), and the Wildfowl Trust counts reported one here (possibly the same bird) from mid-September to mid-November that year. Another drake was seen here on 4 September 1967, and was still about on 12 November that year. In 1984 there were 2 on Loch Gelly 22-28 August, and in 1985 there were reports of several sightings in Fife, including a bird seen on many occasions at Kilconquhar between mid-May and mid-September.

Honey Buzzard *Pernis apivorus*

Rare vagrant

The most recent record of this rare species is a bird seen by Keith Brockie on the East Shore of the Eden on 4 October 1981. One other certain record is that of a pair present near Newport for some months from April 1949. The female, sadly, was shot on 23 July and sent to the Royal Scottish Museum (SB:142 and BB50:142). This was claimed to be the first definite record for Fife, but in the *Vertebrate Fauna of Forth* (1935) another earlier record is mentioned of a bird at Largo on 21 May 1906 (VFF:188), and Dalgleish (1885) had two records of birds shot at Tulliallan, the last one in 1883.

Red Kite *Milvus milvus*

Very rare vagrant

There have been two recent reports of this spectacular bird of prey: one being a bird seen on 4 December 1985 between Boarhills and St Andrews; while another was seen at Buckhaven on 6 January 1982. Before that there had been no records for one hundred and fifty years, when one was shot at Cambo about 1844 (B of S:316), while in *The New Statistical Account* kites were said to occur at Inverkeithing (1836). Kites were mentioned by Dr Harvie-Brown (1906) to have been formerly very abundant, but he also said that many old reports were very confused due to the fact that the most frequently used term for Kite was 'Gled', a term unfortunately also used for Buzzard (FT:195).

One might speculate that 'Gladgate' in Auchtermuchty was so named because 'gleds' were once commonly seen here. In this case it would be likely to refer to Kites, which are scavengers, rather than Buzzards, as Buzzards never come close to towns in the same way.

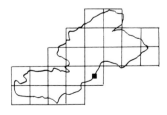

White-tailed Eagle *Haliaeetus albicilla*

There is only one record of the White-tailed Eagle, also called the 'Sea Eagle'. This was a 'very fine female', immature, shot at Kinkell on 29 December 1866 after two days of stormy weather. Geo. Bruce, in the *Land Birds in and about St Andrews,* 1895, related a horrific tale of how this bird was at first only winged, and how it was finally 'squeezed to death' through the efforts of no less than four men, a cloak and a leather strap. Bruce also said that before being stuffed the bird was publicly exhibited in the Town Hall, St Andrews as a great rarity by the bird stuffer—against an entrance fee of sixpence—and was later bought for the College Museum (LStA:72). The record is also included in Robert Walker's list (Scot.Nat.1871:81). Henry Boase mentioned that Baxter and Rintoul regarded the record as doubtful (BNF:45); but Harvie-Brown accepted it, having found the record included in Mr W. Berwick's lists, and also the White-tailed Eagle included in a list of specimens in the said museum in St Andrews (FT:191). There is certainly still a fine stuffed White-tailed Eagle in the Bell-Pettigrew Museum, St Andrews, today.

Marsh Harrier *Circus aeruginosus*

Rare vagrant

In the last twenty years there have been seven records only of this harrier: a female was seen at Lochore on 11 May 1983, and another at East Lomond on 15 May that year. Up to two females were at Morton Lochs 15-24 May 1982, and a male there 15-18 May 1981; a female was at Fife Ness on 5 October 1982, another at Rosyth 6-15 August 1978, and another female was seen at Strathmiglo on 12 May 1973.

Further back one was at Morton Lochs on 8 November 1958, and 2 were seen a few times at Earlshall during the winter 1951-52, a pair having been present here the previous winter. In 1937 there was a report of a pair seen several times at Tentsmuir in the summer and a rather unsatisfactory claim that they may have bred here that year (see SB2:142). There was also a record of a single bird at Earlshall on 29 October 1937.

Harvie-Brown regarded it as rare, and had no specific records for North Fife.

Hen Harrier   *Circus cyaneus*

Regular winter visitor and passage migrant in small numbers

This fine hawk, after a period in which it became very scarce, appears to
be once more on the increase. In the 1980s it has been reported from
several localities in the autumn and winter, especially in East Fife. It
appears annually in the Tentsmuir area, where one at Morton Lochs
from December 1980 until 2 April 1981 bore a wing-tag which
identified it as an Orkney breeding bird. Other recent records have
come from Kinkell, Dunino, Cambo, Randerston, Fife Ness, Crail and
Kilrenny, as well as from East Lomond and Lochore Meadows: almost
all fall between mid-September and early April, with a concentration in
October, but one was seen over the Clune (Lochore) on 28 June 1981.

Further back in the 1960s and 1970s there were one or two reported
sightings most years of individuals—eg. at Tentsmuir, Morton Lochs,
Fife Ness, Dumbarnie Links at Largo, Carriston and Peppermill.

Baxter and Rintoul (1935) regarded it as an occasional straggler, and
could only cite records near Largo and Balcarres within the present
century. Even Grierson, as late as 1962, knew of only 3 records at
Tentsmuir in the previous 13 years (SB2:142), and further back
Harvie-Brown (1906) called it 'exceedingly rare, if not quite extinct',
and knew of only 3 records since 1840, quoting W. Berwick's verdict:
'used to breed in Fife, but now very rare'.

The recent improvement in its status is undoubtedly related to its
renewed spread as a breeding bird in Scotland within the last forty
years, following a reduction in persecution from gamekeepers, and in
recent years it has been suspected of breeding in Fife.

There is an interesting record of a bird ringed as a chick on the Isle of
Bute on 1 July 1982, which was found dead near Cupar on 8 February
1983 (R&M).

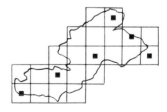

Goshawk　　　　　　　　　　　　　　　　　　*Accipiter gentilis*

Rare visitor

There are very few records of this species in Fife. In 1984 one was seen at Lochore Meadows on 15 January, and 2 at other sites in August; in 1983 a male was seen at Fife Ness on 1 May, and a female at Cameron reservoir on 30 October; in 1982 there were singles at Morton Lochs on 1 May, at Falkland on 25 August and at Gateside on 1 November; a female was at Balcomie on 4 October 1981; a male was found shot at St Andrews on 3 December 1977; and one was reported near Cupar in late August-early September 1975. There appear to be no records for the 1960s.

The Goshawk has always been rare in the area. Harvie-Brown (1906) mentioned only two records: one killed in Kemback wood in 1842, and another—an adult female—obtained at Elie in 1877 (FT:193). Geo. Bruce (1895), in connection with the 1842 bird, said that this had been seen for some weeks flying about Kemback wood in the spring of that year, when it was shot at by a number of people and finally winged. It was then kept in a parrot's cage for several weeks, where its fine plumage deteriorated so much for want of space that the man who shot it gave it away! (LStA:91).

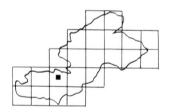

Sparrowhawk   *Accipiter nisus*

Fairly common resident

The Sparrowhawk is much less common than the Kestrel, but it may be seen in most parts of Fife and, in 1983, 5 pairs were reported on the Lomond Hills. After a period of almost total decline, this hawk has been making a comeback since the 1970s and is now reported as breeding in a number of places.

It was mentioned in the *New Statistical Account* of Inverkeithing (1837), and Geo. Bruce (1895) thought it 'so well known, not just about St Andrews, but every wooded district in Scotland, and by every nest-hunting schoolboy, as to need little comment . . ." (LStA:95). Earlier this century W. Berry still thought it common and breeding in North Fife 'though rarely allowed to do so', whereas Boase by 1964 found it scarce (BNF:45). It seems, however, that it was insecticide that nearly exterminated this species in the 1960s, and the banning of DDT especially helped it and similarly hard-hit species to recover their numbers.

Some passage obviously occurs: in the 'Check-list' (SB2:141) Grierson mentioned that the Sparrowhawk was seen yearly at the Eden on passage, and Baxter and Rintoul too said it was much commoner in autumn in East Fife than at any other season (VFF:185).

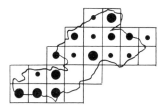

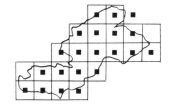

Buzzard   *Buteo buteo*

Scarce but regular visitor

Like all the big raptors the Buzzard is not seen often enough in Fife. Usually only a few birds are recorded each year, and then generally in the autumn and winter, but there are a few spring records too. One individual was seen at Kelty in 1981 as late as 19 June, and another was at Kirkforthar on 17 June 1982, but these are unusual.

In 1984 the first of the autumn sightings was a Buzzard at Kippo on 10 August, and there were other reports from Strathkinness, the Peat Inn area and Kilmany. There were also two spring records: one from Lochore Meadows in March and another from Scotscraig in April.

1982 produced an unusually large number of birds—15 in all—with an exceptional party of 5 soaring above Kirkcaldy on 3 February. Other records in the last ten years have come from New Flisk, Gauldry, Tentsmuir, Morton Lochs, the Eden estuary, St Andrews, Dunino, Kingsbarns, Fife Ness, Kilconquhar, Leven, Wemyss Wood, Lochore, Pitcairn and Culross. In the 1960s and early 1970s there were records from Lindores Loch, Bow of Fife, Morton Lochs, Earlshall, Kingsbarns, St Monance, Arncroach, Kirkcaldy, West Lomond and Tulliallan.

It is difficult to say whether the above records show that it is the Buzzard or the birdwatcher that is getting commoner in Fife, for when a plea was made in *Scottish Birds* (3:199) about the paucity of Buzzard records for Fife, more records materialised within a short time (SB3:320).

Henry Boase (1964) said that the Buzzard had apparently bred in Fife in the 1930s, but there is no mention of where (BNF:44). There have been no records of nesting since.

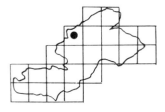 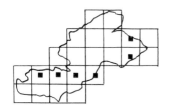

Rough-legged Buzzard   *Buteo lagopus*

Very rare visitor

There are only a very few dated records of this species: 2 birds were at Tentsmuir from 10 December 1972, and one was there on 7 February 1973; while much further back, in 1913, a single bird was seen over Scotscraig in winter (SB2:141). One was in the Glenrothes area in 1955 (Ballantyne, 1982), and Balfour Kirke saw 3 together on Dunearn Hill, Burntisland in autumn 1907. Harvie-Brown said that there were 'Rough-legged Buzzard years', as eg. in 1856 and in 1875, when many birds of this species were shot in the east of Scotland, including one at Largo. Other years of influx were 1894 and 1903-04, when he traced a definite flight path of birds reaching the Scottish coast and turning south: one branch, he thought, passed via Fife along the south side of the Ochils, whereas the main stream, on reaching Fife Ness, turned south (FT:182). Such exciting invasions seem no longer to occur.

Golden Eagle   *Aquila chrysaetos*

Very rare visitor

There are no recent records. The most recent ones are all from the 1950s, when three sightings were made, the second one being less certain, but I will give them all the same: a Golden Eagle was seen being mobbed by a Buzzard over Brucefield—10 miles west of Dunfermline—on 25 May 1958 (EBB8:83); the second report is of an eagle seen by the coastguards at Fife Ness at close quarters (300 yards with binoculars) on 21 May 1956. Chris Mylne commented at the time that it was probably a Golden Eagle, but that the possibility of an immature White-tailed Eagle could not be ruled out (EBB6:60); while an adult bird spent the winter of 1952-53 at Earlshall and was also seen at Morton Lochs (EBB3:26, 40). Further back a Golden Eagle was seen north of Crail on 19 March 1939 (BNF:44).

    In the *Vertebrate Fauna of Forth* (1935) the Golden Eagle is mentioned as having occurred in South Fife, but no details are given. In *Land Birds in and around St Andrews* (1895), however, Geo. Bruce recollects seeing about 1840 'a large bird soaring above Stravithie wood and Prior Moor, all woods and moorland wilds then, which was set down by myself and others as a Golden Eagle . . . about 30 years ago [1860s] 2 were seen in the vicinity of Mount Melville and Drumcarrow Craig. Several people tried to shoot them, but could not get within range, and from observations noted at the time they were a pair of Golden Eagles' (LBStA:53). Credence is given to this account as Mr W. Berwick told Harvie-Brown that one was observed at Stravithie, and two were near Mount Melville 'a good many years ago' (FT:188).

Osprey *Pandion haliaetus*

Scarce passage migrant

There are one or two records of Ospreys on passage most years. In 1984 one was seen at Longannet in late April and another over West Lomond on 19 August. The year before, there were similar records also from the Lomond area and Lochore, while there were 3 sightings in 1982: one at the Eden estuary on 10 May, one at Lochore Meadows on 20 May, and an autumn bird (an immature) at Falkland on 17 September. Other records—few as they are—come from Tentsmuir (1980, 1978 and 1970), St Andrews (1971), Strathmiglo (1979), Fife Ness (1976 and 1971), Kilconquhar (1968 and 1966), Anstruther (1965), Tulliallan (1960) and Peppermill Dam (1960). The earliest date is 8 March (the bird at Strathmiglo) and the latest 17 September (the one at Falkland), with most records falling in May and August.

The Osprey was mentioned in the *New Statistical Account* of Abdie (1836), where it was said to sometimes frequent the banks of Lindores Loch, and Dalgleish (1885) said it occasionally visited Tulliallan Loch. Around the turn of the century it was much reduced in numbers throughout Scotland, a fact much lamented by Harvie-Brown. It died out totally about 1912, but recolonised Scotland in the 1950s, but was apparently not seen on passage in Fife till 1960.

Kestrel *Falco tinnunculus*

Common resident, and migrant visitor

This is without doubt our commonest bird of prey, and it may be seen regularly in all parts of Fife, where it also breeds in many places. In 1983 there were 6 pairs on the Lomond Hills alone.

Grierson (1962) reported it as seen in all parts of Tentsmuir, and Boase (1964) observed that it was a common resident throughout North Fife, though he thought it was becoming rarer. This decline has fortunately halted, and it is now common again in most places.

In autumn and winter migrant birds move in. There are many records of Kestrel arriving at Fife Ness, eg. 20 between Fife Ness and Crail after east winds on 6 October 1968, 14 recorded there in mid-September 1969, 6 there on 6 October 1975, and one was seen actually flying in from the sea—exhausted—on 5 October 1983. There is also an interesting record of a dead Kestrel found at Tayport in late September 1956 which bore a Swedish ring (BNF:47), and Grierson (1962) reported birds seen on passage, mostly in autumn, at Tentsmuir and Shelly points (SB2:143).

These notes of migrant birds are very interesting: numbers of Kestrel seen in winter do not appear to increase, so do our breeding birds move out?

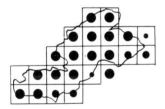 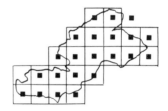

Red-footed Falcon   *Falco vespertinus*

Very rare vagrant

There are no recent records of this species, but in 1941 a male was seen in the Newport area by several observers from 21 November onwards. It stayed for about a month (SB2:142). Much further back a three or four months old female was shot at Kinghorn on 20 September 1880 (B of S:295).

Merlin   *Falco columbarius*

Regular winter visitor and passage migrant

This little falcon is seen quite regularly in Fife. Migrants arrive in August: there were eg. 2 at Fife Ness on 23 August 1980, and birds leave again in February and March, though a few may stay till later, such as a bird recorded at the Eden estuary on 27 June 1981.

The Merlin has been observed in many parts of Fife, especially along the coast from Newburgh in the north-west to Valleyfield in the south-west (19 out of the 23 sightings in 1984 were in coastal areas), but it also occurs inland on the Lomond Hills, Lochore Meadows, Pitcairn and Star of Markinch. A favourite haunt of the Merlin is undoubtedly the St Andrews-Eden estuary area, where it has been recorded on many occasions, and another is Fife Ness to Crail.

In the late 1960s and early 1970s, the Merlin appeared to be decreasing sharply in numbers, but it has made a good recovery recently.

Harvie-Brown (1906) did not think it very common in North Fife, though Baxter and Rintoul (1935) considered it not uncommon in South Fife in autumn and winter. Dalgleish (1885) mentioned that a nest with young had been found a few years earlier on the Lochshaw Moss, West Grange. There have been no breeding records this century for Fife.

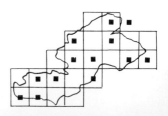

Hobby   *Falco subbuteo*

Scarce passage migrant

This is not a common bird in Fife, but there have probably been more
sightings in recent years than there used to be in the 1960s and early
1970s. It may occur both on spring and autumn passage. There was
one at Fife Ness in May 1985, and the only record for 1984 was a Hobby
chasing swallows at North Haugh (St Andrews) in late April. Other
recent records are from August and September, when it has been seen
over the Eden estuary, St Andrews, Boarhills, Fife Ness, Anstruther
and Kilconquhar.

   According to all the old records, the Hobby has always been scarce
in Fife.

[Gyr Falcon   *Falco rusticolus*

There are no certain records of this falcon in Fife. A bird seen at Fife
Ness. on 24 June 1984 was probably of this species; and another bird
seen by different observers at Tentsmuir Point on 20 February 1955,
and again the following day at Shelly Point, was thought to be a Gyr
Falcon (SB2:142).]

Peregrine   *Falco peregrinus*

Passage and winter visitor

Considering the constant persecution to which this superb falcon has
long been subjected, it is amazing that any survive at all. However, it is
seen regularly in Fife, mainly from September to March. In 1984
reports came from 15 places, mostly coastal areas, and in 1983 it was
sighted 16 times, compared with 11 sightings in 1982. Places where it
has been seen in the last few years are: Tayport, Scotscraig, Tentsmuir
Point, Morton Lochs, Kinshaldy, the Eden estuary, St Andrews,
Kippo, Wormiston, Fife Ness, Shell Bay, Dumbarnie Links,
Burntisland, Cullaloe and Ballo reservoirs, East Lomond, Peppermill
and Ceres.

   In *Birds of Scotland* (1953) it was mentioned that it used to breed on

D

the cliffs at Kincraig, the Lomonds and Benarty (B of S:286), and elsewhere Baxter and Rintoul recalled that it had bred as late as 1903 on the Isle of May, and that it had been observed carrying its prey over there from Fife (VFF:191). Boase (1964) said that Peregrines had tried to nest on the Tay railway bridge in 1908, and again some years later. He also said that Peregrines were 'usual' in North Fife in the region around the Tay estuary in winter, 'kills being the main evidence' (BNF:46).

In recent years, the Peregrine has bred again in Fife.

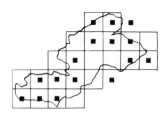

Red Grouse   *Lagopus lagopus*

Resident on the Lomond Hills

The first mention of Red Grouse in Fife is of its being acquired locally for James V's table when he came to Falkland in the 1520s (ExDJV); and in the *New Statistical Account* of Dunino (1837) it is recorded that 'It appears from an old charter that a hundred and fifty years ago, Moorfowl abounded in Kingsmuir (north of Anstruther), but they have been expelled by the progress of agricultural improvements'.

There are no grouse to be found now in the East Neuk, although there are two remarkable records: 2 seen at Largo Bay on 14 April 1976, and one in a hawthorn bush at Boarhills on 4 March 1978—migrating?

The only sizeable area of heather left in Fife is on the Lomond Hills, and here the Red Grouse is fortunately still plentiful, even if this is the only stronghold left. Baxter and Rintoul (1935) thought the Red Grouse was increasing here, and they mentioned that 'the last three years the number shot on Balbirnie has been the largest known. In 1934 the bag consisted of 318 birds' (VFF:345). There are certainly nothing like that number now: 'Small numbers' was the verdict in 1982, and the biggest party in 1984 were 23 on 2 December, which was slightly up on a peak of 18 the year before about the same time.

For south-west Fife, Baxter and Rintoul said that about 1885 a few coveys inhabited Lockshaw Moss north of Culross and Tulliallan, and there were still a good many to be seen here in West Fife in 1935 (VFF:345), but no reports have been received from there in recent years. Red Grouse were also occasionally seen in winter at Burntisland by Mr Balfour Kirk last century.

The Red Grouse was introduced to Tentsmuir in 1876 and shot annually. The highest bag was in 1902 with 64 brace. It has since died out here, the last bird seen on Earlshall being in June 1946 (B of S:725;SB2:143).

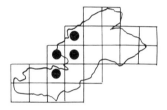 

Black Grouse *Tetrao tetrix*

Scarce resident

The recent reports of a lek in the Cleish Hills were the first for some years. In *Birds of Scotland* (1953) it was mentioned as 'very local' in Fife, and Grierson in the 'Check-list of the Birds of Tentsmuir' stated that the Black Grouse first appeared on Tentsmuir about 1902 and nested there in 1906, but had not done so since 1919. By 1925, according to Boase, they had been exterminated from the new forest here, and thereafter were only very occasionally seen in North Fife (BNF:48). For South and West Fife, Baxter and Rintoul (1935) stated that 'they used to breed on the south side of the East Lomond, but we were told in 1926 that they had ceased to do so, though still nesting at Deveron and Drummie. They also breed about Culross and Tulliallan' (VFF:344).

There had been no reports of breeding from those places for some years, but it now appears that they may not have left the area altogether after all.

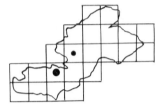

Capercaillie   *Tetrao urogallus*

Scarce resident

A small population has been fairly constant in Tentsmuir in recent years, where Capercaillie have been reported on several occasions, and as late as in 1984. In 1979 there was a maximum number of one male and 7 females, but 5 are more usual. Up till 1970 it was reported in Tentsmuir as 'occasional' only, the sightings being of one or two females, but in 1972 the first male was seen. Capercaillie were probably breeding here at the end of last century: several individuals were reported in the 1890s, and one was shot at Scotscraig in 1901 (SB2:143). There was also a record of a male Caper seen at Lathockar in East Fife in 1874 or 1875 (VFF:431).

The Capercaillie was reintroduced from Sweden at Taymouth in Perthshire in 1837 (FT:282), after having become extinct in Scotland in 1760, and it has since been reasonably successful. Dr Ian Pennie mentioned, in an interesting article in *The Scottish Naturalist* (1951) on the history and distribution of the Capercaillie in Scotland that W. Berry had actually seen a cock Caper fly across the Tay at a great height and settle on the south side of the firth, but no date is given (Scot.Nat.63:4); only one hen was seen on Tentsmuir between 1922 and 1951.

The Capercaillie was also reintroduced at Tulliallan estate in 1864 (VFF:431), and this area subsequently became a stronghold for the species: 33 birds were shot in the season 1913-14. In the years 1935-40, 12 nests here were the usual, but during the war the birds appear to have been illegally removed, and the population by 1951 was down to

3 males and 8-9 females. Devilla forest, too, had a good population before 1925, when 500 acres of pine were felled, but Capercaillies were still breeding here in small numbers in 1951 (for more detail, see Dr Pennie's article).

In Central Fife, Baxter and Rintoul found single females at Teasses in 1920, 1923 and 1924, and also one at Gilston in 1924, while in 1936 nests were found at Norman Law and Mount Melville near Cupar, but the woods here have since been felled.

Outside Tentsmuir the only published record since 1951 is of a hen Capercaillie at Tulliallan on 3 November 1962 (SB2:315), although the *Breeding Atlas* shows a bird present in the Cupar square, and the *Winter Atlas* another present in the Tulliallan/Devilla forest square.

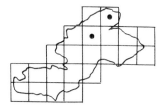 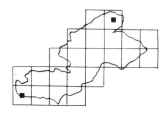

[Chuckar/Red-legged Partridge   *Alectoris rufa*

These are a recent introduction and are mainly hybrids. They are seen regularly at Fife Ness, and there are other records from Kingsbarns, Kellie Law and Kirkcaldy.]

Grey Partridge   *Perdix perdix*

Common resident

The population of the Grey Partridge fluctuates somewhat: 1984 was a
very good year, and larger coveys were seen than had been the case in
recent years: thus 24 were at Lochore Meadows on 15 February, 18 at
Largo Bay on 14 November, and another 18 at Balcaskie in September,
compared with 18 the largest covey recorded in 1983 and 13 the year
before. Low breeding success was generally reported throughout the
1960s, and numbers did not start to increase till 1971 with breeding
numbers 'high' in 1973, only to drop once more about 1975.

Grierson, talking mostly about the 1950s, said that the Partridge was
found in good numbers on all parts of open ground on Tentsmuir, even
on the coastal strips (SB2:143); and Boase (apparently referring to the
1930s) mentioned that up to 300 brace were being shot in North Fife in
good years (BNF:49). Baxter and Rintoul (1935) observed that 'the
improvement in agriculture has been conducive to the well-being of the
Partridge, and the Lothians and Fife are the parts in which it is found in
greatest abundance . . .' (VFF:340).

The earliest mention we have of the Partridge in Fife is in King James
V's Household Book that Partridge was purchased at Falkland Palace
in December 1532. It was also mentioned several times in both the *Old*
and the *New Statistical Account*, and it has obviously been common in
Fife for centuries. It may have become slightly less common during the
last thirty years, but there is no evidence of any real change.

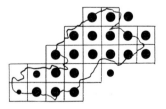

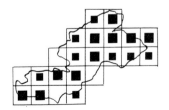

Quail   *Coturnix coturnix*

Scarce visitor

Although never common, the Quail has become positively scarce in recent years. In 1982 there was an exceptional influx with individuals calling at Strathmiglo, Kettlebridge and Guardbridge from July to September, and a brood was seen at Strathmiglo on 17 September, but these were probably tame birds and there have been no records since. Further back, 2 were reported at St Andrews on 4 August 1979; there is a record from Star of Markinch in mid-April 1976, and 1-3 were at Leuchars from 29 June 1972 (SB7:347). There is a lovely description of a Quail hiding under some bushes by St Salvator's Hall in St Andrews on 3 June 1958 (EBB8:111), but Grierson (1962) had no records for Tentsmuir since a Quail was found dead at Leuchars on 6 June 1932 (SB2:143).

Baxter and Rintoul (1935) felt fairly confident that the Quail had nested in Fife last century. They had seen it several times in Fife and mentioned that there were a good many reports of its occurrence there (VFF:341). In the *Old Statistical Account* of St Monance (1793) mention was made of a few Quail there.

The Quail has definitely become rarer this century.

Pheasant   *Phasianus colchicus*

Common resident

The Pheasant was introduced into Scotland in the sixteenth century as game to be shot over. It is now very common everywhere in Fife, where it breeds wild, but no doubt the stock is also augmented by hand-reared birds. They are usually seen in pairs or family parties, but occasionally there are bigger gatherings, such as 18—mostly males—seen near Ceres in June 1983.

There is no change of status.

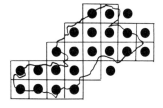 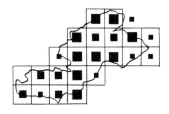

Water Rail   *Rallus aquaticus*

Scarce resident and winter visitor

There are only a few yearly records of the Water Rail, although this
could be partly due to its extremely skulking habits, so that it may be
more common than is suggested by the records. It frequents reedy sides
of lochs and ditches, and comes out only briefly at dawn and dusk. In
1984 single birds were reported from near Tayport on 18 January, at
Lochore Meadows on 23-25 January and again in March; at Cupar at
the end of March, and at Moorloch on 16 April.

   In recent years most records of this species are in autumn and spring
and have been, apart from the above-mentioned places, from Lindores
Loch, the Black Loch, Lochore nature reserve, Morton Lochs and
Kilconquhar Loch. It may have bred at some of these places too.

   On migration, the Water Rail is sometimes found in curious places.
One was for instance hiding—after easterly gales—under the caravans
at Fife Ness on 23 April 1969, and another was seen on dry vegetation
early one morning at Elie Ness on 1 October 1983.

   In the late 1960s and early 1970s the Water Rail was apparently more
numerous in the county, and as many as 7 or 8 birds were found at
Kilconquhar in the winter of 1968 and again in 1971. Baxter and
Rintoul (1953) found the Water Rail mainly a winter visitor, and
described it as less shy when the inland waters were frozen over:
'At such times we have not found it very shy and have often watched it
for quite a long time as it daintily threaded its way through the reeds'
(B of S:707). W. Berry also regarded it as a regular winter visitor to
Tayfield pond in North Fife (BNF:50).

   The Water Rail was mentioned in the *New Statistical Account* as
occurring at Dunfermline (1844).

   There is no evidence of any real change in status, though it has
probably become scarcer.

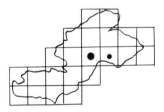
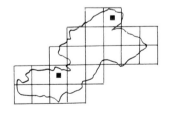

Spotted Crake *Porzana porzana*

Very scarce visitor

There are only two recent reports of this very skulking bird: one was at Moonzie Burn near Guardbridge on 20 March 1985; and one was at the North Loch at Morton on 5 September 1983.

It was mentioned in the *Geographical Distribution and Status of Birds in Scotland* (Baxter and Rintoul, 1928) as an 'occasional passage migrant' to both South Fife and North Fife, but there are no details. Harvie-Brown (1906), however, said that it was 'not really rare, but seldom observed', and put its status as 'regular visitor and an occasional breeder' (FT:287). It could be that it is less rare than recent records suggest, but it has no doubt declined in numbers since Harvie-Brown's days.

[Baillon's Crake *Porzana pusilla*

There is only one—less than a 100% certain—record, and I will quote it *verbatim* from Grierson's 'Check-List': 'On 3 January 1889 a tiny crake was caught at Scotscraig by W. Berry and later released. A detailed description was shown to Dr Eagle Clarke, who reported that the bird was a Baillon's Crake. As the record has never been published, and neither the description nor Dr Eagle Clarke's comments can be traced, it is impossible to be absolutely certain that the bird could not have been a Little Crake' (SB2:143).

According to Dr John Berry, it was his father's insistence that the crake should be released and not killed which unwittingly caused the subsequent uncertainty (Berry pers.com.).]

Corncrake *Crex crex*

Scarce passage migrant

A sad tale of decline. The Corncrake used to be a common summer visitor to all the lower-lying parts of the area: thus it was mentioned in the *New Statistical Account* of Kilmany (1836) that 'The Corncrake's voice is heard during the summer from May to October', and E. S.

Valentine, in *Fifeshire* (1910), has this to say: 'In late spring the summer migrants assemble once more in our land. These are the warblers, the swallows, the cuckoo and the corncrake' (p.44); but in 1935 Baxter and Rintoul noticed that numbers were not what they used to be, although they thought that 'in the last year or two, the birds are becoming more common and we hope that they may return in their former numbers' (VFF:251). Sadly, they have not only failed to do so, but records have become very few and far between: one was heard calling for a few days in late May 1985 at Loch Gelly, but this was the first record in Fife for three years, the previous record being at Fetterdale (Tentsmuir) on 3 September 1982. During the time of the *Breeding Atlas* (1968-72) the Corncrake was reported as 'probably breeding' in 5 squares in Fife and 'present' in another 4 squares. It will be very interesting to see if the next *Breeding Atlas,* planned for 1988-92, will show any present at all.

The Corncrake's dramatic decline is, of course, not just in Fife, but throughout the British Isles, except for the extreme West of Scotland and Ireland, where they are still about. The decline was noted in parts of West Fife by Dalgleish as long ago as 1885, and C. A. Norris, in three articles in *British Birds* (38:142-148, 162-168; 40:226-244), argued that the machine mower, which replaced the cutting by hand of field crops, was to blame for the decline, as it broke the eggs and killed the chicks. Also silage, which involves earlier and more frequent cutting of grass fields, has hastened the decrease, as has the overhead cable,which apparently Corncrakes are unable to see (see ABB:156).

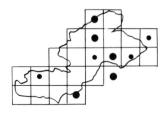

Moorhen   *Gallinula chloropus*

Common resident

This is a common bird throughout the area: during the years of the *Breeding Atlas* the Moorhen was found to nest in every square in Fife

(1968-1972). In winter it often flocks: there were 22 at Rosyth sewage works on 9 October 1982, and 22 on 1 December at Lochore nature reserve in 1981.

In 1962 Grierson observed that numbers of breeding birds at Morton Lochs and Earlshall had fallen over the past fifty years, but also that the winter population had remained the same (SB2:144), and Boase (1964) had a record of 100 Moorhens near Dairsie on 18 February 1914 (BNF:51). It used also to be even more abundant in South Fife in the first few decades of this century: thus Baxter and Rintoul (1935) said that 'during our memory it has increased very much as a breeding bird in South Fife. When we first remember it, it was confined to ponds and lochs and the larger burns. Now we frequently see it far from water and have found its nest twenty feet up in a Douglas fir in a plantation . . .' (VFF:252). This abundance is no longer with us, and the Moorhen is once more confined to the ponds, lochs and burns.

Unlike the Coot it is rarely seen on salt water, even in the hardest of winters.

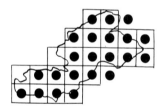 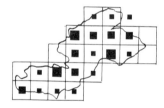

Coot   *Fulica atra*

Common resident

The Coot has been a common breeding bird in Fife for centuries. In the *Old Statistical Account* (1793) it is mentioned as being at Kilconquhar Loch in 'great numbers . . . they make their nest on the flags, and hatch in May . . .'

Baxter and Rintoul (1935) said that Fife and Kinross were the headquarters of this species in the Forth area, and that Coot bred 'in large numbers on Loch Gelly, Loch Fitty, Kilconquhar Loch and in less numbers on all the lochs and ponds in the district' (VFF:254), which still holds true. Twenty years later they also felt that the Coot was increasing (B of S:713), and there has been no decline since.

After the breeding season big flocks may be seen eg. at Kilconquhar, where there were 250 on 1 August 1984, and 407 on 16 September 1968 —'mostly juveniles'—with 870 in September 1972 being the maximum numbers in thirty years.

The largest winter count of Coot in 1984 was at Lochore Meadows, where 436 were reported on 11 January, but big numbers were also at Craigluscar, Loch Gelly, Lindores Loch and Cameron reservoir.

The Coot is regularly seen on salt water in freezing weather: thus there were 114 at Methil docks on 22 January 1984, and others elsewhere, such as at Guardbridge on the Eden estuary.

The Coot is mainly sedentary, but some do migrate, and one was seen off Fife Ness on 14 April 1981.

There is no indication of any change in status.

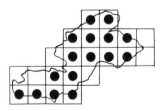

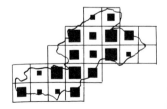

Crane   *Grus grus*

Rare visitor

Cranes have been reported this century only in the 1960s, when there
were 2 present at Dunbog near Newburgh on 27 June 1962 '. . . in a
field, attracted no doubt by the writer's captive cranes . . .' (SB2:422);
and again in 1969, when there were 2 at Leuchars 19-30 March; about
the same time 3 others were seen at Peat Inn on 22 March, while 3—
probably the same birds—were reported at Boarhills on 24 March,
where they stayed till 1 April (SB6:84).

Cranes were probably more common in Fife centuries ago.
Certainly 2 Cranes were donated by two local lairds to King James V at
Falkland Palace on 28 October 1532 (ExDJV:appendix).

Little Bustard   *Tetrax tetrax*

There is only one very ancient record of a female Little Bustard
at St Andrews on 6 March 1840. This record was mentioned by
Macgillivray in the *History of British Birds* (IV:59, 1841).

Oystercatcher   *Haematopus ostralegus*

Common resident and winter visitor

The big flocks of Oystercatcher which may be seen around the coast of
Fife in winter are nothing less than spectacular. At high tide they roost

on sandy shores and estuaries, and flocks of over 3,500 are by no means unusual, with as many as 7,500 reported at Tentsmuir Point on 14 October 1973, and 6,000 at Shelly Point on 21 January 1976. Maximum counts recently have been 3,720 at the Eden estuary on 20 November 1983, and 3,650 on the East Shore there on 7 February 1985; 700 at Tayport on 18 December 1983; and 640 at Burntisland on 22 January 1984.

Most of the wintering birds leave the area in spring, and ringing records give some indication of where they go: thus a bird ringed on the East Shore, Eden estuary on 15 March 1980 was recovered on 12 June 1981 at Mykeness, Faeroes, and another ringed there on 2 April 1981 was found dead on Fetlar, Shetland on 24 June 1982.

But some Oystercatchers also breed here, and it is most probable that breeding numbers have increased in Fife during the second half of this century. Baxter and Rintoul (1935) mentioned that the Oystercatcher nested by the shore and inland 'in small numbers' (VFF:285), and Boase said it did not breed in North Fife till 1963 (BNF:52). The *Breeding Atlas* showed 'confirmed breeding' in 17 squares (1968-72), and even if numbers may be slightly down today, it must indicate an increase over the last fifty years at least.

The size of the wintering flocks on the Eden estuary in recent years is comparable to counts in 1950-55 (SB2:162), allowing for a certain degree of fluctuation, and surveys since 1970 have shown the importance in national terms of the Eden estuary which was considered one of the 9 major wintering areas in Scotland for Oyster-catcher alone, supporting most years more than 1% of the entire British winter population (SB7:392; BTO's Report on the Eden, 1983). Another survey on the wintering waders on rocky shores in the early 1970s estimated a density of 54 birds per square km in North-East Fife (SB8:306).

The Oystercatcher or 'Sea piot' was mentioned by Sibbald in the *History of Fife and Kinross* (1710) and also in the *New Statistical Account* of Inverkeithing (1836).

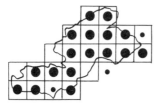 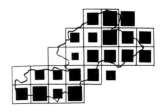

Avocet *Recurvirostra avosetta*

Vagrant

The only old record of the Avocet is of one shot on the sands at Kirkcaldy in the second week of August 1862 (B of S:606). Avocets had nested regularly in the south of England up till about 1840, when they became extinct. In the 1960s the Avocet began a new colonisation of Norfolk and Suffolk, possibly due to a vastly increased population in Denmark and the Netherlands (see ABB:198), and records of Avocets in Fife have echoed this development in a small way: the first available record this century is of a bird found dead at Fife Ness on 25 January 1968 after gales. The next is of one at the Eden estuary on 24 April 1974, this time alive, and again one on 5 August the same year. In 1976 a very late bird was at Morton Lochs in December (J. Cobb), while in 1983 one was at Fife Ness on 8 May; and in 1984 one was on the Eden estuary from 30 March to 5 April. This last bird was apparently part of an influx to eastern Scotland at the time.

It would be lovely if this most elegant of waders was to be seen regularly on our shores in future, but only time will tell.

Stone Curlew *Burhinus oedicnemus*

Very rare vagrant

There are two records only of this species, the first being from last century when a Stone Curlew was shot at Stravithie on 27 January 1858 (B of S:612); and the second of a bird seen at Tentsmuir Point on 12 January 1965 (SB3:417). That both records should be in January, when the bird is a summer visitor to the south of England, is extraordinary.

Ringed Plover *Charadrius hiaticula*

Common passage migrant, winter visitor and scarce breeder

The migratory pattern of this species seems to differ from that of most other waders in that the largest numbers always occur in April or May, and not in the autumn. Maximum numbers are usually found at the Eden estuary: eg. 710 on 21 May 1981, 600 on 15 May 1980, and 580 there on 21 May 1985. Migrant numbers have definitely been increasing here in recent years compared with the numbers mentioned by Grierson in the 'Check-list' (1962) where peaks consisted of about 100 in the autumn, and no spring records were mentioned at all (SB2:144). Big flocks are also seen at Tentsmuir Point such as 292 on 20 May 1981.

The return passage, which takes place from mid-August right up to October (100 at Balcomie on 17 October 1984 were probably migrants, as the wintering population there is only about 50), never produces as big numbers as the spring passage, unlike most other waders. Maximum counts have been 375 at Kinshaldy on 18 August 1982, 105 at Fife Ness on 3 September 1982, and 188 at Culross on 14 October 1977. The reason for the smaller peaks in autumn may be that birds which intend to winter here disperse almost immediately on arrival, and it is certainly the case that the Ringed Plover is a surprisingly common bird on any suitable stretch of sand during this period.

The largest wintering flocks in 1984 were found at Elie harbour (70 on 14 November) and at Kirkcaldy (48 on 26 January), but small numbers may be seen in many places along the coast right throughout the winter. The 'Waders on Rocky Shores Survey in the early 1970s' estimated a density of 10 birds per square kilometre in North-East Fife (SB8:299-308).

It seems likely that our own breeding birds also winter here, as Grierson had noticed that nesting birds at Tentsmuir were back at sites from mid-February, which is well before the migrants arrive. In 1973-74 the first national breeding survey of the Ringed Plover took place, with a follow-up in 1984. Numbers of breeding pairs along the coastal strip from Leven to Tayport in 1973-74 were found to be 23. In 1984 the number was only 11, in spite of the fact that an additional stretch of coast from Leven to Aberdour was examined.

To compensate for this very depressing result, however, some more cheerful news came from 'Inland habitats'. Here a total of 11 pairs were counted, as against only 1 pair inland in 1973-74. Inland habitats included 'industrial wasteland' (one pair), farmland (2 pairs), sand/gravel pit (2 pairs), dockyard (5 pairs) and reservoir (one pair). For full details see Wendy Mattingley's report in the *Fife and Kinross Bird Report* (1984). It is also interesting that there were reports of Ringed Plover trying to nest in a ploughed field a quarter-mile from the coast as early as 1969.

All the old reports agree that the Ringed Plover was a common breeding bird right back as far as Macgillivray (1837), and that breeding numbers have fallen catastrophically in the last twenty-five years is shown by the fact that Grierson could point to nearly 50 nests on Tentsmuir alone. It is much to be hoped that this plover will adapt successfully to new habitats, so that numbers of breeding pairs will rise again. However, it is gratifying that the numbers of migrants have definitely shown an increase in recent years.

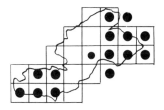 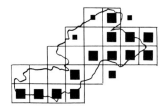

Kentish Plover   *Charadrius alexandrinus*

Very rare vagrant

Two records only for this species in Fife, but both fairly recent: one was reported on the Eden estuary on 22 April 1985; while the first record was another single at Elie Bay on 21 April 1966 (SB4:226).

Dotterel   *Charadrius morinellus*

Scarce passage migrant

The Dotterel has unfortunately become much scarcer in Fife this century. It was mentioned as a bird of passage in the *Old Statistical Account* of Carnbee (1793)—with Woodcock and Swallow—and as an occasional visitor to Dunfermline in the *New Statistical Account* (1837), but even Baxter and Rintoul, writing in 1935, remarked on the sharp decline which had been going on since the turn of the century. The fact that the Dotterel was a much sought-after delicacy has been regarded as being instrumental to their decline.

Recent records have been:

Spring:	*Autumn:*
7 Kirkcaldy 8.5.79	2 Eden estuary 14.8.1982
3 Leuchars 10.5.1974	2 Lundin Links 29.9.1981
4 Leuchars 16-17.5.1973	1 West Lomond Hill 18.8.1976
2 Fife Ness 5.5.1972	
9 Elie golf course 10.5.1960	

R. D. Murray, in an interesting article on the 'Colonization of Scotland by northern birds 1820-1977' (SB:158-174), observed that the Dotterel decreased in Scotland after the 1870s due mainly to man's interference, but that it has been increasing again since the 1960s, having similarly colonised Italy (1950s), the Netherlands (1960s), and also Wales. It is to be hoped that this general increase in Dotterel will result in more birds being seen on passage through Fife.

Golden Plover   *Pluvialis apricaria*

Common winter visitor and passage migrant

Great numbers of Golden Plover arrive in Fife in autumn, some to spend the winter here, and some to pass on to other places when the cold sets in.

The arrival usually begins in August, when as many as 2,000 have been counted at the Eden estuary (eg. on 24 August 1963, with 1,000 there on 10 August 1980). A further increase takes place in September (2,250 on Crail airfield on 26 September 1984), with peaks in October and November (3,400 between Rosyth and Culross on 26 November 1977; and 2,500 at the Eden estuary on 14 October 1984), while a few large flocks are still around in December (2,300 at Tayport on 16 December 1984).

After this, numbers tail off as flocks disperse, and in April most Golden Plovers have left again for the breeding grounds. Baxter and Rintoul believed that many of our autumn visitors were 'Scots bred birds' (VFF:277), and there is no reason to believe otherwise, with the Southern race being a successful breeding bird in the Highlands and the West of Scotland. It is difficult to know how many of the Northern race spend the winter here, as both races look alike in winter, but in late spring they can be distinguished, and on 13 April 1980, 107 Northern Golden Plovers were seen at Fife Ness.

Migrant numbers in autumn have probably increased in the last thirty years: Grierson, in the 'Check-list of the Birds of Tentsmuir', observed that flocks of up to 1,000 were on the Eden from September onwards in the 1950s, which is comparable to today's figures here, but numbers elsewhere appear to be up. Nationally, according to the *Wildfowl and Wader Counts*, there has been an increase in Golden Plover even since 1981.

Dalgleish (1885) said that one or two pairs nested north of Culross and Tulliallan, and Grierson also mentioned that Golden Plover had nested at Earlshall up till 1938. No Golden Plover now nests in Fife.

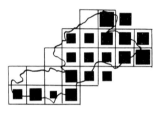

Grey Plover   *Pluvialis squatarola*

Common winter visitor locally

Even more than the previous species, the Grey Plover has been increasing as a winter visitor to Fife. Harvie-Brown (1906) quoted Millais as saying that it was a scarce autumn and winter visitor, and that he never saw them in large flocks on the Tay or the Eden: rarely more than 3 or 4 together (FT:295). Baxter and Rintoul in 1951 remarked that 'we used to think, if we saw one Grey Plover in a day's expedition we had done very well; now we often see 15 or 20' (EBB1:37). The usual wintering flock in the early 1950s on the Eden was 50-60 (EBB1:32), though up to 200 had been recorded on passage (SB2:143). The flock here has steadily increased, with peaks in the late 1960s of about 100; in 1973 there were 120 on 10 December, 200 in the autumn of 1975, and 734 on 18 January 1980. Maximum numbers for 1984 were 650 on 8 November. The importance of the Eden for wintering waders was again stressed in the 1972 midwinter census of waders in Scotland, where it was estimated that out of the total population of 178 Grey Plovers in Scotland, 70 were on the Eden estuary (SB7:391-398). Other big flocks may be found at Tentsmuir (where the numbers have been as impressive as 676 on 24 September 1976); at Tayport (where in the 1950s 'seldom more than 10 have been seen at one time' (SB2:144)); and at Culross where numbers reached 140 in October 1976. Outside these areas the Grey Plover is curiously uncommon.

There are only a few records of the Grey Plover inland: one was with Lapwings at Peppermill on 14 October 1964, and 2 were at Lochore on 22 September 1983. There are also some older records from Morton Lochs, where there were 10 on 20 August 1928, and one on 2 November 1953 (SB2:144). 'Green, gray and golden plovers' were mentioned as occurring at Inverkeithing (1836) in the *New Statistical Account,* and the Grey Plover was also mentioned in the *Old Statistical Account* of St Monance (1793), where it still occasionally occurs today.

Lapwing   *Vanellus vanellus*

Common resident and abundant winter visitor

The Lapwing has been around in Fife for a long time. It was mentioned in the *Old Statistical Account* (1793) as a 'summer visitor' to Anstruther and Kilconquhar, as 'present' at St Monance, and a 'bird of passage' at Carnbee. In the *New Statistical Account* it was said to occur at Kilmany and Inverkeithing (1836), and was 'very plentiful' at Auchtertool, but nothing was said about breeding here.

In 1935 it was reported by Baxter and Rintoul as being 'now a very common breeding bird in the [Forth] area, nesting everywhere except on the highest hills' (VFF:282); while Grierson stated that it had increased as a breeding bird at Earlshall since 1948 with 25 pairs nesting in 1953 (SB2:144). In the *Atlas of Breeding Birds in Britain and Ireland* the Lapwing was proved to breed in every square in Fife (1968-72). A drop in numbers of breeding birds in 1985 may be due to the very hard winter of 1984-85 elsewhere in Britain and Europe, where some of our birds have wintered, and another such temporary crash was mentioned by Boase for 1947 (BNF:54). There is apparently a great variation in the wintering quarters of our breeding Lapwing: a chick ringed at Guardbridge in 1967 was shot at Albufeira in the Algarve, Portugal on 7 January 1968 (SB:321), whereas a brood hatched on Dumbarnie Links, Largo remained there all through the winter (VFF:283).

In autumn and winter, large flocks of Lapwing assemble in Fife: 1,766 were at the Eden estuary as early as 26 August 1980, and good flocks may be seen moving in from the sea in September and October. 1,500 were at Longannet on 9 October 1983, whereas maximum numbers were reached in November and December (2,150 at the Eden estuary on 10 December 1984; 1,850 counted from Balcomie to St Monance on 3 December), with other large flocks at Valleyfield and Guardbridge. By March and April the large flocks have dispersed as the main movement to breeding grounds takes place.

Although the Lapwing has increased its national total (WWC; 1980-84), it does not seem to have increased in proportion in Fife as a wintering bird. Grierson talked of a large flock of 'at least 5,000 on the Eden' in 1953 (SB2:144), which is certainly much larger than anything we see now.

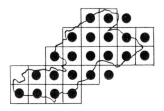
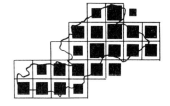

Knot   *Calidris canutus*

Winter visitor, locally abundant

There are few flocks of waders larger than those of Knot in winter.
Maximum counts have in recent years reached 7,150 at Kirkcaldy on 12
December 1983, and 7,300 at Longannet on 18 January 1976.
Numbers, however, fluctuate from year to year. Vast flocks were also
known at the Eden estuary around 1951, when Knot was mentioned as
the most numerous species of the wintering population there, about
5,000 then being normally on the estuary (EBB1:32), and culminating
in a stupendous 10,000 in December 1952 (SB2:162). In 1985 there were
2,960 there on 12 February, which was well up on peaks in the last few
years. Sizeable flocks have also been recorded at Lower Largo (3,000 on
18 January 1981), Methil, Tentsmuir and Tayport.

In addition to the big flocks, small numbers of Knot may also be seen
anywhere along the coast from Tayport to Kincardine, mostly in winter
but also occasionally on passage, when birds may be showing some of
the lovely pink colour on the breast.

Very occasionally a Knot is found here in summer, like one seen on
Tentsmuir in June 1984, but the Knot does not breed in the British
Isles.

It is evident that the numbers of Knot also fluctuate in the longer
term. Harvie-Brown (1906), following Drummond Hay, said that there
appeared to have been an almost universal falling off in the size of the
flocks of many tidal waders frequenting the estuaries of the Tay and
Eden, and that Knot had greatly diminished in numbers of late years,
being formerly abundant on all mudbanks of the tidal Tay (FT:320).
After another period of abundance around the middle of this century
the national total of Knot has dropped considerably since the 1960s (see
Wildfowl and Wader Count), and this seems to be reflected to some
degree in our present wintering population.

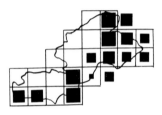

Sanderling *Calidris alba*

Winter visitor

This nice little wader is mainly a winter visitor to the area, but it migrates surprisingly early and may arrive already in July. Thus 44 were seen at Tentsmuir Point on 21 July 1971, and as many as 250 were there on 28 August 1973. Numbers do not seem to increase noticeably during the remaining months, although they may drop somewhat during the coldest time. In April and May most Sanderlings leave the area for their breeding grounds.

However, there are usually a few non-breeders which summer here, eg. at Tentsmuir (SB6:372), and one was at Longannet on 14 June 1960. This habit was also noted by Baxter and Rintoul who in 1912 counted 12 Sanderlings on 5 June in Largo Bay, 5 on 16 June, and one on 13 July, after which the autumn birds began to arrive (VFF:266).

Largest flocks recently have been seen at the mouth of the Eden (270 on 4 February 1984), Tentsmuir Point (248 on 7 October 1984), Tayport (175 on 30 October 1983), St Andrews (206 on 19 November 1984, 130 on 5 March 1978), and Leven (110 on 9 November 1980, 54 on 8 January 1983). There are no records of this wader inland.

Harvie-Brown put the Sanderling down as a regular autumn visitor to the Tay and Eden, and mentioned one obtained on the North Sands of St Andrews in October 1868 (FT:321), whereas Baxter and Rintoul (1935) said it was only an occasional winter visitor, so it appears that Sanderlings have only begun to winter here regularly in the course of this century.

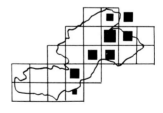

Little Stint   *Calidris minuta*

Scarce passage migrant

There are records most years of Little Stints in Fife, and by far the likeliest time to see this minute wader is in the autumn. The Little Stint occasionally arrives in the last few days of July (one was at the Eden estuary on 29 July 1984), but migrants are more usual in August, with the overwhelming number of records falling in September, tailing off in October, though Dalgleish had a January bird at Kincardine in 1873.

The Eden estuary seems to be their favourite place, where a maximum number of 42 were seen on 17 September 1978, 19+ on 7 September 1975, but 'only' 8 there on 11 September 1983. Other places where it occurs fairly regularly are Fife Ness (as singles or in small numbers, but they are seen here most years August-October), Tentsmuir Point and Kinshaldy (Little Stint was seen here both in 1984 and 1983 in the early part of September). Cult Ness used to be a regular place for stints, but there have been no records from here since 1963. Recent records, however, have come also from Torry Bay and Kirkcaldy, and in the 1960s and '70s from Largo Bay, Crail airfield, Cameron reservoir and Morton Lochs.

There are two spring records of Little Stint, both at Tentsmuir, on 19 May 1973 and 6-8 June 1975.

Harvie-Brown (1906) said it occurred both in the Eden and the Tay estuaries, and Grierson (1962) regarded the Little Stint as 'regular' on autumn passage, single birds as a rule, and said it had occurred at Morton Lochs, but not since 1938 (SB2:147). So a record of 8 there in 1973 on 29 September was unusual.

Little Stints may be slightly increasing in numbers on passage, although the peaks reached in the 1970s have not been matched since.

Temminck's Stint   *Calidris temminckii*

Rare vagrant

This stint is much rarer than the previous species. I have been able to find no old records, but it has occurred twice in the last ten years: one was at Fife Ness on 29 September 1980, and one was at the Eden estuary on 18 August 1976 (SB10:96).

Curlew Sandpiper   *Calidris ferruginea*

Scarce passage migrant

Like the Little Stint, the Curlew Sandpiper occurs on migration in the autumn mostly. Practically all records fall in August, September and October, with the majority occurring in September. Again the Eden estuary provides the favoured habitat: a record 80 were recorded in mid-September 1985, and 30 or more were seen on several occasions in the 1970s. The Curlew Sandpiper also occurs fairly regularly at Fife Ness, but usually in small numbers only. There were 5 on 1 September 1985, but as many as 15 were there on 30 August 1975, which was a very good year for the species in Fife. Outside these two areas the Curlew Sandpiper has been recorded from Longannet, Torry Bay (1984), Cult Ness (not since 1963), Anstruther (1985), Morton Lochs (1980), Tentsmuir and Tayport (1984).

There is only one spring record in the last thirty years of a bird at Fife Ness on 28 April 1982.

A comparison with comments earlier in the century is interesting: Grierson (1962) said that mostly up to 5 birds were seen, but there were 40 on the Eden on 6 September 1953, and it was also seen annually at Tayport, and once at Morton Lochs on 20 August 1912 (SB2:147), whereas Baxter and Rintoul (1935) for South Fife said, 'We see it very occasionally in Largo Bay in autumn and observed one near the East Neuk of Fife [i.e. Fife Ness] on 4 September 1928' (VFF:265). Harvie-Brown thought it was more common on passage in spring about the Tay estuary and the mouth of the Eden than it was in the autumn—'examples of full breeding dress being far from uncommon well into summer' (FT:319). Now most sightings of Curlew Sandpiper are definitely in the autumn, and numbers appear to be increasing.

Purple Sandpiper   *Calidris maritima*

Winter visitor

The Purple Sandpiper does not flock in huge numbers, but it is nevertheless quite a common winter visitor to Fife, where it can be seen on any rocky shore, from St Andrews (40 on January 1984) right along the coast and up the Firth of Forth as far certainly as Kirkcaldy (a maximum of 106 were seen on 7 April 1982).

The Purple Sandpiper usually arrives in September, and it leaves again in April or May. The last birds seen in 1984 were 5 at Fife Ness on 20 May.

It is evident that the Purple Sandpiper has increased markedly this century: Baxter and Rintoul (1935) did not consider it uncommon in suitable locations (VFF:263), but Harvie-Brown (1906) thought it a 'rare winter vagrant', and quoted W. Berwick as saying that it was 'not at all common upon the coast of Fife'. However, he had himself seen a few 'close under the town on the under-cliff below Gillespie Terace, St Andrews' (FT:320).

In more recent years the 'Winter waders on rocky shores' survey in the early 1970s found that between 717 and 489 Purple Sandpipers were present in December and January along the shores of Fife with a calculated density of 55 per square kilometre (see SB8:299-308).

Dunlin   *Calidris alpina*

Common winter visitor, has bred

Like the Knot, the Dunlin gathers in huge flocks in the area in winter: 3,277 on the Eden estuary on 18 February 1980 was the largest count in fifteen years, though in 1950-55 wintering numbers here were regularly between 3,000 and 6,000 (SB2:162); 2,000 was the maximum count in 1984, on 18 January.

The Dunlin may be seen anywhere along the coast in small numbers, from Tayport to Kincardine, whereas the big flocks are usually on the Eden estuary. Baxter and Rintoul (1935) also reported favourite resorts from Kincardine to Torryburn, with other large flocks at Pettycur sands and in Largo Bay (VFF:264).

The wader studies of the 1970s showed that Dunlin as well as Oystercatcher, Redshank and Knot were common on rocky shores in addition to being on the sandy estuaries. The density of Dunlin on rocky shores in Fife was calculated at 41 per square kilometer (see 'Wintering wader populations on the rocky shores of eastern Scotland', SB8:299-308). The Eden, with a wintering population of 3,000, was fourth on the list of important wintering areas in Scotland for this species (see '1972 Midwinter census of waders in Scotland', SB7:391-398).

The Dunlin arrives in September and leaves again in March, some at least to make their way to Scandinavia: birds wintering at Fife Ness in 1968 had been ringed in Finland, Sweden and Denmark (SB5:325), and there are several other ringing records from these countries as well as from Norway. But others move much further afield: an adult ringed at Tentsmuir on 29 July 1977 was recovered on 23 July 1979 at Hurry Fjord, Scoresbysund, Greenland; while some Dunlin have been found migrating in the opposite direction: there are records of birds ringed in the Netherlands which were subsequently found at Fife Ness, and another ringed at Tentsmuir, which was found in Germany. One ringed at Leuchars on 23 July 1976 was found dead on 4 January 1982 at Vila Franca de Xira, Ribatejo, Portugal (2007km), and another, ringed at Guardbridge on 22 August 1981, was recovered on 26 March 1982 at Sida Moussa, El Jadida, Morocco (2654km) (TRG reports).

The Dunlin used to nest in Fife. Grierson (1962) reported the last nesting at Tentsmuir in 1937. Six pairs had been known to nest at Scotscraig before afforestation and 20 pairs at Earlshall earlier in the century (SB2:127). Baxter and Rintoul (1935) reported a few pairs nesting on Dumbarnie Links (VFF:264). Probably no Dunlin now nest in Fife, though in 1984 a pair was seen displaying in June near Tayport.

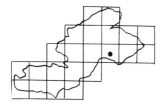
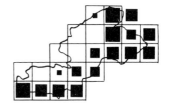

Broad-billed Sandpiper   *Limicola falcinellus*

Rare vagrant

There are no recent records, but one was seen on the Eden on
9 September 1946, and a bird of this species was shot at Morton Lochs
on 12 August 1912 (SB2:147).

Buff-breasted Sandpiper   *Tryngites subruficollis*

Rare vagrant

This American sandpiper is only a very recent addition to the list of
birds seen in Fife. The records are as follows:
1 Eden estuary 18.9.1982
2 Crail 12-14.9.1977
1 Tentsmuir 7.9.1975
1 Tentsmuir 30.9.1973.
   It will be noticed that all records fall in September.

Ruff   *Philomachus pugnax*

Passage migrant and winter visitor

This wader is most commonly seen on passage, and may occur in a
number of coastal places from Tayport to Culross and occasionally on
reservoirs, such as Ballo and Lochore. Migrants usually arrive in
August, and in October numbers tail off. The biggest flocks in the last
thirty years have been 65 at Fife Ness on 23 September 1980; 59 on the
Eden estuary on 28 August 1954, and 42 there on 26 September 1974;
but these are exceptions and numbers are generally much lower.
There were 14 at Wormit on 6 September 1980, 24 at Glenrothes on 20
August 1978, 12 at Cameron reservoir on 18 September 1973, and 22 at
Anstruther on 5 October 1985.
   Another place where Ruff have been recorded on several occasions is
the Rosyth sewage farm/Cult Ness area. This used to be an excellent
place for Ruff and other waders, especially in the 1950s and '60s while
land reclamation was still going on (at least 20 Ruff were seen here on
passage on 9 September 1953 (EBB4:18)), but it still attracts a number

of Ruff both in autumn and spring, and occasionally parties have been seen here even in winter: 20 at Cult Ness on 7 December 1975, 14 at Rosyth on 11 January 1976, and 9 on 5 February 1983. Ruff also often winters in small numbers on the Eden.

Records of spring passage are rather fewer and numbers smaller. The Eden estuary is still the favourite place with 20 there 'lekking' between 15 April and 18 May 1981; but reports also come from St Andrews, Fife Ness, Elie Ness and Culross; and one Ruff was at Lochore Meadows on 9 May 1974.

There is no evidence of any change in status in the last thirty years, though it has certainly increased this century. Baxter and Rintoul (1935) found it only an 'occasional visitor' with single birds occurring irregularly only in July and August (VFF:267), and Harvie-Brown (1906) considered it 'rare', mentioning only one record of a bird shot at Tentsmuir on 27 August 1895 (FT:320).

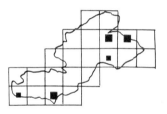

Jack Snipe   *Lymnocryptes minimus*

Scarce winter visitor

Only very small numbers of Jack Snipe are seen in Fife. It usually arrives in late September and stays till April. The area by Cocklemill Burn in Largo Bay is a favourite place for them: up to 3 were seen here in 1984 from 16 September till the end of the year, whereas 7 were recorded here on 28 February 1979, and as many as 12 on 14 November 1965—the maximum total certainly in the last thirty years.

Small numbers, however, also occur elsewhere: there are records from Tayport, Tentsmuir Point, Morton Lochs, Guardbridge, the Eden estuary, Cameron reservoir, Fife Ness, Crail airfield, and Barnyard marsh behind Kilconquhar Loch. Baxter and Rintoul also reported of Barnyard marsh that on 29 December 1923 Jack Snipe were 'very numerous', but two days later all had gone, and they said that the

Jack Snipe was common about Burntisland in some winters (VFF:260). They also noticed that on passage it may frequent quite dry grass land.

The only summer record in the last thirty years was a bird flushed at Peppermill Dam on 27 June 1960.

Harvie-Brown (1906) and Balfour Kirke (1911) considered it fairly abundant, ar d Boase (1964) said that it was generally regarded as a common bird, known mainly by those who shot over rough ground, and was seldom reported (BNF:59). It is, of course, true that the Jack Snipe sits extremely tight and only flies when it is nearly trodden on, so it could be under-recorded, but evidence sadly points to the strong possibility that it has become much rarer in recent times, no doubt due to the fast disappearance of all suitable wet habitat from our countryside.

Snipe   *Gallinago gallinago*

Breeds locally, winter visitor and passage migrant

The Snipe is a fairly common nesting bird where there is a suitable habitat of wet moorland and marsh, and especially in West and Central Fife. Drumming was reported from 7 sites on the Lomond Hills in 1983, and it bred at Lochore Meadows too that year. In 1935 Baxter and Rintoul reported it as a common nesting bird in Fife (VFF:259), and Grierson (1962) said that there were 15 pairs at Earlshall as well as 2-3 pairs at Morton Lochs (SB2:145). There has certainly been a decrease at Tentsmuir since Grierson's time, and although the *Breeding Atlas* showed the Snipe as definitely breeding in almost every square in the area (1968-72), it will be very interesting to see what change has come about in the next *Breeding Atlas* planned for 1988.

In the autumn large gatherings are often seen, such as 22 at Carnbee reservoir on 24 August 1983, 32 at Ballo reservoir on 26 August 1984, 25 at Lochore Meadows on 21 September 1983, 30+ at Fife Ness

2-5 October 1979, and 32 at Longannet-Valleyfield on 22 November 1981. Passage birds are again seen in the spring when 20 were present on Barnyard marsh at Kilconquhar on 4 March 1984.

The Snipe has been around for a long time: it was presented to, as well as purchased for, King James V's table at Falkland Palace between 1528 and 1532 (ExDJV:115 & appendix), and it was mentioned in the *New Statistical Account* as occurring in several parishes (c.1836). There is not enough evidence to indicate any substantial change in recent years, though it has probably become less common.

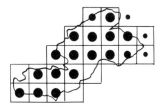 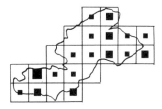

Great Snipe *Gallinago media*

Rare vagrant

There is only one recent record, which is of a bird that was reported by Dr John Berry to have spent a couple of months at Tayfield in winter 1982 (pers.com.). Before that we have to go back to 1951 when Grierson saw one at Earlshall on 28 October; a Great Snipe was also seen by Boase on 3 August 1918, and a bird was shot at Morton Lochs on 28 October 1898 (SB2:145). It is interesting that all the records have been from North Fife.

The 'Large Snipe' was said to visit Kilmany in the *New Statistical Account* (1838)—the author knew both the Common Snipe and the Woodcock from the parish.

Long-billed Dowitcher *Limnodromus scolopaceus*

Very rare vagrant

Only one record, which is of a bird shot on Dumbarnie Links near Largo in September 1867 by the gamekeeper to Robert Rintoul of

Lahill. It was identified as a 'Red-breasted Sandpiper', and the specimen is now in the Royal Scottish Museum (VFF:272). The English name of the species was later changed to 'Red-breasted Snipe' (HBBIV:209), and finally the name 'Dowitcher' was adopted for this North American species. *The Frontiers of Bird Identification* (Sharrock, 1980) mentions this specimen as one of seven authentic records of the Long-billed Dowitcher in Britain. It was an immature with a 70mm-long bill.

Woodcock   *Scolopax rusticola*

Resident and passage migrant

The roding of Woodcock is one of the most pleasing happenings on a spring-evening's woodland walk. Fortunately it is still an experience that may be had in a number of places in Fife because, as a breeding bird, the Woodcock seems fairly well distributed all over the county.

The Woodcock was mentioned both in the *Old* and the *New Statistical Account* (c.1793 and c.1836) as a regular winter visitor or 'bird of passage' to a number of parishes, and Baxter and Rintoul (1935) observed that it was apparently not till the middle of the nineteenth century that Woodcock started to breed in Fife, when a pair was believed to have nested at Tulliallan about 1860. By 1900 it had spread and was fairly numerous about Dunfermline, and about this time it first bred at Gilston. They also mentioned that Woodcock bred sparingly in the coverts of Balcarres, Kilconquhar, Elie, Balcaskie and Airdrie, but they 'are not as numerous as a breeding species in the east of Fife as they are farther west. They nest particularly commonly in the districts about Markinch . . .' (VFF:258).

This breeding distribution seems no longer to be the case. Although the total number of pairs has no doubt decreased, woods have also changed and others matured: eg. the plantation at Tentsmuir—where Grierson mentioned there were only a few pairs in the 1950s (SB:145)—has grown up and is now a stronghold for the species. This must to some extent also be the case of Devilla forest, another stronghold, as well as the plantation on the north slope of the Lomond Hills, where roding is now common.

In autumn, migrant birds arrive in East Fife in October and November, although their numbers vary considerably from year to year. Baxter and Rintoul (1935) noticed that it was usually after prolonged north-east and easterly winds that the Woodcock was seen here in the greatest numbers: thus 'at the end of November 1919 an abnormal number of Woodcock were recorded in East Fife where at least four times the usual number were seen and shot . . .' (VFF:258). Just such an influx took place 10-18 November 1984 when 6 were seen at Fife Ness on 18 November and several individuals further down the coast; eg. one was flushed early in the morning from a woodstack in our backyard at Anstruther.

Only a very small number of Woodcock now winter in the woods of East Fife, where they may occasionally be flushed, as eg. at Tentsmuir, Kippo and Balcarres. These are probably migrants, whereas our own birds seem to leave the area in winter. This migratory pattern was suspected by Baxter and Rintoul, and the fact that two pairs, which had been at Redwalls regularly for several years, were not present in the spring of 1985 supports this theory, as they may have perished in the exceptionally cold winter which the south of England and much of Europe experienced in 1984-85, while the east coast of Scotland got off very lightly.

Migration takes place again in spring, but usually with fewer records and fewer numbers. However, 7 Woodcock were seen at Fife Ness on 28 March 1984.

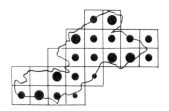 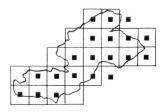

Black-tailed Godwit *Limosa limosa*

Mainly winter visitor to Eden estuary

The Black-tailed Godwit adopted Fife as a wintering place only earlier this century, and as this species is otherwise not commonly seen on the east coast of Scotland in any numbers, it is worth tracing the development in some detail.

Harvie-Brown (1906) put it down as a rare autumn visitor, the only record from North Fife being a bird obtained by W. Berry at Tayport on 3 September 1892 (FT:328), whereas Baxter and Rintoul in 1951 wrote, 'We well remember our excitement when we first saw one [Black-tailed Godwit] on the St Andrews shore on 5 December 1907. Gradually their visits to the estuary of the Eden became more frequent and their numbers increased, and we have seen as many as 200 in a day there in the migrating season, some settled down there as winter visitors, and we have recorded them from other places, such as the mouth of the Tay and Largo Bay . . .' (EBB2:37).

Grierson in the 'Check-list' (1962) recalled that as many as 100 had been there on 28 August 1936, but that 35 had been the wintering average between 1949 and 1955; that birds of this species frequented Morton Lochs, where a maximum of 49 had been seen on 15 July 1952, and a pair in June 1951 (SB2:146). There were reports, too, from other places, usually of singles, such as Longannet (one in August 1960 and 3 there in November 1963), Cult Ness (February and May 1962), Lundin Links (April 1962), Largo Bay (20 in November 1965), and Elie (3 in August-September 1963, 2 in August 1964). But the main flock has always been at the Eden, where peak numbers in 1964 were 73 in April and 60 in August-September; in 1974 there were 80 there in February and 80-112 in August-September, rising in 1984 to 108 in April and 142 in October that year.

Migration obviously takes place, as numbers tend to increase during April (179 on 18 April 1985) and August-October, but peaks may also occur during the winter months: thus 210 in December 1979 was the maximum count reported in the last thirty years.

In the '1972 Midwinter census of waders in Scotland' (SB7:391-398) Scotland's total winter population of Black-tailed Godwit was estimated to be 82, of which 80 were on the Eden. Since then a flock has also been building up in Dumfriesshire. The BTO survey of the Eden (1983) shows that in many years since 1970 this area holds more than 1% of the entire British winter population (BTO: Eden:table 2).

The Black-tailed Godwit no longer frequents Morton Lochs, but it may still be found in small numbers outside the Eden area: thus 3 were at Lochore Meadows in August 1984, one at Fife Ness on 31 July 1983, one at Anstruther on 25-26 August 1985, 4 at Leven on 9 November 1980, 9 at Torry Bay on 1 October 1978, and 4 at Culross in January 1975 with 10 there in August the year before.

It has bred once in Fife within the last twenty years.

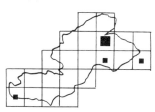

Bar-tailed Godwit   *Limosa lapponica*

Winter visitor, locally common

Although small numbers of this species may be seen anywhere along the coast of Fife where there is mud or sand, the Bar-tailed Godwit tends mostly to flock in huge gatherings in winter, with maximum numbers recorded at the Eden estuary (2,700 on 25 January 1983 and 2,000 there on 17 February 1984); at Tentsmuir Point (2,500 on 5 September 1971, 1,400 on January 1984); at Tayport—especially in early autumn (1,200 on 11 August 1984)—and in the Firth of Forth area at Burntisland (514 on 22 February 1983). Baxter and Rintoul (1935) mentioned that 'hundreds' were sometimes seen at Pettycur (VFF:273), which is still the case.

Our winter visitors begin to arrive in late July, apparently first to gather in the Tentsmuir area, where most of the autumn peaks have been recorded in the last fifteen years: 400 on 7 August 1979 at Kinshaldy, 2,000 along that coast on 28 August 1973, and the 1,200 mentioned above at the neighbouring area of Tayport in August 1984. Numbers here may later decrease as the flocks build up in the Eden estuary, where peaks are reached between December and February.

In 1951 Baxter and Rintoul felt that the Bar-tailed Godwit was decreasing: 'We used to see huge flocks at the mouth of the Tay and in the Eden estuary ... Now we often only see a few and 400 is the biggest count of which we have note in the last few years' (EBB2:37). Grierson, too, gave 700 as usual and 1,000 as maximum for 1950-54 (SB2:162), but it appears that it was only a temporary decline, and numbers began to rise again after 1970.

Most Bar-tailed Godwits leave the area by May, but occasionally some spend the summer here, as eg. in 1972, when a flock of 300 summered at Tentsmuir (SB7:3351).

Although nationally there has been a decrease in the total wintering numbers of this species in the last few years (see WWC, 1980-84), there has been no apparent decrease in Fife, and the BTO survey (BTO: Eden, 1983) shows that since 1970, the Eden supports in most years (and in February in every year examined) more than 1% of the entire British winter population.

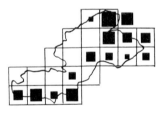

Whimbrel   *Numenius phaeopus*

Passage migrant

The Whimbrel is seen in Fife only on passage. In autumn the first birds usually arrive about the middle of July, when they may be seen and heard anywhere along the coast in East Fife especially, and reports have come from Tayport, the Eden estuary, St Andrews, Kingsbarns, Cambò, Fife Ness and Anstruther, with one or two birds seen as far west as Peppermill Dam and Longannet. Occasionally a bird may arrive in early July, as one reported at Largo Bay on 3 July 1969. The passage usually lasts till the end of September with a few stragglers into October. A very late Whimbrel was at Tayport on 1 November 1984, and, in 1976, 2 birds wintered at Largo Bay. Largest parties have in recent years been 26 at the Eden estuary on 30 August 1974, 21 at Fife Ness on 31 July 1972, and 15 there on 20 August 1983.

The spring passage takes place in late April and May, where reports again come mostly from East Fife, but Whimbrel may occur anywhere from Tayport along to Torry Bay, and also sometimes inland, such as one at Ballo reservoir on 4 May 1984. By the end of May most birds are through, and one at Elie Ness on 2 June 1963 was unusual (SB2:436).

The Whimbrel was mentioned in the *New Statistical Account* of Inverkeithing (1836), and by Millais as being common on migration about the Tay estuary at the turn of the century (FT:329).

There is no apparent change in status.

Curlew   *Numenius arquata*

Resident, passage migrant and winter visitor

The Curlew is a fairly common breeding bird in Fife, the *Atlas of Breeding Birds in Britain and Ireland* giving it as nesting in 12 squares during the 1968-72 period, and there are no signs of change since then. The Lomond Hills are a stronghold, but it is widespread in areas of rough grass and moorland.

The resident population is joined by large numbers of migrants in autumn, when a thousand or more have recently been counted in late July and August on the Eden: a bird recovered in Fife in September 1933 had been ringed in Örebro in Sweden two months earlier. Large flocks also occur in West Fife at this time of year (eg. 469 at Culross on 16 September 1982).

In winter, numbers drop (on the Eden to under 500), but the bird is widespread on all coasts. The winter surveys in the early 1970s indicated a density of 42 per square kilometre on rocky shores (see SB8:299).

Spring passage is less well marked, but an unusual inland flock of 400 was seen at Cameron reservoir on 11 March 1984.

The species was mentioned several times in both the *Old* and the *New Statistical Account,* and there is no evidence of any change in status. There is an interesting record of a bird ringed at Fife Ness on 2 March 1968 which was found dead there fourteen years later in March 1982 (TRG Report).

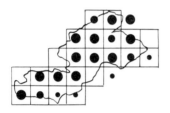
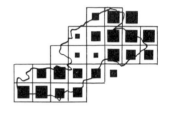

Spotted Redshank   *Tringa erythropus*

Scarce passage migrant

The best time to see this wader is undoubtedly in the autumn, when (in most years) single birds or small parties turn up and may stay for a week or two. There are a few July records, such as one at Wormit on 4 July 1970, but most records fall between early August and the middle of October, with peaks usually in September. One favourite place is the Eden estuary, where there were 6 on 6 July 1984, with a bird reported around till the end of the year. On 29 July 1951 an astonishing flock of 204 Spotted Redshank in summer plumage was seen here (EBB51:71), but 9 on 4 September 1983 has been the maximum in recent years. other good localities are Morton Lochs (with peak counts of 21 on 20 September 1975, and 38 a week later), and Culross, where the Spotted Redshank has several times been known to winter, especially back in the 1970s. Single birds also occasionally winter at the Eden estuary. Spotted Redshanks have also been reported on autumn passage from a number of other places along the east coast from Tentsmuir Point to Longannet, and inland from Cameron, Carnbee, Carriston and Ballo reservoirs, Lochore Meadows and Loch Gelly.

The records of spring migration are far fewer. In the 1950s Spotted Redshanks were seen on several occasions in spring around Cult Ness and High Valleyfield, but in the last few years the only spring records have been from Fife Ness (one on 24 May 1982) and the Eden estuary (one on 6 May 1984).

This bird has evidently become more common on passage during this century. Harvie-Brown (1906) could mention no records for North Fife, and Baxter and Rintoul (1935) had only records of single birds in Largo Bay in July 1912 and August 1930, with one other at Fife Ness on 29 August 1929. Boase (1964), however, could give a number of sightings in North Fife and Edenmouth including a 'first' for Morton Lochs of two birds on 30 August 1916 which stayed for a week (BNF:67).

Redshank *Tringa totanus*

Breeds in small numbers, common winter visitor and passage migrant

Baxter and Rintoul observed in 1953 that 'It is evident that flocks seen now-a-days are very much greater than they were in old days. Macgillivray and Gray say it was not seen in any great numbers, and the latter speaks of a flock of forty as notable . . .' (B of S:580). Certainly Grierson recorded flocks of between 1,000 and 2,500 in winter at the Eden estuary in 1950-55 (SB2:162), rather larger than the numbers seen here today, but nevertheless very big flocks of Redshank may still be seen both at the Eden estuary and elsewhere in Fife, where it is a common bird throughout most of the year. According to Boase (1964), it was absent on the Tay above Flisk (BNF:65), and the *Winter Atlas* has found this still to be the case.

The two surveys of wintering waders in the early 1970s found that the Eden estuary supported the biggest numbers of Redshank on the east coast of Scotland (SB7:395), and also that Redshank was fairly common on rocky shores in winter, estimating a density of 38 birds per square kilometre (SB8:306). It has also been shown that the Eden and the Tay (west of the road bridge), each in a number of years since 1970, support more than 1% of the British winter population (BTO Eden, 1983).

As with many other waders numbers tend to increase in spring and autumn, when the migrants arrive, and peaks recently have been 1,500 at Tayport on 21 April 1984; 1,390 at the Eden estuary on 10 September 1984, with 1,545 there on 29 July 1980, and 600 at Guardbridge on 15 August also in 1984; 214 were at Culross on 27 September 1982; and 175 at Torry Bay on 17 September 1984. The very big flocks of over 2,000 have not been seen in Fife since the early 1970s.

The *Breeding Atlas* had Redshank breeding in most parts of Fife except the most easterly coast (1968-72). In 1983 breeding was reported from Lochore (2 pairs), and it was also mentioned as 'common' around several reservoirs and mires in the Lomond Hills (FRS 1983). Grierson (1962) counted not less than 12 pairs nesting at Earlshall and the coastal strips at Tentsmuir, and said it had also nested at Morton Lochs (SB2:146). The Redshank still nested along the Eden estuary in 1985.

It is difficult to say whether our breeding birds also winter here, but a programme of trapping and measuring, carried out in 1969 in Fife in midwinter, proved that most birds were of the Icelandic race, whereas one trapped at Earlsferry on 14 July 1969 was recovered at Schwenningen, Zuid-Holland on 2 January 1970 (SB6:90).

Baxter and Rintoul (1935) mentioned that the habit of Redshank of feeding inland in ploughed fields and on grassland in winter was a fairly recent development, which they thought had come about with the increase of numbers (VFF:268).

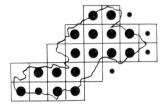 

Greenshank *Tringa nebularia*

Autumn passage migrant; a few winter

The Greenshank visits Fife on passage in the autumn, arriving in July and August. Peak numbers are generally reached in August and September, and in the last ten years maximum counts have been 33 at the Eden estuary on 25 August 1979, and 27 on 30 July 1984. There are other reports from Morton Lochs, Cameron reservoir, Kingsbarns, Fife Ness, Anstruther, Carnbee, Carriston reservoir, Lochore Meadows, and along the shore in West Fife; at Holl reservoir there was an exceptional party of 12 on 2 September 1984.

Occasionally single birds or very small parties winter here: thus 4 birds wintered on the Eden estuary 1984-85, and other places where there have been winter records are Morton Lochs, St Andrews, Boarhills, Kingsbarns, Elie, Culross and Torry Bay. This is not a recent development, as the Greenshank was mentioned as 'by no means uncommon in winter' on the coast of Fife in 1935 by Baxter and Rintoul (VFF:267); and Grierson said Greenshank was an occasional winter visitor to the Tentsmuir area in the 1950s (SB2:147). The '1972 Midwinter census of waders in Scotland' found that 6 out of a total of 35 wintering Greenshank were on the Eden (SB7:391-398).

There are also four June records: a bird was at Morton Lochs on 7 June 1982, and 3 were at the Eden estuary on 18 June 1983; while Baxter and Rintoul had two older records: singles in Largo Bay in late June 1912 and 1934 (VFF:267). It is not easy to say whether these birds were on their way out very late, or back very early. Greenshank, after all, do breed in North-west Scotland.

No change in status is apparent.

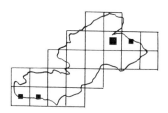

Lesser Yellowlegs   *Tringa flavipes*

Henry Boase recorded that he had seen a small plover with
lemon-yellow legs and other characteristics of this species at Tayport
Bay on 7 February 1961 (BNF:67). This record was apparently not
accepted by the Rare Bird Committee of *British Birds*, but I mention
the record nevertheless, preferring the conviction of a very experienced
ornithologist, who saw the bird, to the judgement of commentators,
who did not.

Green Sandpiper   *Tringa ochropus*

Scarce autumn passage migrant

Practically all records of this sandpiper fall in a period from late July to
late September. Most records are of single birds, and 2 is the maximum
number together in recent years, whereas a record number of 4 were
seen at the Eden estuary on 18 October 1964 (SB3:265). Sightings come
from a variety of places, nearly all in the east of Fife: Wormit, Tayport,
Morton Lochs, Cameron reservoir, the Eden estuary, St Andrews, Fife
Ness, Anstruther, Kilconquhar Loch, Carnbee reservoir, Shell Bay and
Largo Bay; but there are also records from further west at Southfield,
Glenrothes (Ballantyne, 1982) and Ballo reservoir. Baxter and Rintoul
(1935) had also found them here, and added that one was obtained at
Loch Gelly in 1904 (VFF:271). Harvie-Brown (1906) mentioned that
Millais had procured one on the tidal Tay, but gave no date; and Boase
(1964) said the Green Sandpiper was 'now a regular passage migrant' in
North Fife (BNF:64).

Outside this autumn period there are very few records and none in
recent years. In 1972 a Green Sandpiper was seen at Shell Bay on 1
March; for two years running a bird was seen near Kilconquhar Loch
in February 1968 and 1969; and one was at Peppermill Dam in
December 1964.

No change of status is apparent in the last twenty years.

Wood Sandpiper   *Tringa glareola*

Very scarce passage migrant

The Wood Sandpiper is even scarcer than the previous species. Nearly all records are of single birds in autumn, and fall between mid-July and mid-October. It has been recorded most often from Morton Lochs and the Eden estuary, but there are also records from Cameron reservoir, Strathmiglo, St Andrews, Leven, and in the 1950s from Shiremill Pond, Valleyfield and Cult Ness, but none here since.

There are, however, a few spring records too, the most recent being at Morton Lochs on 14 May 1979, and one at Earlshall on 18 May the same year. Another bird was at Morton Lochs in late May 1973; and much further back, Baxter and Rintoul saw a bird at Kinghorn Loch on 10 June 1936 (B of S:575), and they also mentioned one killed at Anstruther in April 1895 (VFF:272).

Harvie-Brown (1906) regarded the Wood Sandpiper as very rare and could give no records for North Fife, whereas Boase (1964) produced two records, both from Morton Lochs, where a single bird was seen on 28 July 1959, and a female there on 1 August 1911.

There is no change of status.

Common Sandpiper   *Actitis hypoleucos*

Scarce breeder and regular passage migrant

The Common Sandpiper is not very common in Fife, but it does occur in some numbers locally. The highest counts are recorded on passage in autumn, when a record number of 29 were seen at Cameron reservoir in August 1972; there were 7 at Guardbridge on 7 August 1984; and elsewhere birds may be seen in ones and twos almost anywhere along the coast and estuaries as well as on reservoirs on passage. Birds usually arrive in April and May, and breeding birds stay till September. In the *Breeding Atlas* confirmed breeding was recorded in 4 squares, all in Central and West Fife, and breeding records recently have come from Lochore Meadows, Lomond Hills reservoirs, Loch Fitty and St Fort. Until recently, the Common Sandpiper used to breed at Kincardine, but there have been no records from here since 1981.

Grierson (1962) mentioned the Common Sandpiper as an autumn

passage migrant in small numbers to Tentsmuir (SB:146); Dalgleish
(1885) said it bred near the Bluther Burn, and it was recorded by Baxter
and Rintoul (1935) as nesting 'occasionally' at Cullaloe reservoir, Loch
Gelly and the Ballo lochs, but they thought it was plentiful on passage:
'We see it by the sea, right out to [Fife Ness] along the sea braes and on
the rocks. We have flushed two or three from every wet spot and tiny
burn as we walked along this stretch of shore in July and August'
(VFF:270).

This could hardly happen today, and records suggest that the
Common Sandpiper is getting less common in the area, both as a
breeding bird and on passage.

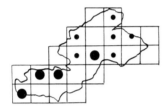

Turnstone						*Arenaria interpres*

Common winter visitor and passage migrant

Turnstones do not flock in the vast numbers that Dunlin or Knot do,
but they are present in smaller parties regularly almost anywhere along
the coast, especially the rockier parts. Flocks usually increase in size as
passage migrants arrive or wintering birds prepare to leave. Thus in
spring we have often watched our winter population at Anstruther
double or treble in spring, when the birds are obviously very restless:
suddenly one day in May there is a great babble of noise and they are
off, first in a spiral as they climb higher and higher, and then they turn
towards the north—and the long journey to the nesting grounds in the
Arctic has begun. It is in fact astonishing how far these small waders
travel. Thus there is a record of a Turnstone ringed at Fife Ness on 14
October 1973 which was found dead on 23 June 1974 at Eureka,
Ellesmere Island, Canada (R&M).

June records are few, but in late July they return again. The largest
flocks in recent years have been in spring (177 at St Andrews on 16 April
1984; and 150 at Fife Ness on 12 May 1983), whereas in the autumn 120

at Balcomie Bay on 19 September 1984 and 109 at Kincraig on 7 October 1982 have been maximum counts.

The 'Winter Shorebird Count 1984-85' showed that Turnstone (with Redshank and Oystercatcher) was the most evenly distributed species of wader along the shore from St Andrews to Kincraig Head, and the wader counts on rocky shores in the 1970s gave an estimated density of 179 Turnstone per square kilometre in NE Fife: more than three times the density of any other wader there (SB8:306), whereas the estuaries count of a total of 667 Turnstone wintering in Fife topped all other east-coast areas (SB7:394).

Baxter and Rintoul noticed that Turnstone frequently lingered on, and that some even spent the summer here, as eg. in 1909 and 1912 in Largo Bay, in full summer plumage, and this led them to hope that 'they may some day be found breeding in Scotland' (VFF:284). James Ferguson-Lees expressed a similar hope in the foreword to *The Atlas of the Breeding Birds of Britain and Ireland* (1976), and although the Turnstone has very recently been suspected of breeding in Scotland, there is as yet no definite proof.

Wilson's Phalarope   *Phalaropus tricolor*

Very rare vagrant

There are only two records of this fine American wader: one at Peppermill Dam on 19 October 1963 (SB3:82) and one on Rosyth mudflats on 11 September 1954 (EBB5:1-3).

This latter record was a 'first' for Scotland, and the bird in 1963 was only the third record for Scotland.

Red-necked Phalarope   *Phalaropus lobatus*

Status unclear

There are no dated records of this species for Fife (see also 'Grey Phalarope'). It was mentioned in the *Birds of the West of Scotland* (1871), where Gray said, 'I have myself met with it in East Lothian and Fifeshire', but no details are given. Harvie-Brown (1906) observed, 'It is said to be a rare occasional visitor to North Fife, but I have no definite notes or actual records' (FT:311).

Grey Phalarope   *Phalaropus fulicarius*

Rare vagrant

All recent records of positively identified birds have been Grey Phalaropes; there are also a few records of birds identified only as 'phalaropes', and these have been marked 'sp'. They could have been either Grey or Red-necked, but the likeliest is that they were Grey too (see also Red-necked Phalarope). All available records are as follows:

1 (sp) Kirkcaldy harbour 4.1.1982
1 (sp) Pathhead 4.1.1981
1-3 (Grey) St Monance 31.1-2.2.1976
1 (Grey) St Andrews 7.2.1976
1 (Grey) St Andrews 22.11.1971
4 (sp) Anstruther 13.10.1970
1-2 (Grey) Lundin Links 22.1.1960
2 (Grey) Fife Ness 28-29.10.1959
1 (Grey) St Andrews January 1952 (SB2:148)
1 (Grey) shot at Tayport October 1885 (FT:311)

It will be noted that all records fall between mid-October and early February.

Pomarine Skua   *Stercorarius pomarinus*

Scarce passage migrant

The Pomarine Skua turns up occasionally along the coast of Fife, usually in ones or twos, on autumn passage. In recent years, however, there have been two or three records every year, and in 1984 there was a bird at Fife Ness on 29 May, which is the first spring records as far as we know. All this suggests that the Pomarine Skua is very much increasing in numbers here. Certainly Grierson (1962) could only mention for Tentsmuir one sighting of 3 Pomarine Skuas off Tentsmuir Point on 14 August 1956; and only one old record from 1930 of one shot for identification, but he also added that many skuas were so far out that proper identification was impossible (SB2:148).

All autumn records up to 1985 have fallen between the end of July (one on 30 July 1983 at Fife Ness being the earliest date) and the end of October, but in 1985 an unprecedented number of Pomerine Skuas were noted, and scores were seen around the coast of Fife from about the second week of November, which were part of a great influx to the east coast. The bulk of records have come from Fife Ness, but birds have also been seen in recent years off Tayport, Kinshaldy, Eden estuary, St Andrews Bay (4 on 10 November 1985), Anstruther, Shell Bay and Leven.

Harvie-Brown (1906) regarded the 'Pomatorhine' Skua as a rare occasional visitor, but 'sometimes in considerable numbers', and mentioned that the autumn of 1879 was such a time. He also quoted Millais as saying that he had noticed it two or three times, and 'in 1886 there was a small visitation, and I killed 3 in St Andrews Bay' (FT:342).

Arctic Skua   *Stercorarius parasiticus*

Passage migrant

This is the commonest skua around the coast of Fife, and there are records from every month of the year, though it is commonest by far in late August and September, when very good counts have been made in recent years: eg. 109 passed Fife Ness in five hours on 10 September 1983; 60 were at Tentsmuir Point on 24 August 1983; 42 at Fife Ness on 24 August 1984, and 26 were counted there in an hour on 19 September 1982.

Spring records are much less common: a single was seen at St Andrews on 20 March 1983, whereas 2 took a shortcut over Kilconquhar Loch on 23 April 1962; and there are other late April and early May records from Elie Ness and Fife Ness, as well as records in June (off Inverkeithing and Tentsmuir Point) with numbers building up in July (eg. 8 in St Andrews Bay on 25 July 1982) to reach the peaks of August and September mentioned above. Then numbers tail off again in October, with a few late birds in November: maximum numbers then have been 3 at Longannet on 2 November 1963, but there are other records such as one at Limekilns on 9 November 1983, one at Boarhills on 28 November 1982, and one at St Andrews on 9 December 1983, while in 1984 one was at Torry Bay on 19 December.

The only winter records have been singles at St Andrews on 27 January 1980, and on 14 February the same year.

As can be seen from the above, the Arctic Skua may occur anywhere along the coast from Tayport to Torry Bay, with the biggest concentration towards the east. It is only rarely seen inland, though one was at Lochore Meadows on 2 August 1984.

It appears that the Arctic Skua has become much commoner this century. Harvie-Brown (1906) regarded all skuas as rare, whereas Baxter and Rintoul (1935) talked about 44 in three-quarters of an hour in South Fife, but they considered that unusual (VFF:308). Grierson (1962) said 9 had been the maximum in the 1950s at Tentsmuir, whereas Boase (1964) felt that the Arctic Skua was 'now' a regular passage migrant to North Fife, seen as far up as Newport, with most records coming from the outer Tay estuary (BNF:74).

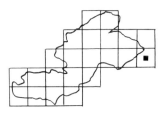

Long-tailed Skua   *Stercorarius longicaudus*

Vagrant

There are not many records of this skua, the most recent ones being set
out below:

1 (imm) at Fife Ness on 16.9.1983—pursuing Sandwich Terns
1 at Tentsmuir on 23 July 1973
1 at Tentsmuir late July 1972
1 at Fife Ness on 12.9.1970—flying south
1 at Fife Ness on 18.8.1969—also going south
1 in Eden estuary area 9-12.8.1965—'very tame'

and three much older records:
1 off Fife Ness on 5.10.1906 (VFF:309)
1 at Newport in 1880
1 at St Andrews 29.4.1868 (Scot.Nat.1871:81)

It may be noted that the earliest record was in spring, but all other
sightings have been in autumn.

Great Skua   *Stercorarius skua*

Mainly autumn passage migrant

The Great Skua, also called the Bonxie, is seen on passage, with
maximum numbers usually in August. Most records are from Fife

Ness, but the Great Skua may occur anywhere along the coast from Tentsmuir, where there was one on 16 October 1983, to Kirkcaldy, where a very late bird was seen on 28 November 1982.

Numbers seem to vary considerably from year to year, so that in 1982, 23 sightings were reported, compared with only one in 1981.

There are also a few winter records: one was seen at Inverkeithing on 22 December 1984; there were 2 at Kirkcaldy on 6 February 1983; and one flew north at Fife Ness on 20 February 1966. The only record for March is also from the 1960s: 3 round the North Carr lightship, then anchored off Fife Ness by the Carr Rock. There are no April records, but several in May, the most recent being at Fife Ness in 1983 and 1985, whereas one off Anstruther on 26 June 1981 is the only record for that month.

Baxter and Rintoul (1935) mentioned that 'the status of the Great Skua in the Forth area has changed considerably within our memory. Whereas formerly it was an event to see one, it is now a fairly common occurrence' (VFF:307); and records suggest that the Great Skua is now seen even more frequently: maximum counts recorded in the 1960s were 8 off Anstruther on 10 October 1969, while 22 at Fife Ness on 29 August 1976 was by far the biggest number reported that decade. Peaks so far in the 1980s have been a passage of 29 at Fife Ness on 24 August 1984, with 14 there the next day; and records on the whole show a steady increase over the last thirty years.

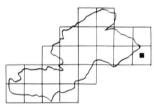

Mediterranean Gull   *Larus melanocephalus*

Vagrant

This species was first recorded for Fife in 1982. There have been three records in all in so many years, and they are:

1 (second winter) at St Andrews on 31.3.1984
1 at Leven on 26.3.1983
1 at Kilconquhar on 26.9.1982.

Little Gull   *Larus minutus*

Visitor in varying numbers

The Little Gull is seen not uncommonly around the coast, from Tayport to Kirkcaldy, especially after strong easterly gales. In the west of Fife it is, however, rare. Usually it is a very maritime bird, keeping far out to sea, but at times on passage it also frequents certain inland waters, such as Kilconquhar Loch, where it comes in towards the end of the day in August and September, to roost but also to feed in a most engaging manner on the abundant insect life over the loch, in graceful swoops or mothlike flutterings.

The last twenty years have seen an extraordinary rise and marked fluctuation in its numbers in Fife. The events were closely monitored at the time in the *Edinburgh Bird Bulletin* and *Scottish Birds,* and it is worth tracing the development.

At the turn of the century Harvie-Brown (1906) called the Little Gull a 'rare occasional visitor', and gave the only occurrence as a bird being at St Andrews (no date). In 1935 Baxter and Rintoul still regarded it as an 'uncommon visitor' to the Forth area as a whole (VFF:298). But about 1950 a change took place, and Baxter and Rintoul could now write that 'the last few years we have seen them in increasing numbers. In 1948 on 30 September, in a two mile walk along the shore in Largo Bay, we saw 68 Little Gulls . . .' (B of S:634); and in 1951 they saw a flock in Largo Bay increase from 12 on 15 September to 100 on 3 October (EBB2:54). This in itself is interesting, as peaks are now reached much earlier on.

Reports, however, also started coming in from other places later in the 1950s, such as from Tentsmuir and Tayport in spring, and single birds at Fife Ness and Cult Ness in autumn 1958.

In 1961 *Scottish Birds* published an article by J. Grierson on 'Little Gulls in Angus and Fife' (SB1:362-367) with detailed tables. The increase in these two areas was discussed, and it was also noted that the distribution of the Little Gull was very local, being mainly confined to the Largo Bay area and Morton Lochs, where it was first observed in early May 1955, building up to a maximum of 30 on 23 May that year.

Numbers kept steadily increasing in the 1960s, when 50 were at Morton Lochs on 21 April 1963, and 40+ on the Eden estuary on 19 May that year (SB2:437), indicating the bird's preference for this north-easterly part of Fife in spring. In autumn 1962 8 Little Gulls were seen frequenting Kilconquhar Loch at the end of August and beginning of September (SB2:259), and the following year a 'first summer' bird was reported there on 21 May 1963. That autumn an extraordinary build-up took place for the first time at Kilconquhar Loch: in early July there was an average of 5 birds there, then 38 were counted on 21 July, with numbers increasing steadily to 318 on 1 August, 412 on 9 August and an amazing 512 on 18 and 22 August. First summer birds now constituted about 60% of the total, while juveniles were first seen on 6 August, comprising about 10% of the total on 18 August (see SB2:490 for more details). It must be kept in mind that Little Gulls nest no closer than Germany and Finland (see BWPIII:733).

All Little Gulls had left Kilconquhar by 28 September (SB3:39), with one or two stragglers seen in October; but after this the Little Gull was seen yearly at Kilconquhar in great numbers for about 15 years, even if they never did exceed the peak of 1963. Little Gulls, however, took to staying around Fife throughout the year; eg. in 1971 *Scottish Birds* said 'reported as usual every month', with peaks such as 31 at Methil on 23 January, and 47 still at Kilconquhar on 7 November (SB3:141).

During the 1960s and '70s reports of flocks of 50-150 birds were also received from other places: Crail, Kingsbarns, Shelly Point and Tentsmuir Point. But in 1976 peak numbers at Kilconquhar dropped below 100 for the first time since 1963. In 1978 numbers were briefly up again (250 on 8 August), but in 1981, 5 was the maximum count at Kilconquhar (5 September), and only one or two birds were seen here between 1981 and 1985, although a few individuals were seen elsewhere during this time.

In 1985, however, the Little Gulls were back at Kilconquhar. Their presence that year was first noted on 7 August when 45 birds were counted, increasing to 140 a fortnight later, with a peak of 175 on 22 August, and 86 still there on 10 September. It will be most interesting to see what numbers the future will bring.

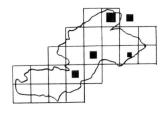

Sabine's Gull   *Larus sabini*

Rare vagrant

This Arctic gull has occurred on passage several times, and always in autumn. It winters in the South Atlantic. The records are as follows:

1 at Fife Ness on 29.8.1976
1 (first winter) at Fife Ness on 8.10.1972
1 (adult) at Shelly Point on 7.9.1952 (EBB3:5)
1 at Largo Bay on 15+17.9.1952 (Scot.Nat.64:58)
1 near Elie 31.8.1907 (VFF:299).

Bonaparte's Gull   *Larus philadelphia*

Very rare vagrant

This North American gull has only once occurred in Fife, when an immature was seen at Luthrie, Cupar on 26-27 February 1972 (SB7:361). It was only the third record for Scotland.

Black-headed Gull   *Larus ridibundus*

Resident, abundant in winter

The Black-headed Gull used to nest in great numbers in Fife, in particular at Tentsmuir, where it was first reported in 1902. The growth of this colony was rapid, and by 1936 it was reckoned to consist of 3-4,000 pairs. Baxter and Rintoul described it as it was then: '. . . the numbers were very large, the birds nesting in rushes, on the sand among the heather, in fact anywhere and everywhere, so many were there they had built two or three nests in the same bush of heather at different heights' (B of S:628). In the 1960s, 8,000 pairs were estimated to nest here, but numbers dropped in the early 1970s, and by 1976 the Black-headed Gull had ceased to nest here altogether (SB10:99), the drastic decline being attributed to the drying out of the moor, but foxes may also be to blame.

Another breeding colony of about 1,000 pairs was discovered on an island off Newburgh (SB5:328), but there is no colony there now. The *Breeding Atlas* had confirmed breeding from 5 squares in Fife, mostly in the central part, and birds continued to nest here for some years in small numbers. The only fairly large breeding colony in Fife in 1984 was one at Redmyre near Auchtermuchty, but even that appears to be dying out.

However, there is no shortage of Black-headed Gulls during the rest of the year. Largest counts in 1984 were 2,500 at St Andrews on 29 November, and 1,700 at Glenrothes tip on 6 January, with 1,260 here on 30 January 1983. Other big winter counts of 800-1,300 have in recent years been made at Tayport, Guardbridge, Kingsbarns and Leven.

Juveniles often spend the summer by the sea, and the first at Anstruther in 1985 appeared on 18 June. Many juveniles, however, leave Fife in October, some to travel a very long way indeed, as is shown by ringing records: of the Tentsmuir chicks, 2 ringed in 1967 were recovered, one at Figuera da Foz, Beira Litorall, Portugal on 20 December that year, the other at La Coruna, Spain on 26 December 1967 (SB5:328).

The Black-headed Gull was mentioned by Sibbald in the *History of Fife and Kinross* (1710), and also in the *New Statistical Account* of Dunfermline, and of Abdie (1836), where the gullery—by then deserted—on the Maw Inch in Lindores Loch had no doubt been Black-headed. It is also reported in the past to have nested at Loch Glow, Miller's Loch, on an island now submerged at Tulliallan, and at Otterston (VFF:293). It is clear that a good deal of changing fortune has always followed these gull colonies, but the decline in recent years has been unprecedented. Soon there may be no Black-headed Gull colonies in Fife at all.

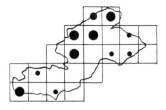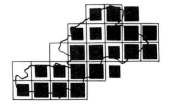

Common Gull   *Larus canus*

Common winter visitor, and passage migrant

The Common Gull is less common in Fife than the previous species, but occasionally very big counts have been made, such as 4,500 at Tentsmuir Point on 22 January 1981, and 1,500 at Tayport on 15 January 1984. Other places where big numbers have been recorded are Glenrothes tip, Lochore Meadows, Burntisland (Ballantyne (1982) reports about 15,000 off here in 'early 1963'), Shell Bay and Carnbee reservoir.

The Common Gull does not nest on the Fife mainland, but some non-breeding birds are usually around right through late spring and summer, while the adult birds and juveniles arrive after the breeding season to spend the winter here. As the Common Gull nests throughout the North and West of Scotland, many of our winter guests are native birds, but others come from overseas: thus a bird picked up dead at St Andrews on 31 December 1969 had been ringed as a chick near Kingisepp, Estonia on 4 June 1968 (SB6:95).

The Common Gull is less a bird of the seashore than the Black-headed Gull, and it is often seen on arable fields well inland. It does also roost on the sea, however, and we have seen a flock of 200 roosting in the bay at Anstruther in cold weather on 2 February 1984, but this was very unusual.

There is no indication of any change in status.

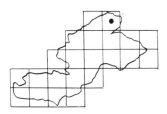 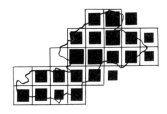

Lesser Black-backed Gull   *Larus fuscus*

Common summer visitor

The Lesser Black-backed Gull arrives in Fife usually about the beginning of March, though some early birds have been recorded, as

eg. 4 at Glenrothes on 12 February 1980. They may be seen anywhere
in the county, but mostly on grass, ploughed fields or flooded areas,
and less often by the sea. Flocks of up to 50 have been reported on the
Lomond Hills in spring and autumn (FRS,83). The Lesser Black-back
does not now nest on the mainland of Fife, but it does nest in some
numbers on the Isle of May, and birds may be seen around Fife
throughout the summer. In 1972 one or two pairs nested for the first
time at Tentsmuir (SB7:360), and the *Breeding Atlas* also showed it
breeding in a very westerly square, but this might in fact not have been
in Fife. Anyway, no breeding records have been had since.

Most birds have left again by the middle of October to winter in the
west, but one or two individuals may winter here. Reports of wintering
birds have recently come from Pittenweem, Glenrothes, Kinghorn,
Kirkcaldy (four years running) and Dunfermline.

There is no evidence of any change in numbers, but winter records
used apparently to be very rare (VFF:292), and it could be that this gull
may be attempting to nest in the area again.

Occasionally other sub-species than the British race *(L.f. graellsii)* are
reported in Fife. Thus in 1983 a bird of the Southern Scandinavian race
(L.f. intermedius) was seen at Anstruther on 30 April, and one of the
Northern Scandinavian race *(L.f. fuscus)* at Shell Bay on 11 December.
Another of the Northern race was at St Andrews on 25 December 1984.

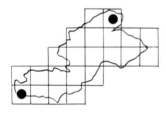   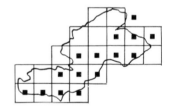

Herring Gull *Larus argentatus*

Common throughout the year

The Herring Gull occurs throughout the year both inland, and along and off the entire coast of Fife, and it may very commonly be seen following the plough in spring in great numbers.

There is little doubt that this gull has increased tremendously in the last hundred years. Baxter and Rintoul (1935) quoted Robert Gray as saying in *Birds of the West of Scotland* (1871) that 'on the eastern shores this bird is nowhere commoner in early spring than Fifeshire . . . on Leven sands they assemble in companies numbering thirty or forty'. The ladies added that 'Now we think nothing surprising to see a flock of three or four hundred there', and also mentioned that the greatest assemblage they had ever seen was on the Forth below Leith '. . . when there must have been thousands . . .' (VFF:289).

Now we could add that flocks of 'thousands' of Herring Gulls are not surprising; eg. in 1984, 6,000 were counted on the West Sands at St Andrews on 28 March, and 5,500 there on 29 November; while there were 3,650 at Glenrothes tip on 22 January that year. It is interesting to note that although most of our wintering gulls are of the native race *L.a.argenteus,* we are also hosts to many overseas birds, especially from Scandinavia. The Scandinavian race, *L.a.argentatus,* is dominant over ours, being nearly as large as the Great Black-backed Gull, and these birds are fairly easy to pick out in a flock of Herring Gulls by their larger size, darker back and heavier streaking on the neck (see also P.J. Grant, *Gulls, a guide to identification,* Poyser, 1982).

The Herring Gull was found breeding for the first time at Tentsmuir in 1955 (SB2:148), but has since ceased to do so. It does, however, nest profusely on the islands in the Firth of Forth, and in particular on the Isle of May, though now a great many are yearly culled here: 15,000 pairs nested here in 1972, as against none in 1880 (SB8:132).

It was mentioned by Sibbald in the *History of Fife and Kinross* (1710).

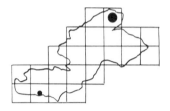 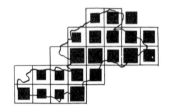

Iceland Gull   *Larus glaucoides*

Scarce visitor, mainly in winter

The Iceland Gull is not common in Fife, but it appears on passage— probably having followed fishing boats and there are records, mostly of immature and sub-adult birds, from every month of the year except June, with the majority of sightings in February, March and April. Places where it has been reported in the last ten years are the Tay Bridge, Fife Ness, Anstruther, Pittenweem, Leven, Methil docks, Kirkcaldy and Glenrothes tip. There is one record from Longannet on 22 February 1962, and it was seen a couple of times at Cult Ness in the 1950s when this area was still being reclaimed (EBB6:58).

In 1932 Baxter and Rintoul saw an immature Iceland Gull at the 'East Neuk' (Fife Ness) on the unusual date of 7 July (the only July record), and they also recorded one on the Tay at Newport on 15 August 1922, 'which had been there about a fortnight and stayed on for a considerable time' (B of S:658). Apparently Iceland Gulls were also present in lesser numbers with Glaucous Gulls in the big immigration of the winter of 1872-73 (see Glaucous Gull).

This gull may have become slightly less rare in Fife if the numbers of records are to be believed and it is not just an increase in observers.

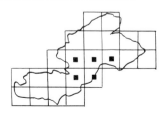

Glaucous Gull *Larus hyperboreus*

Scarce but regular visitor

Like the previous species, the Glaucous Gull is not very common in Fife, and the birds seen are mostly immatures and sub-adults. Very few records seem to exist for the 1970s, but since then several sightings have been reported every year: thus in 1984, 9 individuals were reported: from Tayport, St Andrews/Eden area, Fife Ness, Leven and Glenrothes tip, as well as an early record of a first-year bird at Kilconquhar Loch on 27 August (the first August record). Other recent records come from Tentsmuir, Crail, Anstruther, Pittenweem, Methil, Kirkcaldy; and from Cult Ness, but not since the 1950s. It is interesting that this Arctic gull has more than once been observed following the plough among other gulls (B of S:657 and EBB8:68).

The Glaucous Gull has been reported in every month of the year, with only one record each for July, August and September, and the majority of sightings in winter and early spring.

Apparently last century the Glaucous Gull used to occur exceptionally in huge numbers. Such an influx happened in 1872-73 when hundreds frequented the Firth of Forth which they ascended in numbers as far up as Kincardine. Easterly gales had raged before this great immigration took place, and Harvie-Brown gives the following evocative description of events: 'In the year, or season, of 1871-72, immense numbers of Arctic Gulls appeared upon our coasts; and these numbers were most patent in the Firth of Forth, and also in the mouth of Tay and estuary of the Eden and along the coast of North-east Fife. That these Arctic Gulls had appeared for many years previously there can be little reasonable doubt—indeed there seems to have been plenty of evidence of the fact, but . . . the winter of 1872-73 was previously unsurpassed upon our eastern seaboard. . . . At St Andrews I myself saw literally hundreds—principally Glaucous Gulls—that winter, screaming along the tops and under the shelter of the sandhills which fringe the golf-links, flying low over and almost touching the tops, and hugging the shelter these afforded from the gale from seaward that was blowing. Down along the rocky, cliffy shore under Gillespie Terrace also, these birds continued flying close under the edge of the cliffs over the rocky under-cliff, within half a stone-throw of the tops. It would seem that the great bulk of these Arctic Gulls first struck our coast about the projecting spur of Tents Muir, then followed along the coast till they reached the entrance of the Firth of Forth, and then deviated, as regards a very large proportion of their numbers, and followed that firth as far as Kincardine-on-Forth, and further up . . .' (FT:338-9).

Nothing like this has occurred since, but the increasing numbers of records may suggest that these gulls are recently becoming commoner again around our coast.

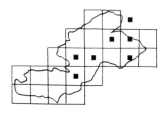

Great Black-backed Gull   *Larus marinus*

Common resident and winter visitor

This is our largest gull and it is present throughout the year, with non-breeding birds around in late spring and summer. In 1972 it nested for the first time at Tentsmuir, but the nest was robbed, and no reports of nesting anywhere in the county have been had before or since this century.

The biggest flocks are seen in autumn and winter, when a maximum of 980 were on the Eden estuary on 29 August 1981, and 850 at Tentsmuir Point the next day. Big roosts are also reported from Longannet (352 on 9 October 1982), and at Anstruther (136 on 4 December 1983). Small numbers are regularly seen inland, eg. at Lochore and on the Lomond Hills.

Grierson (1962) thought that up to 500 could be seen on passage in the autumn, but recent peak numbers are well up on that, so it appears that numbers have increased. An interesting ringing record comes from the Isle of May, where one bird was ringed on 16 December 1974, and was shot on 5 June 1981 at Stormya, Aure, Norway (1002 km; SB 81): it could well be that most of our winter visitors are from Scandinavia.

The Great Black-backed Gull was mentioned by Sibbald in the *History of Fife and Kinross* (1710).

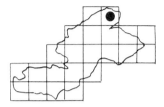 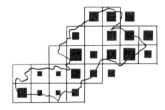

Kittiwake *Rissa tridactyla*

Present throughout the year, but does not breed

The Kittiwake is more maritime in its habits than most other gulls, and it is not commonly seen on our beaches, though young birds in particular may seek shelter inshore in bad weather. For this reason the Kittiwake is also commonest off the east coast, becoming less so further up the estuaries: Henry Boase (1964) said that it was scarce in the Tay above Tayport; and a juvenile as far up as Charlestown in the southwest on 19 November 1983 was unusual. Easterly gales may, however, bring big flocks right up into the Firth of Forth, such as 700 off Inverkeithing on 4 November 1984. There is also an extraordinary record of 3,000-4,000 Kittiwakes for three hours flying high towards the west by the Forth Road Bridge on 16 November 1973—possibly migrating, it was thought, to the Atlantic via Loch Lomond and Loch Fyne (SB8:77-78); and similar events have been reported since, but with varying numbers (SB8:324-25; 13:189-90).

The Kittiwake does not breed on the mainland of Fife, but breeds in large numbers on the Isle of May, and one bird ringed here in July 1976 was recovered near the Eider estuary, West Germany in November 1981, giving some indication of where birds spend the winter.

There are few records of the Kittiwake inland, though juveniles are occasionally found dead inland, such as one at the Peat Inn on 13 August 1968, and there are also records of birds at Kilconquhar, and an unusual record of 12 spending a week at Morton Lochs from 26 May to 8 June 1923 (BNF:81).

Maximum numbers usually occur in spring and autumn along the east coast, where in recent years peak counts have been 1,800 passing north off Fife Ness on 6 May 1984, and 1,400 at Tentsmuir Point on 19 June 1981. In the autumn 1,600 were at the mouth of the Eden on 30 August 1981, and 1,500 passsed east in an hour off Anstruther on 30 September 1983.

Records suggest that the Kittiwake has become much more common recently, Grierson mentioned a maximum count of 750 at Tentsmuir Point and 'small numbers only' in the Eden in the 1950s, whereas numbers are now far above that, no doubt due mainly to the fact that breeding pairs on the Isle of May have increased from 2,000 in 1946 to 3,450 pairs in 1972 (SB8:132).

But the Kittiwake is far from a newcomer to our waters: it was mentioned by Sibbald in the *History of Fife and Kinross* (1710), with a footnote in the second edition of 1803 which says that 'the young birds are a favourite dish with many people, and the shooting of them when they come new fledged, from the nests to the cliffs, is esteemed excellent sport' (p. 133). Dalgleish (1885) thought it was commoner than before about Culross and Kincardine, and in sprat years even 'numerous', as eg. in 1873 and 1885.

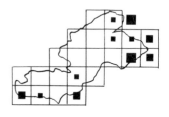

Ivory Gull   *Pagophila eburnea*

Very rare visitor

Very few records exist of this very rare gull from the high Arctic: W. Berry mentioned that an Ivory Gull appeared at the ferry pier at Newport, and it was shot for the Royal Scottish Museum, but no date was given (BNF:75); and Baxter and Rintoul saw one in Largo Bay on 14 September 1904 (VFF:299).

Caspian Tern   *Sterna caspia*

Very rare vagrant

This huge tern was seen for the first time in Fife in 1985 when a bird flew past Anstruther on 8 September.

Sandwich Tern   *Sterna sandvicensis*

Summer visitor and passage migrant: rare in winter

This is our largest common tern, and it is always the first to arrive in spring: one at Fife Ness on 12 March 1981 was exceptionally early, but in most years the first birds come at the end of March, while the main arrival is not till April, when streams of Sandwich Terns can be seen—and heard—cruising along the coast from Culross to Tayport: eg. 30 per hour were counted at St Andrews on 12 April 1964.

The Sandwich Tern does not seem to breed in Fife any longer. As many as 1,000 pairs were said to breed at Shelly Point about 1933, where they had moved after afforestation had driven them away from their previous site at Scotscraig (SB2:123). Although periodically driven away by bad weather (as eg. in 1968), 120 pairs still nested here as recently as 1974, but in spite of voluntary wardens attempting to fend off the worst predators and disturbances, not a single chick was fledged, and Sandwich Terns no longer nest here.

There is, however, little sign of decline in the numbers seen around the coast: 3,000-4,000 were on Pettycur Sands on 18 August 1981, and 2,000 at Goose Pools by Earlshall on 1 August 1984.

In the autumn vast numbers may be seen on their way south, the biggest passage recorded in recent years being 6,000+ seen in four hours flying past Fife Ness on 11 September 1976, and by the end of October most birds are away, while a few stragglers may linger on into November. In the last few years one or two Sandwich Terns have wintered in the Kirkcaldy-Burntisland area. Especially young birds seem to travel far: a young bird ringed at Leuchars in July 1939 was recovered in Angola in May 1941, and a nestling also ringed at Leuchars on 6 July 1936 was recovered on the Ivory Coast on 21 July 1936 (B of S:617), but there are also many records of Fife-ringed birds recovered in England.

Harvie-Brown (1906) considered the Sandwich Tern only as a passage migrant, although he said that Drummond Hay had suspected it of breeding at Tentsmuir towards the end of the nineteenth century. He also mentioned that a flock of about 20 were seen at the Edenmouth on 22 August 1903, which to us does not sound remarkable. Baxter and Rintoul (1953) reported 'huge flocks' seen in autumn, and 'streams of Sandwich Terns passing south at Balcomie' (B of S:617), but it is difficult to assess just how many that meant. Grierson, however, mentioned flocks of 400 off Tentsmuir in spring and autumn in the 1950s, and it therefore appears that the Sandwich Tern has increased on passage certainly since the start of the century and probably even in the last thirty years.

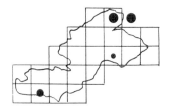 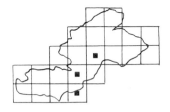

Roseate Tern   *Sterna dougallii*

Scarce summer visitor

This tern has become much scarcer in the last twenty years or so, and now only a few sightings are reported every year, usually of small numbers: 30 birds (3 juveniles) at Kirkcaldy on 10 August 1979 is the largest gathering reported in recent years, whereas 11 (4 juveniles) at Kirkcaldy on 15 August was the largest number recorded in 1984, with the years in between showing a steady decline.

In the 1980s a very small number has again been breeding in Fife. It appears to have bred only twice at Tentsmuir since 1936, when one pair nested there that year, and an amazing 18 pairs were found here in 1956 (SB2:286-293).

The Roseate Tern arrives at the end of April (the earliest being one at Fife Ness on 27 April 1968) and leaves again in late September or October (one with Sandwich Terns at Kirkcaldy on 11 October 1981 is the latest). In between, it is recorded mostly from the Firth of Forth.

Baxter and Rintoul said that it used to breed on the Isle of May last century, but that since 1887 the Roseate Tern had apparently ceased to breed in Scotland altogether: not till the second quarter of this century was nesting reported again, when 2 pairs were found on Tentsmuir in 1927 (B of S:619). A few pairs still breed on the islands in the Firth of Forth, and it is no doubt from these that the visitors to mainland Fife originate.

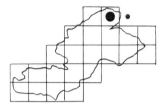

Common Tern   *Sterna hirundo*

Common passage migrant and summer visitor, breeds in decreasing numbers

The Common Tern arrives about the third week of April with the earliest record in the last twenty years being one at St Andrews on 14 April 1968, and it can be seen in small numbers anywhere along the coast from Kincardine to Newburgh, though less commonly west of Balmerino. It may also occasionally be seen inland, and Baxter and Rintoul (1935) related how they had often seen Common Terns feeding on the land, hovering over carrots and potato fields near Largo (VFF:303).

The Common Tern used to breed in several places in Fife, especially at Tentsmuir, where up till quite recently there had been a long and well-established colony. Harvie-Brown (1906) mentioned that the Common Tern had long bred here; and about 1920, 1,200 pairs nested here before afforestation drove them out. Then a new colony was established at Earlshall Moor, which became even more successful eventually, with 2,000 pairs in 1936 and still growing, till Second World War disturbances reduced the numbers drastically (SB2:121). As late as 1973, 300 pairs still nested here with some success, but since then all reports have been of more or less total failure.

Some Common Terns also nested at Longannet in the early 1960s when 97 nests were counted on 1 July 1962, but there have been no

F

records from here since. For several years they have attempted to nest along the shore of the Eden, but spring tides always wash the nests away.

In autumn the Common Tern gathers in huge flocks before departing. Thus there were 4,000 at Tentsmuir Point on 11 August 1983, and 1,550 there on 30 August 1981, whereas 300+ at Kirkcaldy was peak count in 1984. By the middle of October they have all left, though one stayed as late as 18 November in 1978.

Breeding birds have decreased drastically in the last fifteen years, but up to 1983 there was no apparent falling off of migrant birds.

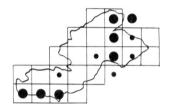

Arctic Tern   *Sterna paradisaea*

Summer visitor, breeds in small numbers

The Arctic Tern arrives about the same time as the Common Tern, in the third week of April, but is less common. It too used to breed on Tentsmuir. Harvie-Brown (1906) considered it uncommon, but mentioned that 12 nests were found on the shore of Tentsmuir in 1885, and that it had been breeding here certainly twenty or more years prior to this date (FT:333). In 1924, 50 pairs bred here, and after the Second

World War the colony increased again in size to reach, in 1953, a maximum of 350 nests on Earlshall as well as 150 on the east shore (SB2:120). Since 1973, when about 175 pairs attempted breeding in the Kinshaldy-Earlshall area, not a single chick has been fledged here, nor from the Eden estuary area, where a few optimistic terns yearly lay their eggs, only to be washed away by high tides.

The Arctic Tern also gathers in flocks in the autumn: maximum counts in recent years have been 800 roosting at the mouth of the Eden on 17 July 1982, and 700 at Tentsmuir Point on 31 July 1983. The largest count in 1984 was 165 at Leven on 20 August. There is an interesting ringing record of a chick ringed on 21 June 1976 at Roomassaare (Kingiseppa), Estonia SSR which was picked up dead on 15 August 1976 at Leven.

This tern appears always to have been less common on the east coast of Scotland than the Common Tern, but though it has decreased markedly as a breeding bird on the Fife mainland, it may still be seen in some numbers about the coast. It is, however, more maritime than the Common Tern and is rarely seen as far up the estuaries, and never inland.

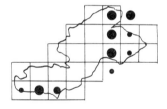

Little Tern   *Sterna albifrons*

Scarce summer visitor, no longer breeds

All our terns have declined as breeding species, but this beautiful little bird has been wiped out from all its Fife colonies due to increased disturbance from leisure activities on all our beaches. A few still visit the coast from thriving colonies in Angus and East Lothian, arriving from the end of April or mid-May, and leaving in August and September: Tentsmuir is the most frequented site, but within the last five years they have also been seen at the mouth of the Eden, Fife Ness, Elie, Shell Bay, Leven and Kirkcaldy. A maximum of 4 together were seen in 1984.

The last occasion on which breeding was attempted was in 1979, when 3 pairs failed at Tentsmuir. The colony there was recorded at 30 pairs and was said to be 'increasing' by Harvie-Brown in 1906: it fell to 16 in 1924, rose to 70 after the Second World War, but by 1958 had fallen again to 20-30, and continued to fall. Pairs used to breed at many other sites along the coast—I recall them at Kingsbarns in the early 1970s, and Baxter and Rintoul (1935) mentioned that it bred on the south side of the Eden and at Largo. The loss of so charming a bird from our breeding species is greatly to be lamented.

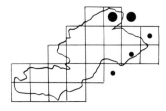

Black Tern   *Chlidonias niger*

Scarce migrant

This tern is seen most years in very small numbers, with the majority of records from the autumn. The Black Tern usually occurs singly, and 3 at St Andrews on 17 October 1963 was the largest number together since 1950. The earliest autumn record in the last twenty years was an adult with Little Gulls at Kilconquhar Loch on 9-24 July 1968, but that was unusual. Most records fall in August and September, and come from a variety of coastal places from Torry Bay to Tayport (not infrequently Fife Ness); but also from inland lochs, such as Lindores Loch, Morton Lochs, Carnbee reservoir, Kilconquhar Loch, Loch Gelly and Peppermill Dam.

There are rather fewer records in spring, and it is interesting that all but one of the available records at this time come from inland waters: Lindores Loch, Morton Lochs, Kilconquhar Loch and Peppermill Dam (here not since the 1950s) from late April till mid-June. A bird was also seen along the shore at Shelly Point on 13 June 1976.

The Black Tern has always been an uncommon visitor, and there is no sign of any change in status.

Guillemot *Uria aalge*

Common throughout the year

The Guillemot does not breed on mainland Fife, but it nests in large numbers on the Isle of May, and it may be seen offshore at all seasons, especially off East Fife but also further west; eg. 5 were recorded at Kincardine Bridge on 25 August 1983 after strong westerly gales. Henry Boase said it used to be common in the Tay up to the railway bridge from November to March, but 'it is now [1964] a casual up to Tayport' (BNF:88).

The Guillemot suffers badly in any oiling incident, and Grierson (1962) observed that about 60% of all oiled birds on the east shore of Tentsmuir were Guillemots. It is nevertheless a very successful species, and numbers are increasing around Fife. About 1,000 were counted going south at Fife Ness on 4 June 1984. The breeding population on the Isle of May has increased from 1,000-1,500 pairs in the 1880s to 3,500 pairs in 1972 (SB8:132).

The 'plane' as well as the 'hooked-beaked marrot' was mentioned in the *New Statistical Account* of Inverkeithing (1837), which presumably refers to Guillemots and Razorbills.

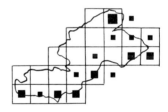

Razorbill   *Alca torda*

Resident

Rather rarer than the previous species, this bird also nests in increasing numbers on the Isle of May (a few hundred in the 1880s—600 in 1972). It occurs in the Tay as far up as Newport, and it is seen rather more commonly in St Andrews Bay than anywhere else. The largest flocks in the last few years have been 200 on 1 August in St Andrews Bay, and 100 at Tayport on 9 December both in 1983.

This species is also badly affected by oiling, and 282 were found oiled on the beaches in Fife alone in 1970 (SB6:235-250).

The Razorbill or 'Marrot' was mentioned by Sibbald in the *History of Fife and Kinross* (1710), and also in the *New Statistical Account* of Inverkeithing (1836). Harvie-Brown (1906) recorded the Razorbill as 'common' for North-east Fife, whereas Baxter and Rintoul (1936) thought it had decreased as a breeding bird on the Isle of May about 1924 but, as can be seen from the above records, it has been increasing here again in recent years. The Razorbill is also more inclined to come to the upper reaches of the Firth of Forth than the Guillemot, and there were 30 at Kincardine on 6 March 1983.

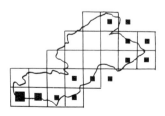

Black Guillemot   *Cepphus grylle*

Scarce visitor

The few records there are of this bird in the last twenty years are distributed between all the months of the year except July, and they are practically all of single birds, with the majority of sightings coming from St Andrews Bay and Fife Ness, but there are also records from Kingsbarns, St Monance, Elie, Burntisland and Kirkcaldy. The Black Guillemot is sometimes found dead from oiling.

Harvie-Brown (1906) said that it was occasionally found in St Andrews Bay, which is still one of the best places, and Baxter and Rintoul (1935) mentioned that it used to breed on the Isle of May, possibly up to 1850. They also recalled having seen several full-plumaged Black Guillemots about the May as late as in May 1934, though they never found any eggs (VFF:313).

This bird has obviously become rarer, at least in the second half of this century.

Little Auk   *Alle alle*

Scarce winter visitor

A large proportion of the records of this tiny auk is unfortunately of dead birds, and generally they are not close enough to the shore to be seen unless there have been prolonged easterly or NE gales to drive them into our bays in some numbers. Such a 'wreck' was caused by NE gales in late January 1983, when Little Auks were found all the way down the east coast of the country, and in Fife there were 19 reports alone, including 98 passing north at Fife Ness in two hours on 8 February, 14 at Crail, 3 at Inverkeithing and 3 at Newport, all on 11 February, with 7 in St Andrews Bay the next day. An even more recent influx of Little Auks took place in November 1985, when 200 were reported passing at Fife Ness, and smaller numbers of birds were seen at Largo Bay.

Harvie-Brown as well as Baxter and Rintoul mentioned such great wrecks or 'irruptions'; eg. there was a particularly memorable one in 1894-95 when 'many Little Auks were driven on to our shores and the Firth of Forth was full of them. On 13 January 70-80 were seen off

Aberdour . . .' (VFF:315). During these big wrecks Little Auks are occasionally blown far inland, and there is a record of a bird found alive but exhausted at Ladybank in late November 1958 (*Dundee Courier* 23.11.58).

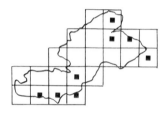

Puffin   *Fratercula arctica*

Summer visitor

The Puffin tends to keep well out to sea, which gives the impression that it is rarer than is really the case. It does not breed on mainland Fife, but the population on the Isle of May has positively exploded in recent years, so that now there are something like 14,000 pairs breeding here, compared with 3,000-4,000 in 1972, and anyone taking a boat trip in these waters will find an abundance of Puffins just a little way out.

The Puffins arrive in early April, and 12 were seen at North Queensferry on 24 April 1983. The nesting places are deserted again in late July, but many may be seen around the coast till October: eg. one was off Fife Ness on 5 October 1983. Occasionally birds are reported during the winter months: in 1983 one was seen off Anstruther on 9 January, and another at the Eden estuary on 13 February the same year.

Harvie-Brown (1906) called the Puffin 'occasional' to the Tay estuary; and Grierson (1962) said there were not many records for the Tay area since 1949, and all the most recent records were of dead birds (SB2:150). Baxter and Rintoul (1935) observed that they had been unable to trace any older records of this species breeding on the Isle of May, saying that it could of course still have done so. In 1880 not more than 20 pairs bred there, and in 1934 there were only 8-10 pairs

(VFF:316). The Isle of May now constitutes one of the major breeding sites for Puffin in the British Isles.

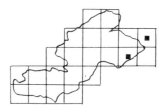

Pallas's Sand-Grouse *Syrrhaptes paradoxus*

Irrupted twice last century

In the second half of the nineteenth century two big migrations of Pallas's Sand-Grouse took place. The first was in 1863, before which the Sand-Grouse had never been recorded in the Forth area. The second great irruption was in 1888, when it was reckoned that no fewer than 1,500-2,000 Sand-Grouse visited Scotland in May, June and July. Baxter and Rintoul (1935) wrote that 'In the last ten days of May and early June small flocks were repeatedly seen between Elie and Crail, and three were shot on the Isle of May on 30 May out of a flock of about forty which were on the island for several days' (VFF:339). W. Berry (in his unpublished notes) recalled being told by Admiral Maitland Dougall that there were about 200 in a flock which visited the rough ground adjoining the heather on Tentsmuir, and 4 were shot for identification. Berry also shows on a map of the area exactly which area of the dunes was most favoured by the Sand-Grouse, but of course Tentsmuir has changed greatly in the years between. Geo. Bruce, reporting the same irruption in the *Land Birds about St Andrews* (1895), said that 'about 50 were seen on our links in first of June, others on Tentsmuir, Cambo, Pittenweem and Priormuir'. He also mentioned that one bird, which was killed by flying into the telegraph wires near the Eden, was found to be a female and had embryo eggs in its ovary (LBStA:553). Harvie-Brown (1906), however, said that there was not enough evidence that any of the birds had bred (FT:267-71).

This irruption was only part of a much bigger migration: Baxter and Rintoul (1952) mentioned that flocks of many hundreds began to move from their natural habitat in the steppes of Central Asia and South-East

Russia at the end of February that year, and spread out over Europe, north as far as Norway, west to Ireland, and south to Spain (B of S:530). The mind boggles as to the numbers which must have been on the move.

Rock Dove   *Columba livia*

Used to breed, ancestor to Feral Pigeon

It is not possible to say when the last pure Rock Doves bred in Fife, but it is undoubtedly quite some time ago. Harvie-Brown (1906), quoting W. Berwick, said it was rare in North Fife, and Baxter and Rintoul (1935) found that the Doo's Cave on Kincraig cliffs was inhabited by feral pigeons, as were the caves at Wemyss, where they believed Rock Doves used to breed 'in old days' (VFF:337).

In two most interesting articles on Rock Doves in Scotland (SB2:22-25; SB4: 359-365), Raymond Hewson said that the Rock Dove was first domesticated in Persia as long ago as 500 BC, and in Scotland probably about the same time as duck and geese, though he does not venture to say when that was. Hewson mentioned that it had been suggested that sea caves, such as the Wemyss caves, were fitted up with accessible nesting places, whence young pigeons could be harvested, and that this preceded the building of dovecots nearby (there is certainly an old dovecot at Macduff's Castle by East Wemyss), though Hewson could find no other records of such caves in Scotland. Whatever gave rise to the dovecot, it is a fact that enormous numbers of these were built in Fife between the fifteenth and nineteenth centuries. It was estimated by Thomson in the *General View of the Agriculture of the County of Fife* (Edinburgh, 1800) that 360 dovecots held 36,000 pairs of pigeons here which, as Hewson said, must have outnumbered by far the wild coast-dwelling pigeons. Hewson also suggested that as dovecots became ruinous (which was probably mostly last century), some pigeons continued to nest in the ruins, but most no doubt went to join their wild cousins, and as he said, 'The effect on the pigeons of the sea caves of recruitment from displaced dovecote pigeons must have been considerable'.

The *Winter Atlas* below shows the distribution of the Feral Pigeon. No attempt has been made to separate feral pigeons that are obviously descendants of the Rock Dove from others (eg. the Pied) which are not.

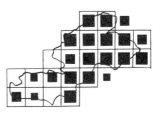

Stock Dove   *Columba oenas*

Common resident

Stock Doves breed in holes in trees or on the ground; they are particularly common around Tentsmuir and the fields at the back, where it would indeed be difficult not to see them most of the year. The East Neuk also has a good population, and small parties may be seen in all parts of Fife, either by themselves, or feeding with Woodpigeons.

The Stock Dove colonised Scotland only in the latter half of last century; Dalgleish (1885) recorded that it was first found breeding in Fife at Tulliallan in 1878. Harvie-Brown (1906) stated that it 'Formerly appears to have been unknown, then it was recorded as an "exceedingly rare bird", and finally it became almost suddenly abundant' (FT:259).

In fact, the development parallels the more recent spread of the Collared Dove to a remarkable degree. Dr. John Berry says that at one time the Stock Dove was even commoner than Woodpigeons in North Fife, after which it became very rare again, before stabilising at a much lower level (pers.com.).

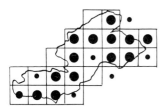 

Woodpigeon   *Columba palumbus*

Common resident

This is one of our commonest breeding birds, reported from every
possible square in the *Breeding Atlas,* and it may be seen anywhere and
everywhere. In winter, as the weather turns colder, our resident
population is joined by migrants, apparently mostly Scottish-bred,
seeking milder climates near the coast (see *Bird Study* 9:7-41), and vast
flocks are then seen in Fife. Just such a movement was described in
Scottish Birds: 'Great numbers of Woodpigeons were moving in the East
Neuk of Fife on 30 December (1961), a day of intense cold and north
wind. Flocks of 200-300 began to pass eastwards on a broad front over
Largo, Kilconquhar, Elie, and further east from about 10.30 a.m. For
an hour they went on almost without a break and there must have been
many thousands. After an interval the birds began returning westwards
in the same endless stream, possibly having failed to find sufficient
open ground in the East Neuk to sustain such numbers' (SB2:105).
    In 1984 similar huge flocks were seen of about 15,000 near Chance
Inn by Craigrothie, and 10,000 at Dunino.
    The Woodpigeon appears always to have been common in Fife,
indeed Harvie-Brown (1906) reported that professional pigeon-
shooters were employed to shoot and trap a great number during
winter and early spring, but also that Woodpigeons did not seem as
common then as they used to be (FT:258). They appear, however, to
have recovered from this set-back a long while ago, and there is no
evidence of any change in status in the last fifty years.

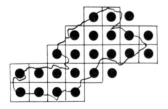
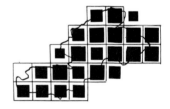

Collared Dove   *Streptopelia decaocto*

Common resident

It was only in 1959 that the first Collared Dove was seen in Fife, and the following 'Short Note' appeared in *Scottish Birds:* 'On 23 and 25 August 1959 I observed a Collared Dove which was calling regularly and lustily from a poplar in a garden near the park above Lower Dunfermline Station. It was very shy and kept to the treetops so that it was extremely difficult to get good views of it among the foliage. I had suspected its identity from the call-note . . . ' (SB1:189). Another bird was reported from Methil that autumn, which was thought to be an escape, but in 1965 the first article appeared in *Scottish Birds* (3:292-301) outlining the spread of this dove in Scotland, and listing all known records up to the end of 1964, which in Fife came from nine places, excluding the two above-mentioned: by October 1964, the Collared Dove had spread as far east as Crail, and as far north as Dunbog and St Andrews, and it was breeding at Dunfermline. After that numbers increased by leaps and bounds: the *Breeding Atlas* found Collared Doves breeding in nearly every square in the period 1968-72, and flocks of 200+ were reported at Wormiston from January to March 1971, increasing to 350 the following year, with 200 at Strathkinness in mid-March 1974. Interestingly enough such big flocks are now rare, the biggest numbers recorded in the 1980s being 65 at Kilrenny on 14 November 1981, and the total population of Collared Doves has probably fallen and stabilised since the first concentrated influx.

The explosive spread of the Collared Dove can be compared to that of the Stock Dove last century.

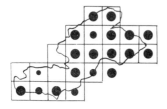 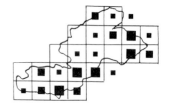

Turtle Dove   *Streptopelia turtur*

Scarce passage migrant

Most records of this species in the last thirty years are in May and June and come from Fife Ness, the earliest being one here on 30 April 1968. But there are also records from every month between May and October, practically all being sightings of single birds. Apart from Fife Ness, places where it has been reported since 1960 are Morton Lochs, Dunino, Crail, Kilrenny, St Monance, Kilconquhar, Largo Bay, Thornton and Culross.

It has never been common in Fife: Harvie-Brown (1906) called it rare, but also 'Occasional visitant in autumn and winter' (FT:267). He did not, however, support this remarkable last statement with any concrete examples, October being the latest date he mentioned. The only old record for North Fife was a bird shot at Boarhills in August 1863 (FT:267). All Baxter and Rintoul's records in the Forth area were between May and September too, although they mentioned none specific for Fife, whereas Dalgleish (1885) mentioned a young bird shot at Tulliallan in September about 1872.

There is no change of status.

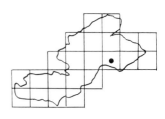

Ring-necked Parakeet *Psittacula krameri*

Scarce vagrant

There are not many records of this bird in Fife, the most recent being one of a juvenile at Fife Ness on 18 September 1984; a male spent some weeks near Glenrothes in autumn 1977 (Ballantyne, 1982), and there was an adult, again at Fife Ness, on 1 November 1975.

These birds are now flying free, notably in the London area, and the species has been included on the British List (class C). Ballantyne also mentions a bird observed flying out over the Firth of Forth from Dunbar towards Fife Ness in April 1976.

In his unpublished notes, W. Berry said that he had known the Parakeet in a semi-feral state since 1875.

Cuckoo *Cuculus canorus*

Summer visitor in small numbers

The Cuckoo arrives in late April or early May, the earliest record since 1960 being one at Mossmorran on 21 April 1984. It may then be heard calling till mid-June, and departs again in August, the latest record in recent years being a juvenile at Anstruther on 6 September 1985.

It is difficult to know how many birds do actually breed in Fife, but it appears that the Cuckoo moves in across Fife and may breed anywhere where there are Meadow Pipits. Thus a juvenile was seen at Sauchope caravan park (Crail) with Meadow Pipits on 14 June 1984. The stronghold is no doubt the Lomond Hills, where 7-8 males were heard in May 1984. Other places in the west, where it has been heard, are Lochmill Loch, Gauldry, Strathmiglo and Lochore Meadows, while in the east reports have come from Tentsmuir, Reres Wood, St Andrews, the Eden estuary, Fife Ness and Kilconquhar in the last few years.

Harvie-Brown (1906) did not consider the Cuckoo very abundant in North-east Fife, whereas Grierson (1962) said that it bred at Tentsmuir and was reported from all parts including Morton Lochs. Baxter and Rintoul (1935) said numbers varied from year to year, but that there were very few in East Fife, and that sometimes several years went by without them hearing one (VFF:163). Dalgleish, however, did not find it uncommon in West Fife around 1885.

It is almost entirely the Meadow Pipits that act as foster parents for Cuckoos in the area, but for three years running (1980-1983) a particular pair of Blackbirds in a garden in St Andrews also became foster parents. Their nest was in a dense, inaccessible thicket of ivy, and the parent Blackbirds were frequently observed totally exhausting themselves trying to feed their monstrous, ever-expanding nestling.

There is no real evidence of any change in status.

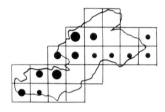

Barn Owl *Tyto alba*

Scarce resident

The Barn Owl has become rare in recent years, though in 1984 there were more reports than usual, including a pair at Buckhaven, with other records from East Balrymont, East Wemyss, Dunshalt and Dunfermline, suggesting that a few pairs are still left in Central Fife.

The Barn Owl has not always been quite so scarce: it was mentioned in the *New Statistical Account* of Inverkeithing, as well as nesting in the woods of Dunbog and Ayton; and Harvie-Brown (1906) said it was fairly common, though he gave no details specifically relating to Fife. Baxter and Rintoul (1953), however, said that the Barn Owl decreased seriously in the second half of the nineteenth and first decades of the twentieth centuries, but also that it had reappeared in Fife in 1910, had increased for a time, but was decreasing again (B of S:278). Grierson (1962) also found that very few had been seen this century at Tentsmuir (SB2:151); but elsewhere there are a number of records in the 1960s from the Crail-St Monance-Colinsburgh area, where there are none now; and also from Longannet.

The Barn Owl is usually very nocturnal in its habits, though it is occasionally about in full daylight, as when feeding young or on winter afternoons, and one was seen on 4 October 1981 frequenting the Lochore nature reserve in full daylight.

All owls seem to have got scarcer in recent years, but the Barn Owl more so than most. It does, however, appear from past records that numbers have always fluctuated, and it would be very pleasing if—after a period of decline in the 1970s—another upward swing was on the way.

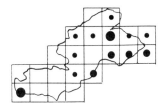 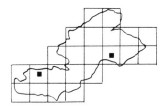

Scops Owl   *Otus scops*

Very rare visitor

Only one record, of a female shot at Montrave, near Lundin, on 16 May 1909 (VFF:177).

[Eagle Owl   *Bubo bubo*

Pennant, in his *Tour of Scotland* 1777, mentioned an Eagle Owl shot in Fife, but gave no other details except that it was 'probably a migrant from Norway'. This might in fact not have been a truly wild bird, and Harvie-Brown (1906) related how a friend of his had obtained a young Eagle Owl in Norway, 'taken from the nest', which he had subsequently brought back to Scotland alive (FT:177).]

Snowy Owl   *Nyctea scandiaca*

Very rare visitor

Very few records in Fife. The most recent was a bird seen on the West Sands, St Andrews, in late September 1982. It was found sitting on the beach and was very tame, allowing the observer to approach within yards of it, when it took off and circled low before disappearing over the golf course. This record has not been published before, but the observer knew Snowy Owls well from the zoo, and gave a perfectly satisfactory description.

Another bird was seen on the Eden golf course, St Andrews on 31 January 1936 (Scot.Nat.1936:45), while Baxter and Rintoul mentioned a Snowy Owl, which had been shot by the keeper at Lahill about 1875, and which was subsequently stuffed and preserved for a time at Lahill House (VFF:177).

Little Owl   *Athene noctua*

Very rare visitor

Only one record, which was a bird caught at East Grange, six miles west of Dunfermline, on 9 November 1910. This was mentioned by Baxter and Rintoul (VFF:178).

Tawny Owl   *Strix aluco*

Fairly common resident

The *Breeding Atlas* found this owl breeding in 13 squares and present and/or possibly breeding in the remaining squares, and although there are signs that it may have become rather less numerous in the 1980s, it is still a common bird throughout Fife.

Owls have been much persecuted down through the centuries, having often been classed as 'Vermin', and trapped or destroyed on sight: Harvie-Brown (1906) eg. related a shocking incident of 22 Tawny Owls—all adult birds—hung up by their feet on a large hoarding as recently as January 1900, and although that was in Perthshire, there is little reason to suppose that similar things did not happen in Fife.

Both Dalgleish and Baxter and Rintoul (1935) thought the Tawny Owl common in South Fife, and Grierson (1962) said it was present all the year at Tentsmuir, and that it had nested in a nest box at Morton Lochs (SB2:151). Tentsmuir is still a favourite area for this species, but its hooting may be heard almost anywhere, and frequently in built-up areas, as eg. St Andrews and Anstruther.

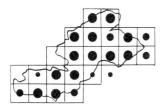 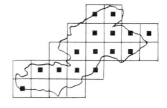

Long-eared Owl   *Asio otus*

Scarce resident

The Long-eared Owl is generally found in small woods, in particular coniferous ones, but it may also hunt over open country. The *Breeding Atlas* recorded it breeding in 7 squares in the five-year period 1968-72, and 'present' or 'probably breeding' in another 6, but since then there have been many reports of poor breeding success, and in 1977, 8+ pairs were reported to have disappeared from their territories. In 1981 and 1982, however, a pair was reported to have nested at Morton Lochs with some success, and in 1983 another pair bred at Gauldry. There are also other recent summer records of birds at Tayport, Scotscraig, Kirktonbarns (Tentsmuir), Redwalls, Fife Ness, Lochore Meadows, Star and Inverkeithing; and there are several records of Long-eared Owls at Fife Ness in May, and in October/November, which suggests migration, but it could also be owls coming to Fife Ness to prey on newly arrived and exhausted migrants.

In winter the Long-eared Owl may roost in some numbers: there was a winter roost in 1982-83 at Port Laing by Rosyth with a maximum of 4 birds in December and February, and there was a roost at

Inverkeithing the following year, with a maximum count of 3 birds on 30 January 1984; while in 1952 a flock of as many as 10-11 birds in a blackthorn thicket was reported near Burntisland (EBB3:23).

Dalgleish (1885) for West Fife, Harvie-Brown (1906) for North Fife, and Balfour Kirke (1911) for Burntisland, all described the Long-eared Owl as common, whereas Baxter and Rintoul (1953) said that it had decreased in Fife. Grierson (1962) could still say that it nested on Tentsmuir, both in the new forests and at Earlshall (SB2:151), but records indicate that this owl has decreased markedly in recent years.

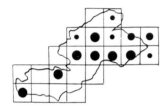 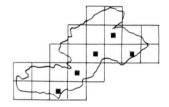

Short-eared Owl   *Asio flammeus*

Winter visitor, sometimes breeds

The Short-eared Owl generally hunts in daytime over open ground or young forestry plantations, and it is not uncommon in winter, when it may be flushed from patches of rough grass and stones: in 1984 there were over 30 reports from all parts of the county, from January to 2 May, and again from 5 August onwards; 2-3 birds spent the winter of 1984-85 at the disused airfield at Crail.

The Short-eared Owl used to breed in Fife. H. Boase (1964) said it first nested in North Fife at Earlshall in 1936, that it had nested here several times since, and also that a pair had spent the summer of 1953 at Morton Lochs, though breeding was not proved (BNF:92). The *Breeding Atlas* shows it as definitely breeding in 3 squares during the survey years 1968-72, but no breeding has been proved since. Ballantyne (1982) speaks, however, of the species breeding 'on the lower slopes of the Lomonds' without giving details.

Harvie-Brown (1906) observed that the Short-eared Owl used to breed in North Fife, and mentioned Kinshaldy and Priormuir, but also that it was 'many years ago'. Baxter and Rintoul (1935) also remarked that it 'used to breed' in South Fife. On migration they noted that some autumns 'great numbers arrive from overseas', and in late autumn they had often flushed Short-eared Owls, sometimes in considerable numbers, when riding through the old cadgers' roads of East Fife (VFF:175). But it is difficult to say what 'great' or 'considerable' numbers meant, and there is no real evidence that the wintering numbers of this owl have changed substantially.

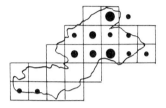 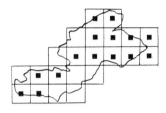

[Tengmalm's Owl   *Aegolius funereus*

Professor Heddle wrote a note on 28 January 1886 to the *Citizen* that he had seen one or other of the two rarest owls known in Britain, the Little Owl or Tengmalm's Owl, on a visit to St Andrews:

'Passing the west gable of St Leonard's Chapel at dusk, my notice was attracted to the perfectly noiseless flight of the owl, by the chattering of three birds which were teasing it. The owl settled on the laburnum near the chapel . . . Though I got within seven feet of the bird, immediately beneath it, I was unable to ascertain to which of the above pigmy species it belonged—partly from want of light, and partly from its ruffling its breast feathers, in which it muffles its bill in a slumbrous manner. I was thus unable to note the chequered colour of the breast, which is one of the best points of distinction between the species. Disturbed either by myself or its assailants, the tiny *strigid* made off with the usual fluffy flight of its order to the tree before the Ladies' School . . .' Professor Heddle goes on to say that he had shot a *Strix Tengmalmi* in Wales (Orkney?) in 1857, and that this was placed in the Museum in Kirkwall, and at the same time he condemns the senseless persecution of owls.

The whole charming letter is produced in full in Geo. Bruce's *The Land Birds about St Andrews* (1895). I would agree with Bruce, who thought it a Tengmalm's Owl from Heddle's description, and that the large head, short neck, and full, downy plumage of this species would give it the appearance of 'ruffling its breast feathers, etc.' In addition the

Handbook of British Birds mentions a record of Tengmalm's Owl at
Peterhead in February 1886, whereas no Little Owl was recorded in
Scotland till 1902, but, of course, there is no way of being absolutely
certain.]

Nightjar   *Caprimulgus europaeus*

There are no recent records of this bird in Fife. It was mentioned in the
New Statistcal Account of Cupar (1836), and of Dunfermline (1844),
where it was an occasional visitor. Harvie-Brown (1906) quoted W.
Berwick as saying, 'I hear one often here [i.e. Pathcondie] at night', but
also that he considered it not very common in North Fife (FT:159). W.
Berry thought it was a visitor on passage in autumn to the Tayport area,
though he never saw it on Tentsmuir and did not think that it bred
anywhere in the area (W. Berry's unpublished notes, 1872-1947);
Baxter and Rintoul (1935) mentioned an old record of one shot on
Benarty in 1870, and that in South Fife it was a regular summer visitor
to Cullaloe and Tulliallan districts in 1885. They also quoted Balfour
Kirke as saying as late as 1926 that the Nightjar was increasing and
breeding in one or two suitable places about Burntisland, and that it
was not uncommon about Cullaloe. They added, 'We have no record
of the bird having bred farther east in Fife, though it occurs on
migration in this district [Largo?] as in other parts of the area'
(VFF:171).

    It is not known when the last Nightjar was seen in Fife.

Swift *Apus apus*

Common summer visitor

The Swift usually arrives about the first day of May, with the earliest record in the last thirty years being 28 April 1968, when 6 were seen at Kilconquhar Loch. It nests in high buildings such as the castle of St Andrews, or on high crags, eg. on the rocks near Burntisland. It is possibly our finest flyer, spending almost its entire life airborne, except for the period when both parents brood the nest. In early morning and late evening big screaming parties may be seen high in the air from late June onwards, as they feed on insects: eg. 350 were counted over Kilconquhar Loch on 5 August 1985, and 230 there on 4 July 1982.

In autumn the Swift leaves quite early: in 1968 numbers peaked at Kilconquhar at 500 on 6 August, but they had all left by 25 August nearly three weeks later, whereas a passage of Swifts was noted off Fife Ness on 3 September 1974. Swifts are unusual after the middle of September, though one or two stragglers may stay till later and one, seen at Fife Ness on 1 November 1975, is the latest record in recent years.

Harvie-Brown (1906) quoted W. Berry as saying that the Swift was rare or at least not very common in North Fife, but in Berry's unpublished notes there is a reference to the Swift in 1948, when it is said to be 'widespread but not dense'. Boase, too, thought it uncommon till 1911, certainly at Newport; whereas Baxter and Rintoul (1935) mentioned for South Fife that Kilconquhar was by then a favourite haunt, 'where they are found in numbers'; Loch Gelly also was visited by 'great assemblages' (VFF:168). It is therefore evident that the Swift has spread and possibly increased this century: the *Breeding*

Atlas showed it breeding in Fife in every square but two between 1968 and 1972, and there is no reason to suppose that this is not still the case.

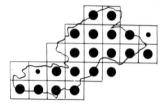

Little Swift   *Apus affinis*

Very rare vagrant

The first record of this species in Fife was a bird seen off Castle Cliff, St Andrews, on 29 May 1985. This record has not yet been considered by the Rarities Committee.

Kingfisher   *Alcedo atthis*

Rare resident

The Kingfisher's incredibly vivid colours ensure that it is not easily overlooked, but unfortunately it is not a very common bird in Fife. It nests mostly along banks of rivers, and in 1984 a pair bred successfully at Glenrothes on the River Leven; there have also been reports of possible breeding from one or two other places recentiy.

During the rest of the year birds may be seen in a number of places where they do not breed, eg. right down by the sea at St Andrews, where a Kingfisher was seen on a number of occasions between 2 October and 23 December 1984, or at Leven power station in December 1981; there are also recent reports of sightings from the Kenly Burn (Boarhills), Edenside, Morton Lochs, the Bluther Burn and Black Devon in the west; and, earlier, at Gartmore Dam and Shiremill Pond, but not since 1953.

The Kingfisher was mentioned in the *New Statistical Account* of Cupar and of Monimail (1836). Geo. Bruce (1895) said he had seen it along the Kinness Burn, close to the shore, and also on the Kenly, the

Cameron, the Kinaldy, and other burns in the district, as well as on the Eden up at Dairsie and Dura Den, which he thought were favourite resorts, but he did not think they were common (LSTA:226), and although Bruce is not always accurate, there is no reason to disbelieve him here.

The *Scottish Naturalist* (1905) reported that a Kingfisher was shot at Tayport on 29 October 1904, and because it was already then under the Protection of the Birds Act, the shooter was fined half a crown by the sheriff. W. Berry in his unpublished notes reported the Kingfisher as a not infrequent visitor to Tayfield, though he had not seen it for a year or two (1940s); and Boase (1964) mentioned a record of as many as 4 at Morton Lochs on 14 August 1928, two records from Tayport shore in the 1920s, and a stunning passage of about 30 Kingfishers in all, in small parties, passing south along the shore at Tentsmuir Point on 1 October 1927. However, there had been no records for some years from North Fife (BNF:93).

For West Fife, Baxter and Rintoul (1935) observed that it bred or had done so at Peppermill Dam, and also at a burn near Keavil, whereas in Central Fife it nested at Milnathort and on the River Leven, as well as on the Balbirnie Burn, and had done so on the River Ore. They stressed, however, that it had never been numerous, and that numbers fluctuated considerably.

In spite of this fluctuation of numbers, the Kingfisher appears sadly to have become much rarer in the last thirty years. There were practically no sightings in 1982 or 1983, and there had been no records of confirmed breeding anywhere in Fife for many years till 1984.

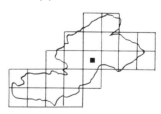

[**Roller**   *Coracias garrulus*

Baxter and Rintoul mentioned a record of a bird of this species which was 'got' at Auchmeden, near Aberdour, Fife, on 9 September 1905 (VFF:164). *The Ordnance Gazetteer of Scotland*, 1884, however, gives the only 'Auchmedden' as near Aberdour, Aberdeenshire, which makes this species very doubtful for Fife.]

Hoopoe   *Upupa epops*

Occasional passage migrant

There are only a few published records of this exotic bird in Fife. In the last thirty years they have been as follows:

Spring:	*Autumn:*
1 Guardbridge 12.6.83	1 St Andrews golf course 14.10.82
1 Kingsbarns 17.5.75	1 Boarhills 12.9.78
1 Kirkcaldy 14.4.74	1 Fife Ness 2-3.10.76
1 Lower Largo 23.5.68	2 Fife Ness 1.9.68 (as a pair)
1 (heard) Largo 1.6.68	1 Cupar 9.9.68
(same bird?)	1 Anstruther 20.9.67
1 Kilmaron Castle 10.5.66	
1 Elie golf course 16.5.60	

Ballantyne (1982) writes that 'a small party was seen north of Kirkcaldy in the early 1950s' and of older records, Baxter and Rintoul (1935) mentioned that there were several from coastal areas in South Fife, but gave no details, except that one was shot below Barnsmuir between Crail and Kilrenny in 1844 (VFF:164). Harvie-Brown (1906) had only two records for Fife: one shot at Birkhill on 8 October 1892, and another at Elie House on 8 May 1875.

It is interesting to note that the Hoopoe has been seen in a much wider number of places in Fife compared to eg. the Wryneck, of which nearly all sightings have come from Fife Ness. This could be due to the differences in the brightness of plumage, where the Hoopoe is indeed difficult to overlook anywhere, even by non-birdwatchers, whereas this is hardly the case with the Wryneck.

There is no apparent change in the status of this species.

Wryneck *Jynx torquilla*

Occasional passage migrant

In the last thirty years the following sightings have been reported:

Spring:	*Autumn:*
1 Fife Ness 26-30.4.83	1 Fife Ness 1-3.9.84
1 Fife Ness 10-11.5.75	1 Fife Ness 22.8.83
1-2 Fife Ness 29.4-4.5.74	1 St Andrews 16.9.83
1 Fife Ness 10.5.70	1-2 Fife Ness 31.8-1.9.80
	1 Fife Ness 29.8.76
	2 Fife Ness 19.9.76
	1 Fife Ness 26.9.76
	1 Crail 10.10.76 (dead)
	1 Fife Ness 31.8.74
	1 Fife Ness 16.9.73
	1 Fife Ness 23.8.70
	2 Fife Ness 16.9.69
	1 Fife Ness 15.9.68
	1 Eden estuary 5.9.63
	(first for the area)
	1 Fife Ness 5.9.63
	1 Newport 29.9.56
	(inside a car!)

It is apparent from the above that the Wryneck is commonest on passage in autumn, and has been seen far more often at Fife Ness than elsewhere in the county compared eg. to the Hoopoe. This could well be due to the Wryneck's relatively inconspicuous plumage (see article in *Fife and Kinross Bird Report* (1983).

The Wryneck was considered an occasional passage (autumn) migrant in the older accounts; Harvie-Brown (1906) only mentioned a bird shot in Gilston wood, but gave no date; and Baxter and Rintoul (1935) said there were several records for South Fife, but again mentioned only one record of a bird visiting Elie on 30 August 1905.

There seem to be no records for the early 1950s or the years leading up to this period, and it therefore appears that the Wryneck has become commoner on passage, coinciding with the first breeding records in Scotland in the late 1960s (SB6:154 & SB10:158-174).

Green Woodpecker   *Picus viridis*

Common resident locally

The Green Woodpecker inhabits parkland and deciduous woodland, especially where the trees are well scattered. It nests in holes in trees, which it makes new every year, and in 1984 it was reported present—though not necessarily breeding—in 22 areas, distributed all over Fife, detected, no doubt, in many cases by its mad laughter.

The spread of the Green Woodpecker northwards from England, not just to Fife, but to much of Scotland in the last fifteen to twenty years is truly remarkable. Harvie-Brown (1906), quoting W. Berwick, said that it was an irregular visitor to North Fife last century, mentioning that one was shot at Fiddinch near St Andrews in August 1887, and others in 1888 at Cambo, Gilston and St Fort woods. However, he had not been able to verify these (FT:164). *The Handbook of British Birds* (1943) reported it as a rare vagrant to Scotland as a whole, and Baxter and Rintoul (1953) had only one record of a Green Woodpecker visiting Fife in spring 1933.

Throughout the 1960s, however, reports were coming in of sightings at Tulliallan and Burntisland, and then 2 juveniles were found at Burntisland (7-11 August 1969). In 1971 the Green Woodpecker was recorded breeding at 7 sites, and in 1973 at Tentsmuir for the first time. In 1976 the report in *Scottish Birds* reads, 'Continue increase, now common in some areas. 5 pairs at Tentsmuir'.

This is a most excellent addition to our regular breeding birds in Fife.

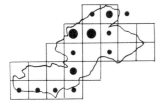 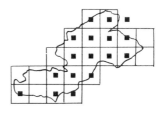

Great Spotted Woodpecker   *Dendrocopos major*

Scarce resident

The Great Spotted Woodpecker has never been common. It frequents wooded areas and parkland, where its 'drumming' may give it away. It seems to prefer rather larger trees than the Green Woodpecker.

Since 1981, breeding has been proved only at Morton Lochs and Falkland (1982), at Devilla forest (1983), and at Star Moss (1984), but other places where it has been reported 'present' in recent years are Gauldry, Balmerino, St Fort, Birkhill, Scotscraig, Tentsmuir, St Andrews, Balcaskie, Kilconquhar and Limekilns. It could well be that some of these records are migrants of the continental or 'Northern' race (see Jim Cobb in *Fawn* 3:7).

The Great Spotted Woodpecker apparently bred in the county early last century, but about 1850 it became extinct as a breeding bird in Scotland (HBBII:286). Harvie-Brown (1906) referred to it only as an autumn and winter visitor. He mentioned a very old record from the *Scots Magazine* (vol. lxxix:95) of a fine male shot at Melville House in February 1817, and also that a few pairs apparently bred yearly then in the old woods of Melville and Rankeillor. Of autumn and winter records he mentioned that the Great Spotted Woodpecker turned up almost every year, but that in 1868 a 'rush' took place and two specimens in the St Andrews museum were dated 1868: one from Boarhills and the other from Kittocks Den. There were also records at the end of the century from other places in North Fife such as Cambo, Leuchars and Scotscraig (FT:160). Dalgleish (1885) called it rare in West Fife, but mentioned one shot at West Grange on 3 April 1871.

Early in the present century it began to breed again in small numbers: thus Baxter and Rintoul (1935) reported that it had bred at Brucefield near Dunfermline in 1909. Boase mentioned a pair breeding at Birkhill in 1924, and W. Berry said that it bred at Tayfield in 1946 and 1947 (unpublished notes). It bred again at Brucefield in 1951 and 1953 (EBB3:71), and a few breeding records were forthcoming in the 1960s from Wormit and Morton Lochs, but reports were generally that the breeding population fluctuated from year to year. A note in *Scottish Birds* (6:106) stating that the Great Spotted Woodpecker was absent from much of Fife in 1969, still holds true in 1985.

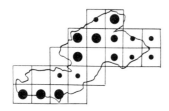   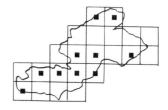

Wood Lark   *Lullula arborea*

Very rare visitor

There is only one old record of this species in Fife, which is of a Wood Lark found at Balcomie on 7 April 1924 (BNF:94).

Skylark   *Alauda arvensis*

Common resident and winter visitor

The Skylark nests from the middle of April in fields of growing crops or grass, where it lays its eggs in a hollow. It is one of our commonest breeding birds, with the *Breeding Atlas* showing confirmed breeding in every possible square between 1968 and 1972, and there is no reason to suppose that this is not still the case.

In the autumn a substantial migration takes place. It is difficult to determine how many of our own breeding birds leave the area, but it is likely that a substantial number of immigrants from North Europe spend the winter here; and especially in October big movements of Skylarks can be observed in East Fife, when eg. 200 per hour were passing north at Fife Ness on 25 October 1980, and 180 were seen moving south-west over Anstruther on 8 October 1983.

The really huge flocks, however, occur in winter, when cold weather may send the Skylarks moving to milder temperatures, especially to coastal areas. Such a spectacular weather movement at Longannet on 4 February 1961 was vividly described in *Scottish Birds*: '... There was an inch of snow on the ground: in the $2\frac{1}{2}$ hours before midday 30 flocks were noted, totalling nearly 4,500 birds. The largest flock totalled nearly 500 birds; they were swarming westwards along the north shore of the Forth with smaller flocks coming across the water from the Grangemouth side' (SB1:12). The biggest recent flock recorded were 1,000 at Crail on 6 January 1982.

Baxter and Rintoul (1935) noted the fact that these movements of Skylarks are often passing in different directions on the same day, either to our snow-free shores, or on their way to milder districts elsewhere (VFF:96).

By March and April our breeding birds are back at their sites. The Skylark is no newcomer to our area: on 4 December 1532, 80 Skylarks were procured at Falkland for King James V's table (ExDJV:appendix), and Skylark was also mentioned in the *Old Statistical Account* of Kilconquhar (1793). Harvie-Brown (1906), however, considered it less common as a breeding bird than was generally supposed, a statement which was also corroborated in W. Berry's unpublished notes for Tayfield in North Fife, and by H. Boase (1964), though he found it a common nesting bird on Tentsmuir. Baxter and Rintoul (1935) had always found it common in South Fife. There is no evidence of any change in status in the last twenty years, though records suggest a somewhat patchier distribution than is immediately obvious from the *Breeding Atlas*.

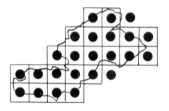 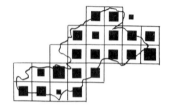

Shore Lark *Eremophila alpestris*

Uncommon winter visitor

There are only a few records of this species, and they are as follows:

1 at West Sands, St Andrews in March 1985
1 at Tentsmuir on 13 October 1977
2 on the Eden estuary on 5 October 1976
3 at Fife Ness on 6 October 1976
2 at Tentsmuir on 20 October 1976
1 at St Monance on 3 January 1970
1 near Cellardyke bathing pool on 1 January 1963, feeding on the verge of the road
2 (a pair) spent a week at Shelly Point from 25 November 1951 (EBB1:3)
3 at Tayport on 7 January 1924 (SB2:152)
1 in Largo Bay on 13-14 January 1911
1 at St Andrews on 31 December 1869 (Scot.Nat.1871:81)
2 caught near St Andrews in winter 1865 (ibid.).

There is little evidence of any change in status.

Sand Martin *Riparia riparia*

Summer visitor, breeds locally

The Sand Martin nests in banks of rivers, quarries and sea cliffs, and it is one of our earliest summer visitors, arriving often at the end of March, the earliest record in the last thirty years being one at Kilconquhar Loch on 20 March 1983; and the main arrival in the middle of April.

Sand Martins are very gregarious, always nesting in colonies, which have been recorded in a number of places in Fife, as is evident from the *Breeding Atlas*. But in recent years many of the old sites have either disappeared or more often simply been deserted, and the number of Sand Martins has dropped dramatically: eg. a big colony at Leslie Quarry had only 12 pairs breeding in 1984, dropping to 6-10 pairs in 1985. Similar reports have come from Cocklemill Burn, where Sand Martins were mentioned as breeding as long ago as 1935 by Baxter and Rintoul, but this colony was deserted in 1984, and only one pair bred at St Monance in 1985 where 6 pairs had been the year before, with other small colonies along this part of the coast having been deserted within the last five years. A colony at St Andrews near the harbour was deserted in 1984, when the cliff had to be repaired and the nesting holes were covered up. The local BTO survey in summer 1985 showed, however, that there were 55 pairs at two sites at Wormit sand pits in 1985, and 46 pairs at a new site at St Michael, the only major sites now left in Fife. Smaller colonies were found at Straiton (near Lucklaw) and Saline in the west, whereas a good site at Kirkforthar, which was used by a large colony for over thirty years, has been destroyed, the sand pit being reclaimed.

In autumn Sand Martins flock before migrating south again, and 50+ at Lochore Meadows was the peak count in 1984, compared with a peak of 200 here on 27 July in 1983. The last birds usually leave in late September, with the latest record in the last thirty years being on 11 October, when one was seen at Kilconquhar in 1970.

In 1947 Baxter and Rintoul had found several pairs breeding in small ventilator pipes in the wall of an old byre in Upper Largo (B of S:243), and they mentioned other small colonies at Culross and Tulliallan (VFF:158). Boase (1964) thought the Sand Martin scarce in North Fife, though Grierson, writing about the 1950s, mentioned a colony at Guardbridge and another larger one at St Michael (SB2:153). It has thus probably never been very numerous in Fife, but all through the 1970s the reports were of poor breeding seasons, and it is still getting scarcer every year. The decline here, as elsewhere in Britain, is believed

G

to be related to drought conditions in the Sachel in West Africa, through which the birds are obliged to pass on migration.

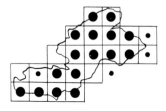

Swallow   *Hirundo rustica*

Common summer visitor

The Swallow nests in rafters in sheds, in outhouses and other buildings, and it arrives in early April, usually first in the easterly parts of Fife: thus one was seen on 1 April at Fife Ness in 1984, but the earliest record in the last thirty years is of one at St Andrews on 23 March 1982. It is common throughout the area, and there is no reason to suppose that the general picture has changed since the *Breeding Atlas* survey (1968-72) set out below.

The Swallow is not a colonial nester in the same way as the Sand Martin, though several nests may be built near one another if the site is suitable: a number of pairs were thus nesting in an old engine house near Tayport in 1952, where an unexpected mortality was described in the *Edinburgh Bird Bulletin*: although the engine house had been reroofed and windows put into the upper floor, there was open access through the lower floor, and the adult Swallows were seen to fly in and out with perfect ease and in good health, but when the mill was visited again after a holiday, a large number of Swallows were found dead—52 in all—which had apparently all died at the same time, all with their wings open in various degrees. It was thought unlikely that they had died because they could not get out, seeing there had been no difficulties earlier, and Dr. Berry suggested that the hot weather might have vapourised the oil, with which the building was saturated, thus poisoning the birds (EBB3:Aug.).

Occasionally Swallows feed in large flocks after arrival, such as when 150+ were seen over Kilconquhar Loch on 20 May 1984, but the really big flocks gather in autumn prior to birds leaving: eg. 1,000 were seen at

Kilconquhar in the evening of 10 September 1985, 500 were roosting at Guardbridge in late August 1972; while 300 were seen flying south at Fife Ness on 8 September 1984.

Many Swallows rear two broods, and the feeding of young may well go on till mid-October, though many birds have already left for the south by then. November Swallows are thus by no means rare, and the latest record in the last thirty years was a bird at St Andrews on 24 November 1980. A map in the *Handbook of British Birds* (1943) shows that our British population mainly winters around the Cape and Transvaal in South Africa.

The Swallow was mentioned for several parishes in both the *Old* and *New Statistical Account,* and all the older accounts agree that it has long been common. Although numbers may vary from year to year, there is no evidence to suggest that any real change has taken place in their status this century.

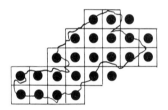
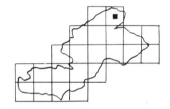

House Martin   *Delichon urbica*

Common summer visitor

This is usually the last of the hirundines to arrive, the earliest date in the last thirty years being 12 April, when singles were seen at Morton Lochs and at Lochore Meadows in 1981, but the main arrival is often not till May, and pairs have been known to arrive in late June, when they immediately began to build the nest (VFF:157). As the name suggests, the House Martin builds its nest on houses under the eaves, often with several nests in clusters together, and Baxter and Rintoul mentioned a house in Crail where they had seen nests built close together all round under the eaves. The House Martin may also nest on cliffs, and in 1983 a big colony was reported at Kincardine power station under the conveyor belt system.

On arrival the House Martin may flock, eg. 150 were reported at Morton Lochs on 9 June 1982, and like the Swallow it is double-brooded, with the second brood not flying till well into September or later. Thus birds may be seen about as late as November, with the latest record in the last thirty years being 23 November 1960.

In the autumn, House Martins gather like Swallows together on telegraph wires before leaving, and birds may also be seen on passage, usually in family parties or small flocks, but occasionally in very big flocks: thus Baxter and Rintoul described how, on 16 September 1925, they watched House Martins pass NE to SW over Kilconquhar Loch from 3-4 p.m., when they reckoned thousands must have passed during that hour (B of S:238). The peak count in 1984 was 140 at Cullaloe reservoir on 19 August. Numbers seem to fluctuate, however, and the House Martin, even more than the Swallow, is commoner in some years than others.

Compared to Baxter and Rintoul's numbers, the House Martin has decreased today. W. Berry also in his notes on Tayfield (1872-1947) said that it used to breed all round the house, when he was a boy, but that it had only done so once or twice during the last twenty years. H. Boase (1964), too, thought it had declined so that in North Fife it was 'now possibly less numerous than the Swallow' (BNF:96). This decline has undoubtedly to do with some very worrying evidence put forward in *Scottish Birds* by D. W. Oliver. For a number of years he had been involved in ringing House Martins and noticed a decline. He continues: 'On 11 August 1973, John Clark and I visited a colony at a farm in Crail, to attempt a pre-dawn catch of the House Martin colony. We were rather disappointed to find only two birds flying around, where there had been a dozen pairs earlier in the season. In the courtyard there were several pools of bright blue-green liquid and around their edges the ground had become muddy. On asking the farmer, he told us that the substance was fentin hydroxide . . . a tin-based fungicide, which is used for the control of potato blight. This compound is mixed with water and then sprayed on the crops, but in this instance the liquid had spilled out of the mixing tank, presumably a fairly common occurrence. He assured us that he had seen the martins drinking, and collecting mud thereafter. Inspection of nests showed there to be dead adults and chicks or eggs in four nests, some of the adults though dead for some time, showed grotesque distortion of the mouth, as if dying in great pain. . . .'

This unhappy experience was repeated when he went to another colony near Kilconquhar the same day: there had been 23 pairs earlier in the season, but only 2 nests now had live birds in them, and all other nests contained dead adults, chicks or eggs. The farmer, when asked, said he had used fungicide on his potatoes earlier. In late August 1974 Oliver rang the farmer in connection with another site which had previously held 30 pairs, only to be told that the martins had already left. His worst fears were confirmed when he arrived to find dead birds in every nest, mostly adults, some unfledged young and some juveniles of the year. Again the farmer had been mixing fungicide solution some weeks before. Oliver adds that, of course, this mortality was not deliberate, that it was due to lack of care in the mixing process, and also that all the farmers in question were fond of House Martins (SB8:325-327).

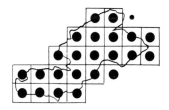

Tawny Pipit   *Anthus campestris*

Very rare straggler

Only one record: a single was seen at Leuchars on 1 May 1979 (SB:1979 report).

Tree Pipit *Anthus trivialis*

Passage migrant, breeds in West Fife

The Tree Pipit arrives at the end of April and early May, when it is fairly regular on passage in East Fife. Twenty at Fife Ness on 4 May 1969 was the biggest number in the last twenty years.

In Fife the Tree Pipit breeds only in the central and western sections, where there is suitable habitat of heaths or commons with scattered trees and open woodland, such as at Devilla forest (12 pairs in 1983), and Lochmill Loch by Newburgh (2 pairs in 1985). It may also breed at Pitcairn, Clune and on the Lomond Hills.

Return passage takes place in the autumn, and peak counts in the last twenty years have been 16 at Fife Ness on 24 August 1971, and 15 there on 15-16 September 1973.

Harvie-Brown (1906) did not mention it for Fife, though he thought it fairly common in the Tay basin as a whole, while Boase (1964) had seen only 2 Tree Pipits in North Fife, both on Tentsmuir: one on 26 July 1925, and the other on 18 July 1925, and he considered both birds to be on passage (BNF:114). Baxter and Rintoul (1953) mentioned that it bred in West Fife, extending as far east as Markinch (B of S:106).

Records therefore suggest that the Tree Pipit was always scarce as a breeding bird except in the west, and that its status is little changed.

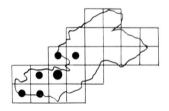

Meadow Pipit *Anthus pratensis*

Common resident and passage migrant

This is our commonest pipit, nesting throughout the area where there is rough grassland, moor, heath and sand-dunes, and it is particularly abundant on the Lomond Hills. It lays its eggs in a depression in the ground, and breeding pairs are usually present at their sites from early April.

In spring and autumn big migrations take place: 2,000 in one hour seen passing over St Andrews on 20 April 1975 is by far the biggest spring passage recorded, whereas the autumn passage is heaviest in September with eg. 500 in a field in fog at Fife Ness on 10 September 1968; 400+ at Fife Ness on 24-25 September 1972, and 308 in one hour moving SW at Anstruther on 17 September 1985. At Anstruther the passage regularly peaks in the morning a good hour before that of Skylarks.

In winter only comparatively few Meadow Pipits stay in Fife, moving to the coastal areas when the weather gets cold, and about the end of March our breeding population is back on the sites.

Baxter and Rintoul (1953) mentioned that the Meadow Pipit fluctuated greatly in numbers, and that it was, for instance, scarce as a breeding bird in Fife in 1940. There is no evidence, however, that our breeding population has varied appreciably in recent years.

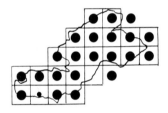 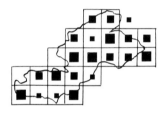

Rock Pipit   *Anthus spinoletta*

Common resident and winter visitor

The Rock Pipit nests on rocky shores, as its name suggests, and it is therefore commonest in the east of Fife: in 1983 there were 7 pairs on the 5½ miles of coast between Crail and Pittenweem. Baxter and Rintoul (1953) quoted Harvie-Brown as saying that in 1867 Rock Pipits bred as far up the Forth as Kincardine, but they had never found them west of North Queensferry, and this absence was also confirmed by the *Breeding Atlas*.

In winter our resident population is joined by migrants, and 41 birds were counted in 2 miles from Cambo to Fife Ness on 9 January 1983. Birds of the Scandinavian race *A. spinoletta littoralis* are occasionally recorded on passage, such as 2 at Fife Ness on 29 March 1981, and one at Ballo reservoir on 17 September 1984. The Rock Pipit is solitary and does not flock as Meadow Pipits do; the largest party in recent years has been 25 on 19 October at Kilrenny in 1982.

Boase (1964) thought the Rock Pipit only a winter visitor to North Fife, and had looked in vain for nests along the shore from St Andrews at least as far as the Rock and Spindle in May 1948 (BNF:115), but it is common in the St Andrews area today. Their choice of rocky shores has probably saved them from the reduction of numbers in other breeding species of our shores as modern leisure activities expand.

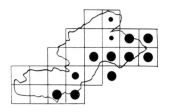 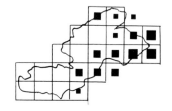

Yellow Wagtail   *Motacilla flava*

Scarce passage migrant, has bred

This is our rarest wagtail, and practically all records in the last thirty years are from the east coast of Fife, where it has been reported on passage in various places from Tayport to Elie Ness. Most records are from spring in April and May, with fewer autumn sightings in September and October.

Breeding at Fife Ness was suspected in 1982, when sightings kept being reported at various times throughout the summer, and breeding was proved the following year in 1983, being the first time for Fife, but in 1984 there were no sightings after 14 June, so they probably did not breed here again. In 1983, however, a pair was also seen at Lochore Meadows on 4 May, as well as singles at St Andrews on 8 May, and at Anstruther on 10 June.

There is no doubt that the Yellow Wagtail has become less rare in recent years. Baxter and Rintoul (1935) knew of only two records for South Fife: one in May 1883 (no location given), and 2 at Largo on 3 September 1929 (VFF:101). For North Fife, Boase (1964) also reported two sightings: one at Newport at the end of August 1938, and one at Earlshall in March 1950 (BNF:117), but since the 1960s the Yellow Wagtail has been reported in Fife every two years or so, and since 1981 there have been several sightings every year, including birds well inland, such as the above-mentioned pair at Lochore, and a bird of the Blue-headed race at Clune on 10 May 1983.

The British race is the *Motacilla flava flavissima,* but other sub-species are occasionally seen in Fife, such as the Blue-headed *M. flava flava,* which is usually found in Denmark and mid-Europe, and the female of the pair at Fife Ness in 1982 was suspected to be of this race.

An Ashy-headed Wagtail *M. Flava cinereocapillo,* or South European race, was identified at Cult Ness on 30 April 1959, and birds of the Grey-headed race *M. flava thunbergi,* from East Scandinavia and Russia, have also been seen: one at St Andrews on 8 May 1983, and an older record of an adult present at Rosyth mudflats from 31 July to 14 August 1955 (EBB5:80).

Grey Wagtail   *Motacilla cinerea*

Local resident

The Grey Wagtail nests by rivers and streams in holes in banks or on ledges. It has never been abundant, and numbers seem to vary a great deal, as it is very vulnerable to frosty weather: thus the cold winter of 1981-82 wiped it out as a breeding bird over much of Fife, but 1984 was a good year for the species, and it was reported breeding in many parts of the county.

Birds may also be seen on passage, especially in autumn at Fife Ness, where there are several records of ones or twos between mid-August and mid-October.

Harvie-Brown (1906) called the Grey Wagtail resident but very local in North-East Fife, no doubt following W. Berry, who had found it nesting at Tayfield in 1899, but none since; Grierson (1962) had only one record from Tentsmuir of a bird at Morton Lochs on 12 August 1919, whereas Boase (1964) could add that he had seen a couple of individuals—probably on passage—on Smithy Burn at Newport in spring, and a pair at Dura Den in 1948, which were not there the following year. For South Fife, Baxter and Rintoul (1935) found it nesting 'sparingly', which they put down to lack of suitable burns (VFF:99).

During the *Breeding Atlas* survey of 1968-72 the Grey Wagtail was proved breeding in a number of squares, and it could be that it has increased slightly as a breeding species in Fife as a whole in the second half of this century.

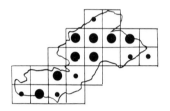
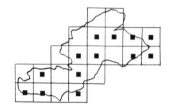

Pied Wagtail *Motacilla alba*

Common resident and passage migrant

This is our commonest wagtail, present all the year round (although in smaller numbers in winter), frequenting all manner of habitats throughout the area. It is at home in towns as well as in the countryside, often near streams and the coast, and it nests in trees, shrubs, sheds and holes.

In autumn and spring a considerable passage takes place; thus 45 were seen at Fife Ness on 5 August 1984, and 40 were there on 2 September 1982. Last century Dalgleish (1885) reported 'immense' flocks on autumn migration at Tulliallan lochs.

From autumn to spring the Pied Wagtail also roosts gregariously:

Baxter and Rintoul (1935) found it roosting in the ivy at Balcaskie House (VFF:98). About 100 roosted at Lochore Meadows in mid-September 1984, and another roost was reported at Dunfermline about the same time, but this had dropped to 22 in December that year.

Various wagtails are mentioned in the *Old* as well as in the *New Statistical Account,* but it is difficult to tell which species. The Pied Wagtail was reported as more abundant in summer than in winter by Harvie-Brown (1906), and Grierson (1962) said it nested on most parts of Tentsmuir, where good numbers were also seen on passage (eg. 95 moving south over Shelly Point on 2-4 October 1954). There appears to be no change in status this century.

The sub-species *Montacilla alba alba,* or White Wagtail, is a regular passage migrant, especially to the east of the county: 90 at Earlsferry on 23 September 1977 is the biggest count; but one White Wagtail was also found as far west as Holl reservoir on 1 April 1984. W. Berry reported that a pair of this species was seen with 3 young in the grounds of Tayfield in 1946 (unpublished notes).

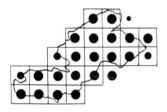 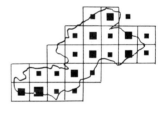

Waxwing *Bombycilla garrulus*

Erratic winter visitor

The Waxwing usually only occurs locally in very small numbers, but in some years a considerable invasion may take place to parts or the whole of the east of Scotland. Such a 'Waxwing Year' happened in November 1959, which was described in detail in *Scottish Birds* (1:241). Arrival was first noted of single birds on 2 November at St Andrews, but within a week there were also reports from Elie, Cupar, Dysart and Crail, and on 8 November 30 Waxwings were seen at Kirkcaldy. During the whole of November that year reports of small flocks were received from many places, mostly coastal areas, from Newburgh all round to Inverkeithing, but also inland at Rathillet, Cupar, Gateside, Lochore and Colinsburgh. An estimated 199 birds were thought to have visited Fife, with as many as 45 at St Andrews alone. That year, too, a dead Waxwing was picked up at Kirkcaldy which bore a Swedish ring, having been ringed as an adult in Norbotton district in northern Sweden. Another smaller invasion took place in 1961, this time in the second half of November and December (SB2:85-89), where all reports (apart from 7-9 birds at St Andrews) were from the stretch between Longannet and Kirkcaldy. Other recent Waxwing years have been 1963 (95 birds in North Fife, and 85 in South Fife), 1968, 1970 and 1974, when a maximum of 185 Waxwings were recorded at Guardbridge in November. A much smaller invasion took place in 1976, and since 1982 only occasional birds have been recorded in Fife.

The Waxwing or 'Bohemian Jay' was mentioned as an occasional visitor to Anstruther in the *Old Statistical Account* (1792) and in the *New Statistical Account* of Anstruther and Monimail (1836). All the older reports also talked about these periodic invasions, and it appears that St Andrews has long been a particularly favoured spot for Waxwings. H. Boase mentioned other years when big invasions had taken place: in January (1922 and 1928); in February and March (1937); and that in 1946-47 a big influx took place around St Andrews, where there were about 100 on 22 November, with the last seen on 26 January, when a few Waxwings were also reported at Tayfield (BNF:117).

There have been no big Waxwing years for over ten years now.

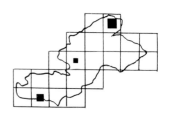

Dipper   *Cinclus cinclus*

Local resident

The Dipper typically frequents stony, fairly fast-flowing and unpolluted streams, where it nests in holes in banks, and under tree roots, bridges or stones, and it has recently been reported as present and probably breeding at Boarhills, St Andrews, Colinsburgh, Riverside Park (Glenrothes), Strathmiglo, Gateside and Bluther burn.

In winter, birds may also be seen on the shore and in other places where they do not breed, such as Anstruther (from 17 October to 11 November 1984), Harperleas reservoir, Lochore Meadows and Morton Lochs.

The Dipper, or 'Water-ouzel', was mentioned in the *New Statistical Account* of Cupar (1836); Harvie-Brown said, 'At the present time (1904) Dippers are known to be abundant on the Kenley Burn and elsewhere in the east of Fife' (FT:68). W. Berry, however, said that the Dipper was only seen on the burns around Newport in hard weather, whereas it used to breed freely on the Moultrie under the farm road bridges (unpublished note, 1872-1947); and Boase (1964) could only add one record of a Dipper at Cupar, on the River Eden in early summer 1943, but noted that it had ceased to breed at St Andrews by 1950 (BNF:102). For South and West Fife, Dalgleish (1885) said it was rare, but increasing, and Baxter and Rintoul (1935) found it nesting on most of the burns; but also that it used to nest on the Balbirnie Burn, but by 1926 had ceased to do so (VFF:151).

It therefore appears that the Dipper population fluctuates somewhat. The *Breeding Atlas* had it definitely breeding in 9 squares (1968-1972), but recent records suggest that it is rather rarer today.

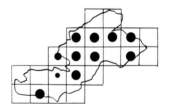
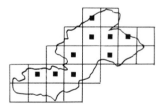

Wren   *Troglodytes troglodytes*

Common resident

The Wren is one of our commonest birds, and nests in a wide variety of places from gardens to woods and anywhere with some kind of low cover. Although the Wren is sedentary, there is some evidence that it moves away temporarily in very cold weather, eg. at Kippo wood where, in the cold winter of 1981-82, 13 birds had been present before the frosts: only one Wren could be found in January, but 5 pairs nevertheless bred here the following summer.

Grierson (1962) in his 'Checklist' also noted that the Wren was found more commonly on the coastal strips at Tentsmuir in winter.

The Wren was mentioned in the *New Statistical Account* of Inverkeithing (1837), and it appears always to have been very common, being quick to recover its numbers after hard winters.

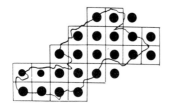 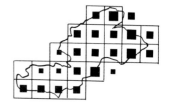

Dunnock   *Prunella modularis*

Common resident

The Dunnock, or Hedge Sparrow, is common through the area. It nests mostly in hedges and bushy places. In autumn and spring a definite passage takes place: thus about 100 Dunnocks were at Fife Ness on 29 September 1971, and 50+ there on 11 October 1978, with 14 passing SW over Anstruther on 26 September 1984. Spring numbers have peaked at 30 at Fife Ness on 29 April 1974, with 15 there on 1 May 1984.

When cold weather sets in, our resident Dunnocks move to the coast: 20 were counted between Buckhaven and Macduff's Castle, East Wemyss, on 13 January 1984. Baxter and Rintoul (1935) also noted that Dunnocks move about far more than one would expect.

Boase (1964) thought it was rather patchy in distribution in North Fife. The *Breeding Atlas*', however, reported it breeding in every possible square in Fife, and this is undoubtedly still the case in the 1980s, where the Dunnock is abundant everywhere in the area.

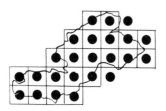 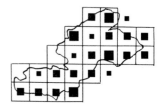

Robin   *Erithacus rubecula*

Common resident and passage migrant

The Robin breeds commonly throughout the area in a variety of places such as hollows in banks, tree stumps, thick hedges, sheds and even old tin cans. It is uncertain how many of our local breeding population are fully sedentary: there is a marked passage which takes place especially in autumn, when 100 birds at Fife Ness are not unusual, and where as many as 500 were seen on 11 October 1982 during the big autumn rush that year, falling to 200 the next day. Another big rush was in 1976, when there were 300 there on 30 September, and 400+ on 28 October; and big arrivals of migrants have been noted elsewhere along the east coast, such as at St Andrews, where there were 50 in a coastal garden on 3 October 1983. Baxter and Rintoul (1935) also reported a number of autumn migrants: at Crail, and right along to Lahill in Largo Bay on occasions.

The passage is less well marked in spring, when maximum numbers in the last twenty-five years have been 30 (all apparently of the continental race) on 23 April 1969.

In winter the Robin continues to be common in Fife, but birds often move to the coast to spend the coldest part of the season here: we usually have at least 2 Robins in our garden by the sea in Anstruther throughout the winter, where there are none in summer.

No change in status.

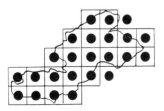
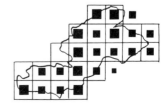

Thrush Nightingale   *Luscinia luscinia*

Very rare passage migrant

There is one record of this East European species: seen in Den Burn
wood at Crail on 15 May 1985. This record is still to be considered by
the Rarities Committee.

   Another nightingale (sp), but probably of this species, was seen at
Balcomie on Fife Ness on 13-14 October 1982. Certain identification at
that time of the year is virtually impossible, except in the hand.

Bluethroat   *Luscinia svecica*

Uncommon passage migrant

Most of the Bluethroats seen here on passage are of the Red-spotted
race   *(L.s.svecica)*,   but   the   rarer   White-spotted   Bluethroat
(L.s.cyanecula), or middle-European race, has also been recorded (see
below). The majority of records are birds on spring passage, but there
are also some in autumn. It can fairly be assumed that birds not
otherwise specified have been Red-spotted. They are as follows:

Spring:
1 R.sp. Knockhill 11.5.85
15 R.sp. Fife Ness 14-15.5.85
  4 still there a week later
1 R.sp. Crail 17.5.85
1 Wh.sp. Fife Ness 18.5.85
1 Wh.sp. Kingskettle garden
  16-17.5.82
1 R.sp. Kingsbarns garden
  10.5.81
1 Fife Ness 13-15.5.81
1 R.sp. male Fife Ness 16.5.79
1 Fife Ness 15.5.70
1 Boarhills 14-15.5.70
1 female Kilconquhar 4.5.69
1 R.sp. Fife Ness 7-9.5.69
1 Fife Ness 6-7.5.68
1 R.sp. male Fife Ness 14.5.67

Autumn:
1 (trapped) Fife Ness 24.9.72
1 male Fife Ness 17.9.69
1 Fife Ness 14.9.68
1 St Andrews garden 3.9.58
1 Fife Ness 23.9.56

As can be seen from the above, a quite unprecedented fall took place on 14-15 May 1985. It is not known how many Bluethroats were in Fife during this time, but for several days Bluethroats were the commonest little birds at Fife Ness. There is also no reason to suppose that new arrivals did not take place throughout the week.

The Bluethroat was not mentioned by Harvie-Brown (1906), and Baxter and Rintoul (1935 & 1953) had no records except from the Isle of May of either race. It therefore appears that the passage of Bluethroats is of quite recent origin.

Red-flanked Bluetail *Tarsiger cyanurus*

Very rare passage migrant

There is only one record: of an individual at Fife Ness on 28 October 1976. This was only the fourth record for Scotland.

Black Redstart *Phoenicurus ochruros*

Scarce passage migrant

There are slightly more records of this species in spring than on autumn passage, mostly of singles, and a maximum of 3 were present at Fife Ness on 9-10 May 1970. Birds are usually seen in April and May, and occasionally as early as March, such as one at St Andrews on 28

March 1980. In autumn the earliest record is of a male at Fife Ness on 15 August 1971, but most birds are found from late September till early November. Reports in recent years have come from Tayport (the meteorological station), St Andrews, Kingsbarns, Fife Ness (the majority), Crail, Anstruther, Dalgety Bay and Dunfermline.

Very occasionally a Black Redstart may spend the winter in Fife: thus one wintered near St Andrews Castle from December 1984 to January 1985; a female was at Crail from 1 January to 19 March 1975; another was mist-netted at St Andrews on 17 January 1964, whereas a male was seen at Longannet on 24 January 1960.

Harvie-Brown (1906) had only one record for Fife, of a bird obtained by himself at Kincardine on 10 November 1876; Baxter and Rintoul (1935) mentioned one at Elie in August 1897, and another at Fife Ness on 25 September 1933, but it was clearly unusual; and Valentine in *Fifeshire* (1910) called the Black Redstart 'the rarest of all migrants'. In North Fife the Black Redstart was recorded near Guardbridge in November 1926, and there was one at Shelly Point on 28 October 1951 (BNF:107).

This species has definitely become much more regular on passage since the 1950s.

Redstart   *Phoenicurus phoenicurus*

Passage migrant in small numbers, rare breeder

There are very few breeding records of this species in recent years: a pair reported to have bred in a wood on the Lomond Hills in 1983 was the first record for several years. This is obviously a decline since the *Breeding Atlas*, which found the Redstart definitely breeding in 6 squares in the five-year period 1968-72. Before that there was a record of 6 nestlings being ringed in June 1960 at Peppermill Dam, which was the first local record of breeding there. Baxter and Rintoul (1935) mentioned the Redstart as breeding as far east as Burntisland in South Fife, whereas Harvie-Brown (1906) found it breeding only in very small numbers in North Fife, and thought it was getting rarer (FT:72).

The Redstart is also a passage migrant to the coastal areas, especially in East Fife, where the vast majority of records come from Fife Ness, but where there are other records from Tentsmuir Point, Morton Lochs, St Andrews, Kilrenny and Elie Ness in the last twenty years, as well as one record from West Fife of a bird at Dunfermline on 4 May 1984. Passage in spring is usually in April and May, the earliest in the last thirty years being 10 April, with a maximum of 9 at Fife Ness on 15 May 1985. Largest numbers are reported in autumn: 30 at Fife Ness on 17 September 1969 is the maximum number on record, with the earliest autumn bird on 6 August, and the latest on 3 November. Autumn 1976 was a particularly good year for migration, and Redstarts were about at Fife Ness from 24 August to 30 October, with 15+ on 3 October. That year, too, a male bird of the eastern race *P.p.samamisicus,* or Ehrenberg's Redstart, was at Fife Ness on 23 September 1976. This was the first record for Scotland and only the second for Britain.

Though never common, the Redstart has declined markedly as a breeding bird in Fife this century, and it is too early to say whether it is making a comeback. There seems to be less change in the numbers of passage migrants.

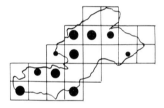

Whinchat *Saxicola rubetra*

Passage migrant, breeds locally in the west

The Whinchat frequents open country with rough grassland, where it nests on the ground. There have been good reports of breeding in the last few years, all from Central and West Fife: thus 30+ bred on the Lomond Hills in 1984, and 20 pairs at Glenvale in 1983, with other pairs reported from Lochore Meadows, Pitcairn, Kirkforthar and the Loch Glow area. It used to breed in the Scotscraig-Morton Area, but not since 1938 (SB2:155).

Spring and autumn passage also occur, when records are mostly from Fife Ness; at Largo Bay a Whinchat was recorded as early as 30 April in 1965, and one was at Anstruther on 12 May 1982. A maximum number of 10 were at Fife Ness on 4 May 1969, although there are slightly larger numbers in autumn: 20 at Fife Ness on 5 September

1968 is the biggest count on record; with as many as 14 at Kingsbarns on 31 August 1975. One on 16 November at Fife Ness is the latest date.

The Whinchat was mentioned in the *New Statistical Account* as uncommon, but occasionally found at Carnock (1843), and it was not considered common in North Fife at the beginning of this century (FT:70). Baxter and Rintoul (1935), too, thought it very local in South Fife, where they found it nesting in the higher parts above Culross and Tulliallan, above Burntisland, and once near Largo, where on 20 June 1911 they found young Whinchats newly out of the nest (VFF:146).

Unfortunately there are no old reports of the Lomond Hills area, so comparison with the past of this most favoured area is not possible. It may be that the Whinchat has become commoner as a breeding bird in Fife.

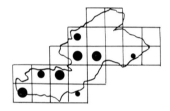

Stonechat   *Saxicola torquata*

Scarce resident and passage migrant in small numbers

The Stonechat frequents rough hillsides and coastal areas with scattered gorse bushes in particular, but very few records have been reported in the last few years: a pair bred at Fife Ness in 1981 (but none here since), and another pair at Glenvale in 1983. In 1984, 2 pairs were present at East Lomond in June, but breeding was not proved. This is a drastic decline since the *Breeding Atlas* survey, when Stonechats were found breeding in 12 squares (1968-72). Records, too, suggest that it was much commoner back in the 1950s, when eg. they bred between Anstruther and Pittenweem, and there were 3 pairs alone on the short stretch from Crail to Fife Ness in 1956 (EBB6:48). Baxter and Rintoul (1935) observed that numbers of this species fluctuated greatly, the Stonechat being very vulnerable in severe winters and slow to recover: thus they noted, eg., that the Stonechat had been very scarce after the cold winter of 1917, when they did not see it again in Largo Bay till 1923, but by 1934 birds were apparently back in their usual numbers as a 'common breeding bird' from Fife Ness to Culross and Tulliallan (VFF:144). Harvie-Brown (1906) said that the Stonechat was less common in North-East Fife, but also that it bred at Tentsmuir, where there are none now. It was mentioned in the *New Statistical Account* as occurring at Inverkeithing (1837).

Winter records are usually from the coast, and in recent years have come from the West Sands (St Andrews), Sauchope Links (Crail), Earlshall, Shell Bay, Limekilns, but also inland at Lochore Meadows.

There is also a marked passage, especially in autumn, of migrants, usually of small numbers, but an amazing 50+ were reported at Fife Ness on 24 September 1972, with 20 there the next day. Three on 10 November was the maximum count in 1984.

That Stonechats are so slow to recover their numbers was put down, by Baxter and Rintoul, to the fact that they are very aggressive towards other Stonechats, vigorously keeping these away: they thought young birds in particular left the area, and a bird ringed as young at Largo in 1929 was recovered at Johnstone, Renfrew on 19 January 1933 (VFF:145).

Very occasionally one of the Siberian races *S. t. manta* or *S. t. styngeri* comes to Fife Ness: thus one was there on 15 May 1985; another from 30 September to 1 October 1983; and one or possibly two there on 5 October 1979 (Jim Cobb).

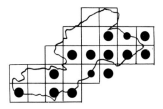 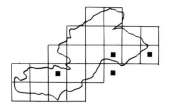

Wheatear   *Oenanthe oenanthe*

Summer visitor and scarce breeder

The Wheatear is one of our earliest summer visitors, with first arrivals usually towards the end of March, and main arrival in mid-April: a male at Fife Ness on 17 March 1971 is the earliest date in thirty years. Wheatears may often stay along the shore for several days before moving on, and not just in East Fife, for it is more dispersed and less concentrated at Fife Ness than many other migrants. Seventeen at Fife Ness on 1 May 1982 represent the largest count in recent years.

Only a few pairs breed in the area, mostly on the Lomond Hills (7 pairs in 1983), or in West Fife, where it nests on the ground on hillsides and upland pastures. In September our birds leave, and the return journey of migrants also takes place with stragglers well into October: one at Billow Ness on 1 December 1985 is the latest date.

The *Breeding Atlas* had Wheatears breeding in 10 squares, and Grierson said that at least 12 pairs bred at Earlshall in the 1950s. A few pairs still bred here about 1980. Baxter and Rintoul (1935) considered the Wheatear common, but mentioned no specific records for South Fife, but Dalgleish (1885) considered it 'rare and local' in the west.

It may be that the Wheatear has decreased somewhat as a breeding bird in the area in recent years, but it is probably under-recorded; it is certainly common on passage.

The Greenland race, *O.o.lencorrhoa*, is seen fairly regularly on passage in East Fife.

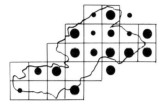

Ring Ouzel   *Turdus torquatus*

Passage migrant in small numbers

A few Ring Ouzels are usually seen every year on passage in East Fife, especially after easterly winds. The earliest record in the last thirty years was a male near Anstruther on 27 March 1967, but most spring records fall in April and May, with a maximum of 9+ reported at Fife Ness on 2 May 1974, and 8 birds there 2 days later. In autumn the main migration takes place in October, with only a few September records, and the latest record is a bird at Tentsmuir Point on 8 November 1976. Other places where it has been reported are Pittenweem, Kingsbarns, St Andrews and Cameron reservoir, and there is an interesting record of a male seen on 16 April 1952 at Saline in West Fife, at an altitude of 500 feet in a district where there are very few records of the Ring Ouzel on passage.

There are no published records of the Ring Ouzel having bred in Fife. It was mentioned in the *New Statistical Account* as an occasional visitor to Dunfermline (1844). Harvie-Brown (1906) quoted W. Berwick saying it was 'rare', though seen on passage in North Fife, which was also the opinion of W. Berry (unpublished notes 1872-1947). Baxter and Rintoul (1935) knew it on passage only in South Fife.

No change in status.

Blackbird   *Turdus merula*

Common resident and passage migrant

One of our commonest birds, the Blackbird is at home in most habitats, and nests in bushes, trees, sheds, even on the ground if necessary. Every garden has its pair, and one pair may raise several broods in a season.

A substantial migration takes place in spring and especially in late autumn, when eg. 'thousands' were reported as coming in 'all day on a wide front in east winds and fog' in East Fife on 19 October 1968 (SB5:343). In 1982, 800 were counted at Fife Ness on 17 October, with 350 there on 5 November the same year, when scores were also reported in cliffside gardens in St Andrews. Ringing records show that some of these migrants come from North Scandinavia. Migration may easily go on well into November, when eg. there were 140 at Fife Ness on 11 November 1984, and 220 at Mossgreen in West Fife a week later on 18 Noember. In winter there are occasional roosts, such as one of 500 at Glenrothes from January to March 1980.

The Blackbird was mentioned in the *New Statistical Account* of Inverkeithing (1836), and all the old reports agree that it was common and increasing, though W. Berry, in the 1940s said it was not as common as it used to be about Tayfield. There is, however, no evidence of any decline in recent years.

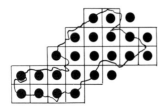   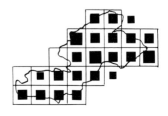

Fieldfare   *Turdus pilaris*

Common passage migrant and winter visitor

In autumn huge flocks of Fieldfares (often mixed with Redwings) arrive in Fife, most of which do not stay but pass over the area, either immediately or after a short stay. In some years they are very much more plentiful than in others. The first birds may arrive already in August, when there was one recorded at Fife Ness on 24 August 1970, but the main arrival is not till later, when eg. 'thousands' were reported passing over East Fife on 16-17 October 1982; and in 1959, 2,000-3,000 were seen in fields between Kincardine and High Valleyfield on 25 October. Some years the main arrival is even later, as when a large influx took place between Crail and Kingsbarns on 11 November 1978.

Some flocks stay in the area throughout the winter, feeding chiefly on berries and roots, and as the cold weather sets in, numbers may move about in search of alternative feeding grounds: thus flocks of 50-100 were noted passing west at Kirkcaldy on 3 January 1984, flying low along the coast: a total of 2,250+ was estimated to have passed that day. Other big winter flocks have been 600 at Inverkeithing on 11 November 1984, 500 at Guardbridge on 8 December 1982, and 314 on the Lomond Hills on 30 December 1983, with flocks of 'several hundred' at Cameron and Airdrie in 1984.

In spring large numbers again pass over Fife on their way north: 200 per hour moving north at Cupar on 24 March 1972 were early; whereas 1,000 at Crail on 10 May 1981 were late.

The Fieldfare was mentioned as a migratory bird at Inverkeithing in the *New Statistical Account* (1836), as well as at Burntisland and Anstruther. There is no evidence of any change in status this century.

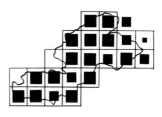

Song Thrush   *Turdus philomelos*

Common resident and passage migrant

The Song Thrush frequents gardens, woods and thickets, where it builds its nest off the ground, and it was reported as breeding in every square in Fife during the *Breeding Atlas* survey of 1968-72, although, of course, no numbers were given.

A marked migration takes place in September and October when 100 at Fife Ness is not unusual, while 2,000 there on 2 October 1970 is the biggest number in the last thirty years. The movement in spring is more dispersed, and 20 at Fife Ness on 15 April 1972, and 20 there on 29 April 1974, are the biggest counts.

In winter there are very few Song Thrushes about, and nearly all are by the coast, but how many of them are local birds, and how many winter visitors from other parts or abroad, is uncertain, though ringing records show that birds may move a very long way: birds ringed at St Andrews have been recovered as far away as Algeria and France, but strangely enough, there are also several records pointing to Fife birds spending the winter in Aberdeen (J. Cobb). Harvie-Brown (1906) noted that the Song Thrust was 'locally migratory', and Baxter and Rintoul (1935) mentioned that in severe weather the shore was much frequented by the British Song Thrush, and described how, on 19 December 1925, in frost and snow, quantities of birds of the British race were feeding by the edges of the tide all the way along Largo Bay: ' . . . the sands and rocks were alive with them, and several small parties came in from over the Forth flying NNE and pitched so quickly that the next wave washed round their feet . . . some were eating winkels'. They did, however, also observe large flocks of the continental race on passage here, but mostly in October (VFF:133).

Such an influx in winter as described above has not been recorded since the 1950s, and there is evidence that Song Thrushes are declining in numbers: Dr. J. Cobb's view is that the species has declined heavily in East Fife in the last twenty years as a breeding species, though it is still generally distributed.

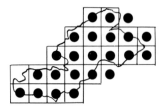 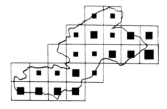

Redwing *Turdus iliacus*

Common passage migrant and winter visitor

In autumn the first Redwings may arrive in mid-September (2 at Fife Ness on 16 September 1973 being the earliest in recent years), with the main arrival in October, and then often mixed with Fieldfares and Song Thrushes: eg. 3,000 Redwings were reported passing south at Fife Ness on 17 October 1982; and 2,000 thrushes were there on 6 October 1966—the majority Redwings, with a good portion of Song Thrushes —while in October 1969 a massive protracted arrival was noted with a heavy passage over St Andrews a foggy night with east winds. 400 per hour were coming in over Fife Ness the next day, followed by heavy migration during the rest of October. Redwings, like many thrushes, tend to migrate at night, when only their call ('zieh') gives them away, but passage takes place usually over a very wide front, so that they may be seen or heard almost anywhere, especially in the coastal districts.

A few of these migrants stay in Fife, when they may be seen in fields or in shrubby trees, as eg. hawthorns, often with Fieldfares. Like the Fieldfare, the Redwing moves on when the frosts set in: 300+ were passing at St Andrews on 14 January 1984, whereas in January 1982 the area was reported 'largely deserted'. Baxter and Rintoul also reported a roost near Largo House in December 1951, when they found a constant stream of Redwings (and a few Fieldfares and Blackbirds) arriving from about 4 p.m. in small parties, till there were 'hundreds' roosting in an evergreen thicket, being very noisy; 'they were evidently drawn from a wide extent of country' (Scot.Nat.64:55).

The return journey takes place in April, but it is far more dispersed, and no big flocks have been reported: 157 at Cameron on 18 March 1984 is the biggest spring flock in recent years.

The Redwing was mentioned in the *New Statistical Account* of Inverkeithing (1836). Numbers on passage seems always to have fluctuated, and there is no change in status this century.

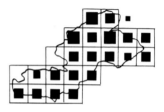

Mistle Thrush   *Turdus viscivorus*

Fairly common resident

This large thrush nests mostly in woods, both coniferous and deciduous, where it breeds as early as February, though some not till April. It is widely but thinly distributed throughout the area, and there appears to be little change since the *Breeding Atlas* (1968-72). Baxter and Rintoul (1935) said that it had increased considerably in South Fife last century, and quoted Balfour Kirke writing in 1900 that a big increase about Burntisland had taken place in the previous twenty-five years (VFF:129). But it was apparently quite scarce in North-East Fife around the turn of the century, and Grierson (1962) thought it had increased at Tentsmuir, after a period of decline in the 1940s, when several pairs bred at Earlshall in the 1950s. Numbers therefore obviously fluctuate, and in 1980 it was reported only as 'possibly breeding' in Tentsmuir, whereas 12 Mistle Thrushes were reported present at Kinshaldy on 3 March 1984, though breeding was not mentioned. Post-breeding flocks on the Lomond Hills numbered 50 from May to August in 1984, compared to 30 the year before.

In winter many birds leave the area: a young Mistle Thrush ringed at Largo on 2 May 1932 was recovered on 5 December 1932 near Masseube, Gers, France; but some also stay, probably mostly adult birds, and 12 were seen at Morton Lochs on 1 January 1984.

There is no apparent change in status over the last thirty years.

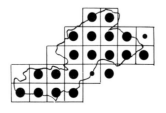

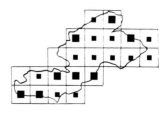

Grasshopper Warbler   *Locustella naevia*

Scarce summer visitor

This warbler favours wet reedy places and rank grass, but only a few Grasshopper Warblers visit Fife each year, when their reeling may be heard from late April onwards. There are records in the last thirty years from Tayport, Morton Lochs, Tentsmuir, Nydie Mill (near Cupar), Magus Muir, Cameron reservoir, St Andrews golf course, Kingsbarns, Fife Ness, Kilrenny, Kilconquhar and Elie; and further west from Largo Bay, Wemyss wood, Cult Ness, Tulliallan (1950s), Lochore Meadows, Rossie Bog, Carriston and Glenrothes.

By the end of September it has left again: one at Fife Ness on 28 September 1985 is the latest date.

Harvie-Brown (1906) found it local, but not abundant in North Fife; Baxter and Rintoul (1935) reported in breeding 'just to the north of our boundary line in Fife' in 1905, but had no other records.

The Grasshopper Warbler is still very scarce, and there is little apparent change in status this century.

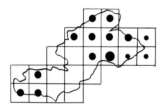

Sedge Warbler   *Acrocephalus schoenobaenus*

Common summer visitor

This is one of our commonest warblers, widely distributed as a breeding bird throughout the area where there is a suitable habitat of reed-beds and thickish vegetation along streams and inland waters. It may also frequent quite dry areas with thick gorse, such as Fife Ness, and the scolding, vigorous song advertises its presence. Early birds come in late April (20 April 1980, when 2 were at Morton Lochs, is the earliest date in recent years), with the main arrival usually about the second week in May; and by the end of September most are away again, though a few late birds may be picked up. There are two very interesting ringing records of late birds: one ringed on 15 October 1966 at Fife Ness was recovered on 21 November that year in the Cordoba district in Southern Spain, and another, ringed at Guardbridge on the same day, was recovered on 22 November at Bayonne, Basses Pyrénées, France (J. Cobb).

Harvie-Brown (1906) said that in North Fife the Sedge Warbler was fairly common in suitable situations, and believed it was increasing; Baxter and Rintoul (1935) thought it was a common nesting bird in South Fife, and also on passage, occurring in places where it did not nest, though Dalgleish (1885) found it 'rare' in West Fife.

The Sedge Warbler appears to have increased, if anything, during the earlier part of this century, but there has been no change in status in recent years.

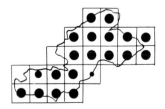

Marsh Warbler   *Acrocephalus palustris*

Very scarce straggler

Only one record of this species in Fife, which is of a bird ringed at
Kingsbarns on 14 October 1982 (J. Cobb). It is, however, possible that
some sight records of Reed Warbler in fact refer to this species.

Reed Warbler   *Acrocephalus scirpaceus*

Rare passage migrant

The following are the only recorded sightings of this warbler in Fife, all
within the last ten years:

Spring:	*Autumn:*
2 Fife Ness 4.5.1983	3 Fife Ness 31.8.1980
	1 Fife Ness 29.8.76
	2 Fife Ness 26.9.76
	(1 there the next day)
	2 Fife Ness 2.10.76
	(1 the next day)
	1 Kingsbarns halt 3.10.76
	1 Kingsbarns halt 10.10.76

1976 was obviously an exceptional year. The birds at Kingsbarns
were ringed, but some of the sight records at Fife Ness could have
referred to Marsh Warblers. The species are extremely difficult to tell
apart in the field.

Great Reed Warbler   *Acrocephalus arundinaceus*

Very scarce straggler

Only one record of this large European warbler, which was a bird
singing at Kilconquhar on 17 June 1970 (SB6:337).

Icterine Warbler   *Hippolais icterina*

Rare vagrant

The following birds have been recorded in Fife:

Spring: *Autumn:*
1 Fife Ness 1.6.1984   1 Fife Ness 16-21.9.1984
1 Fife Ness 6-7.5.83   1 Fife Ness 1-4.9.83
1 male Tentsmuir Point 15.5.81   then 2 there till 8.9.83
                                       1 Fife Ness 23.9.80
                                       1 Fife Ness 6.10.77
                                       1 Fife Ness 26.8.76
                                       1 Fife Ness 24.9.76
                                       1 Kilconquhar 14.9.75
                                       1 Fife Ness 9.10.75
                                       1 Fife Ness 1.9.74
                                       1 Fife Ness 22+27.8.68
                                       1 Fife Ness 22.9.67

There appear to be no earlier records of this colourful Scandinavian warbler in Fife, though a bird identified as either Icterine or Melodious was seen at Elie on 8.9.65 (SB3:429). The pattern of recent records suggests that it may be increasing.

Subalpine Warbler   *Sylvia cantillans*

Very rare vagrant

A male bird was at Fife Ness 3-9 May 1983, when it was seen by a number of observers. It was possibly joined by a female on 7 May. This is the first record for the Fife mainland.

Barred Warbler   *Sylvia nisoria*

Uncommon passage migrant

This warbler is extremely skulking in its habits, and it has never been recorded outside Fife Ness in the area. Records are of one or two birds, all in autumn, and falling between 16 August and 2 October. It has only been reported in Fife since 1946, when 2 birds were found at Fife Ness on 5 September, and up to 1953 only one other Barred Warbler had been recorded on the mainland of Scotland. There are records every two years or so since 1967, and every year since 1982, so it appears to be increasing.

Lesser Whitethroat *Sylvia curruca*

Passage migrant, has bred

This warbler is seen most commonly on passage at Fife Ness: in spring the earliest date in recent years is 23 April 1983, with as many as 10 at Fife Ness on 10 May 1970, and 7 there on 16 May 1983, but spring migrants have also been recorded at Crail, Kilconquhar, East Wemyss wood and Burntisland. The Lesser Whitethroat favours thickets of hawthorn, and it was first found breeding in Fife in 1974, when a fledgling was seen at Priormuir on 13 July. It was again suspected of breeding in 1984, when a pair was present in May and June at Cults Hill; males were also singing at three other sites that year: Lindores, Falkland and Charlestown.

In autumn passage migrants are present on their return journey, all records in recent years falling between 17 August and 11 November. Autumn numbers are usually smaller: 3 at Fife Ness on 7 October 1979 is the maximum autumn count in twenty-five years.

The Lesser Whitethroat has definitely increased this century. Harvie-Brown (1906) had no records of the species for North Fife, even on passage; whereas Baxter and Rintoul (1935) called it an occasional passage migrant to South Fife, and mentioned that they had watched 2 at Kilminning near Crail on 4 May 1920, and one at Fife Ness on 15-16 September 1934 (VFF:118). In the *Birds of Scotland* (1953) they could add a note of an unusual fall on 7 May 1936, when 30 Lesser Whitethroats were in the gorse at Fife Ness. Since 1968 it has been recorded every year except 1977.

H

Whitethroat   *Sylvia communis*

Common summer visitor

This is one of our commoner warblers, nesting throughout the area, where it frequents thickets, untrimmed hedges and gorse bushes. It arrives in late April, and one on 24 April 1971 at Fife Ness is the earliest in twenty-five years. Other April records have come from Kilconquhar, Lundin Links and Craigluscar reservoir, with the main arrival being in May. In autumn birds leave from mid-August: there were 7 at Fife Ness on 19 August 1971, with the latest record being one there on 17 October 1975.

Harvie-Brown (1906) found the Whitethroat a common summer visitor to North Fife. Baxter and Rintoul (1935) said it was very common in East Fife, nesting 'even in the rose and blackthorn bushes and meadow sweet along the seashore' (VFF:117), which is still the case in the 1980s. Grierson mentioned it as common in the Tentsmuir area in the 1950s, with 4-5 pairs at Morton Lochs and others at Earlshall (only since 1953) and Tayport (SB2:156). Numbers fluctuate, however, and in 1969 the Whitethroat was reported in *Scottish Birds* as 'virtually disappeared as a common breeding bird in Fife', and it was not till 1973 and 1974 that reports were coming in of increased breeding. More recently it was considered common in the Lomond Hills area in 1983; and 12 were singing at Balmerino on 30 May 1984. A local BTO survey in 1985 came up with only 42 breeding pairs, widely distributed throughout Fife. This could represent an under-recording, and it would be interesting to run this survey for a few more years.

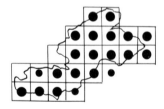

Garden Warbler   *Sylvia borin*

Summer visitor

The Garden Warbler mainly favours woodland edges in the breeding season, as well as large gardens, where it nests in bushes and shrubbery. The first birds may arrive in late April (one at Kippo on 25 April 1981 is the earliest record in recent years), with the main arrival in May. In the last few years it has been reported as present in an increasing number of places: as many as 10 pairs were found at Devilla forest in 1983, and it has also been heard at Dunfermline, Lochore (several), Cults Hill, Lindores, Norman Law, Wormit, Tayport, Morton Lochs, St Fort, Magus Muir, Dura Den and Balcaskie.

The return journey takes place from August (single birds at Fife Ness from 16 August 1980, and 15+ on 26 September 1976), with the last birds on 17 October 1982.

Harvie-Brown (1906) found the Garden Warbler very rare in North Fife; Boase (1964) could only add that it was known to have nested at Lindores and Myres Castle. W. Berry said a pair had been at Tayfield, but breeding was not proved (1930s); Grierson had a record of a pair at Earlshall in 1951, and a single bird there on 10 June the same year (SB2:156). For South Fife, Baxter and Rintoul (1935) said that 'in the Forth area we are nearing the northern limit of the breeding range of the Garden Warbler in Scotland. We do not, therefore, find it very numerous anywhere . . . ' It had, however, been known to nest as far east as Gilston, 'though its breeding east of Burntislands is an exceptional occurrence' (VFF:119).

There is therefore no doubt that the Garden Warbler has extended its breeding range this century, and especially in the last few years.

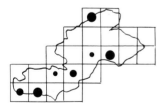

Blackcap   *Sylvia atricapilla*

Summer visitor and passage migrant, a few winter

The earliest record of spring arrival in the last thirty years was a male at
Kilconquhar on 21 April 1968, and migrants may be found at Fife Ness
and other coastal areas in East Fife in late April and May. The Blackcap
frequents open woodland and old gardens, and it often sings from a
more elevated position than the Garden Warbler, whose song is very
similar and may possibly be confused with that of the Blackcap.
The *Breeding Atlas* (1968-72) showed it breeding in 3 squares only, with
'probably breeding' in another 12, and records of breeding birds are
still very scattered. In the last few years, singing birds have been
reported at Devilla forest, Lochore, Lindores, Tayport, Scotscraig,
Kilconquhar, Balcaskie and Colinsburgh.

Our breeding Blackcaps leave the area in September, but passage
migrants may be seen along the east coast, increasingly so in October,
with a few stragglers into November. There is an extraordinary record
of 100 Blackcaps at Fife Ness on 5 October 1979, but peak numbers
otherwise recorded are between 10 and 15.

Most years one or two birds stay behind, and wintering records in
recent years have come from Gauldry, Kinshaldy, St Andrews, Crail,
Burntisland and Limekilns. This appears to have been a development
of the last thirty years, though Boase referred to a 'Marsh or Willow
Tit', described to him, in an old garden in West Tayport in the winters
of 1915 and 1916, which could well have been a Blackcap.

Harvie-Brown (1906) quoted W. Berwick as saying that the Blackcap
bred in North Fife; though Grierson found it a rare casual to Tentsmuir
in the 1950s, with one record only of a bird seen at Earlshall in August

1950. For South Fife, Baxter and Rintoul (1935) had only one definite record of breeding, which was at Burntisland in 1926, with a 'probable breeding' at Pittencrieff Glen, Dunfermline in 1915.

In the 1950s several reports of successful breeding came from High Valleyfield and Longannet, but none since. A pair at Kilconquhar, with 5 eggs on 12 May 1964, was mentioned as the first breeding record for East Fife (SB3:148). Records therefore show that the Blackcap, like the Garden Warbler, has increased in numbers this century, but probably only slightly so in recent years.

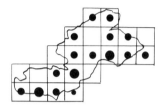
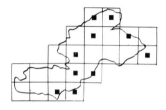

Greenish Warbler *Phylloscopus trochiloides*

Very rare vagrant

A bird seen at Fife Ness on 18 September 1976 is the only record of this rare Scandinavian and East European warbler.

Pallas's Warbler *Phylloscopus proregulus*

Very rare vagrant

One Pallas's Warbler was seen at Fife Ness on 11 October 1982, and 2 there the next day. This was part of a big fall of migrants (especially Goldcrests), and many Pallas's Warblers were reported elsewhere along the east coast of Britain. The species breeds east of Moscow.

Yellow-browed Warbler   *Phylloscopus inornatus*

Rare autumn migrant

The following are all the published records of this rare Siberian species. They have all been in the autumn between 14 September and 28 October:

2 at Fife Ness 23-28.9.1985
1 at Fife Ness 25-28.10.1981
2 at Fife Ness between 23-28.9.1976
2 at Fife Ness 9-10.10.1975
2 at Fife Ness 7.10.1973 (one the day before)
1 at Fife Ness 1.10.1972
1 at Fife Ness 14.9.1971
1 at Fife Ness 27.9.1971
1 at Fife Ness 5-6.10.1968
1 at Lahill near Largo 23.10.1922 (VFF:128)

It was recorded on many occasions on the Isle of May between 1922 and 1968, but apparently not on mainland Fife.

Radde's Warbler   *Phylloscopus schwarzi*

Very rare passage migrant

A bird of this Central and East Asiatic species was first recorded at Fife Ness on 5 October 1979. Jim Cobb identified another bird of this species at Fife Ness on 14 May 1985 which, if passed by the Rarities Committee, will be the first spring record for Britain.

Wood Warbler   *Phylloscopus sibilatrix*

Scarce summer visitor, has bred

This warbler is fairly rare. The earliest arrival in spring is one found at Inverkeithing on 26 April 1984, whereas other spring passage Wood Warblers have been recorded at Cults Hill, Star of Markinch and

St Andrews. It has been recorded at Fife Ness occasionally in spring and autumn.

As the name suggests, the Wood Warbler frequents woods, especially tall deciduous trees such as beech, and in 1984 a pair breeding at Falkland was the first record in many years. Baxter and Rintoul (1935) mentioned that they had occasionally seen it on passage in East Fife, and that it bred in West Fife, as far east as Burntisland. They had found it in the woods at Culross and Tulliallan, although it had apparently not been common here in 1885 (VFF:127). Dalgleish, however, recorded it breeding at West Grange in 1874. For North Fife Harvie-Brown (1906) quoted W. Berwick as saying that the Wood Warbler (or 'Wood Wren') was not common, but bred in the woods by Stravithie (FT:82); and Boase (1964) only had records of the species on passage in North Fife.

It therefore appears that the Wood Warbler has always been scarce.

Chiffchaff *Phylloscopus collybita*

Mainly passage migrant, breeds in small numbers

The Chiffchaff is usually the first warbler to arrive: 2 at Morton Lochs on 25 March 1984 is the earliest record in recent years, but there are several other March records, such as one at Falkland on 29 March 1982. Numbers usually increase in April, and an unprecedented count of 40 Chiffchaffs was made at Fife Ness on 30 April 1983, though few birds stay to breed in Fife. The first record of breeding in South Fife came from High Valleyfield in 1958 (EBB8:91), and a pair fledged 6 young here in 1960. A Chiffchaff had been present here already in 1952, when a 'migrant' was reported on 1 May (Scot.Nat.64:115). There were no breeding records of Chiffchaff in the *Breeding Atlas,* although it was 'probably breeding' in 10 squares (1968-72). More recently, records of birds singing in summer have come from Lindores, Wormit, Tentsmuir, Magus Muir, Balcaskie, Kilconquhar, Kelty, Balbirnie Park (Glenrothes), the Lomond Hills, Falkland, Peppermill and Devilla forest.

The return journey takes place in September and October, when a maximum of 20 were at Fife Ness on 11 October 1982, and the latest record was a bird at Fife Ness on 17 November 1984. Occasionally an individual spends the winter in the area, and there are wintering records from Strathmiglo, Dalgety, Largo Bay, Kirkcaldy and St Andrews.

None of the older accounts mentions more than a few migrants at Fife Ness and St Andrews, and it therefore appears that the Chiffchaff has increased on passage in the last twenty years and that, although it bred in Fife for the first time in 1958, it is still a very scarce breeding species here.

Occasionally a bird of the pale˙ Scandinavian and Baltic race *P.c.abietinus* is seen on passage, such as one at Denburn wood, Crail on 10 November 1984.

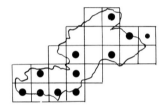

Willow Warbler   *Phylloscopus trochilus*

Common summer visitor and passage migrant

This is by far our commonest warbler. It frequents a variety of habitats, as long as there are trees or bushes with some undergrowth, and it breeds widely throughout the area. In spring the Willow Warbler arrives later than the Chiffchaff, in the second week of April or later: 4 at Morton Lochs on 10 April 1981 is the earliest date in recent years, with other early birds at Kilconquhar, St Andrews, Kirkcaldy, Star of Markinch, Lochore, North Queensferry and Limekilns. The main arrival is in May: thus in Kippo wood there was one on 15 April 1981, 20 on 23 April, and 100 on 9 May. About 30 pairs bred here that year.

In autumn, migration takes place from mid-August onwards: there were 30 at Fife Ness on 18 August 1969; and one at Fife Ness on 20 November 1970 is the latest in the last thirty years. A juvenile ringed at Kingsbarns on 27 August 1967 was recovered at Algarve, Portugal on 19 September 1968.

It appears that in North Fife, at least, the Willow Warbler increased as a breeding bird around the middle of this century for, although Harvie-Brown called it common here, he gave no numbers; Grierson said it had increased remarkably in the Tentsmuir area in the early 1950s; whereas Boase (1964) found it had not been present earlier this century in a number of places where it was now common, as eg. at Lindores (BNF:110).

In the south it was always more common. Baxter and Rintoul (1935) mentioned that, at the end of July and August, large numbers of Willow Warblers, both old and young, appeared in their gardens in Largo, obviously on the move after nesting (VFF:125).

The Willow Warbler has, if anything, increased in recent years, but unlike the Chiffchaff it has never wintered here.

The 'Willow Wren' was mentioned in the *New Statistical Account* of Cupar (1836).

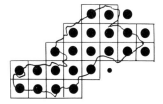

Goldcrest   *Regulus regulus*

Common resident and passage migrant

The Goldcrest is common throughout the year in suitable habitats of coniferous woods and clumps of fir trees. It also occurs on passage in very varying numbers, especially in autumn. In October 1982 a quite extraordinary invasion took place, when an estimated 1,500 Goldcrests were at Fife Ness alone on 11 October, where they sat on the gorse bushes so closely together that they literally weighted down the branches. Several hundreds, possibly new arrivals, were there for the next few days, and large numbers were also observed elsewhere in East Fife, eg. at Cambo, where there were reports of birds so tame they could be picked up in the hand; and many were killed on the roads in these parts. A week later, Tentsmuir was bubbling with Goldcrests (see article in *Fife and Kinross Bird Report* 1982). In 1983, 300 Goldcrests were at Fife Ness from 29 September to 1 October, and parties of up to 30 were reported from Elie to St Andrews during this time. Another 30 were at St Andrews golf course on 21 November the same year. Before that time, the biggest recent count was 150 at Fife Ness on 8 October 1977. Numbers in spring are quite small: 8 on 8 April 1974 has been the maximum in the last twenty-five years.

The Goldcrest was not mentioned as a bird of passage either by Harvie-Brown or by Grierson; and Boase had only one late September record (for Fife Ness in 1957), but they all considered it a common breeding bird in North Fife. Baxter and Rintoul (1935) thought the Goldcrest had greatly increased in the nineteenth century, given that it was mentioned only once in the *Old Statistical Account,* of St Monance (1793), as very rare, whereas it was mentioned in a number of places in the *New Statistical Account* (Cupar, Burntisland and Kilrenny in Fife), and they considered it still increasing in South Fife. They did, however, note a considerable passage through the area, and especially a fall of migrants from 19-21 October 1908, when there were 'very great numbers in the East Neuk [Fife Ness]; at Crail the trees in the Nethergate were full of Goldcrests; there must have been hundreds there' (VFF:107). The dramatic autumn invasions are not, therefore, a novel phenomenon.

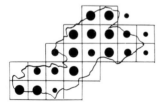
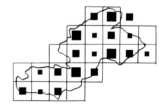

Firecrest *Regulus ignicapillus*

Very rare migrant

There have been two sightings of this southern relative of the Goldcrest in Fife, both fairly recently: at least 3 were at Fife Ness on 3 October 1976; and one was at Kilrenny on 24 April 1973 (SB8:81).

Spotted Flycatcher *Muscicapa striata*

Summer visitor

The Spotted Flycatcher favours woodland and parkland with scattered trees. It appears recently to have become rather scarce in Fife: the *Breeding Atlas* recorded 'confirmed breeding' in 15 squares in the 1968-72 period, which would scarcely be the case today. In 1983, 5 pairs bred on the Lomond Hills, with pairs present in summer at Clune, Balcaskie, Kilrenny, St Andrews, Leuchars and Tentsmuir; but there are even fewer records in 1984. It may, however, be under-recorded.

The Spotted Flycatcher arrives in May, with the earliest date being one at Kilconquhar on 28 April 1963, and a few individuals may be seen in East Fife on passage, such as one at Denburn wood on 18 May 1985; and it leaves again in late September and October: 5 were at St Andrews on 2-5 October 1984, with the last bird recorded at Fife Ness on 5-7 October 1973.

The Spotted Flycatcher was probably never very common in the area: of the older reports only W. Berry found it always common about Tayfield right up to 1946 (unpublished notes 1872-1947); whereas Grierson said it was never numerous in Tentsmuir in the 1950s, but it had nested in the past at Fetterdale and Earlshall, and it had bred at Morton Lochs in 1952 (SB2:156). In the 1980s it was still breeding in Tentsmuir. Both Dalgleish (1885) and Baxter and Rintoul (1935) found it not very abundant but regular in West and South Fife.

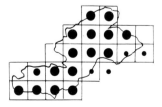

Red-breasted Flycatcher   *Ficedula parva*

Scarce passage migrant

Practically all records of this Baltic species are from Fife Ness, of one or
two birds. There are only two spring records; all the rest fall between
7 September and 19 October:

Spring:
1 female Fife Ness 16.5.1982
1 female Fife Ness 7.5.1968

Autumn:
4 Fife Ness 22.9.1985
1 Denburn wood 22.9.1985
1 Fife Ness 22-23.9.1980
1 Fife Ness 1.10.1979
1 Fife Ness 19.10.1977
1 Fife Ness 23.9-1.10.1976
1 Fife Ness 29.9.1975
2 Fife Ness 16.9.1973
1 Fife Ness 4-7.10.1973
1 Fife Ness 7-14.9.1968
1 Fife Ness 16.9.1967
1 Elie Ness 16.9.1964
1 Fife Ness 11.2.1962
2 (1 male adult) Fife Ness 18.9.1960
(first for mainland Fife SB1:337)

Pied Flycatcher   *Ficedula hypoleuca*

Passage migrant

Since 1968 a few birds have been reported every year, with records
in spring falling between 28 April and 20 May, and a maximum of
6 birds on 7 May 1970; autumn records fall between 16 August and
27 November, with a maximum count of 25 at Fife Ness on
17 September 1969, but this was unusual. Most records are from Fife
Ness, but birds have also recently been reported at Morton Lochs,
Wormiston and Denburn wood. Up to 1968 this species was reported
in Fife every few years only, but from a wider area, such as Tulliallan, St
Andrews and Newport. W. Berry observed that it had occurred at
Tayfield about 1874, and that he and Dr Eagle Clark had watched one

at the edge of a pine wood at Tentsmuir on 9 May 1904 (unpublished notes); for South and West Fife, Dalgleish (1885) called it 'very rare to Scotland', but mentioned one shot at West Grange on 23 April 1881, while Baxter and Rintoul saw single birds at Gilston on 8 May and at Largo on 12 May also in 1904 (Scot.Nat.1905:53).

This species appears to have become rather less scarce on passage in the last twenty years or so.

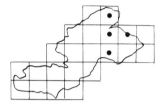

Bearded Tit   *Panurus biarmicus*

Very rare vagrant

All records of this reedbed species are from 1972: a male, trapped at Guardbridge on 5 November, was released at Kilconquhar where it was present until at least 10 November; 2 were seen at Morton Lochs on 9 December, and one (a female) was at Earlshall on 10 December (SB7:370).

Long-tailed Tit   *Aegithalos caudatus*

Fairly common resident

This tit moves around in small flocks frequenting the edges of woods, tall bushes and thickets. It is generally distributed throughout Fife, but not in any great numbers, which may be due to its vulnerability in cold winters. Good places to see them are eg. Morton Lochs and Kemback woods in the east, Lochore Meadows in central Fife and Devilla forest in the west. On the evening of 27 September 1952, a large congregation was observed at Cameron reservoir when more than 77 individuals were moving through (Scot.Nat.65:57). All the old reports agree that the Long-tailed Tit was always sparsely distributed, but also that it had long been known here: it was mentioned in the *New Statistical Account* of Cupar and of Dunfermline (1836 and 1844).

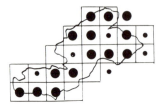 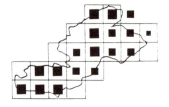

Willow Tit   *Parus montanus*

Formerly a scarce resident, now extinct

The only records are undated and before 1935, when Baxter and Rintoul observed that the only place they knew in South Fife to be inhabited by Willow Tits was the district about Burntisland and Aberdour, but they had also seen them out of the breeding season around Largo (VFF:112). Dalgleish (1885) as well as Balfour Kirke (1911) spoke of 'Marsh Tits' as being uncommon in South and West Fife, but Baxter and Rintoul (1935) considered that all records of Marsh Tits did in fact refer to Willow Tits (see also 'Blackcap').

Coal Tit   *Parus ater*

Common resident

The Coal Tit favours coniferous woods and well-established plantations, and it is present and common throughout the area. Grierson (1962) said it was the commonest tit on Tentsmuir. Baxter and Rintoul (1935) mentioned that it suffered badly in severe winters, when they had often found it dead after spells of hard frost, and said it has never really recovered after the disastrous winter of 1916-17. There seems, however, to be no change of status in recent years.

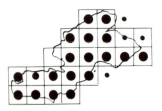 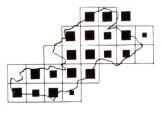

Blue Tit *Parus caeruleus*

Very common resident

The Blue Tit is one of our commonest birds throughout the year, when it is present in gardens, hedgerows and thickets, as well as in woodland, especially deciduous. In autumn there are also a fair number that visit Fife Ness, probably on passage, and it is not unusual to find parties of 20-40 here in October or early November. The Blue Tit was mentioned as very common in all the older reports, and it seems to suffer less in severe frosts than many other resident small birds, which could partly be due to the fact that it is an avid visitor to bird tables and nut feeders.

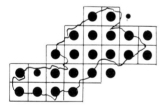 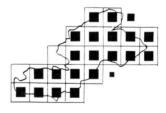

Great Tit   *Parus major*

Common resident

Although less common than the Blue Tit, the Great Tit is nevertheless widely distributed in the area, especially in gardens, hedgerows and mixed woods. It appears always to have been common, if fairly local, and there is no evidence of any change in status.

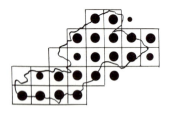
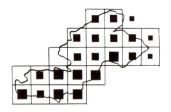

Treecreeper   *Certhia familiaris*

Fairly common resident

This bird frequents mature woodland and parks; Grierson (1962) thought it nested freely on Tentsmuir, which is still a good place to find it. The Treecreeper was reported as 'streadily increasing' in 1969, and the *Breeding Atlas* showed it breeding in 17 squares during the 1968-72 period, but recent records point to a decline. No doubt numbers fluctuate, and the older reports never found it very common anywhere in Fife.

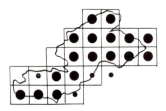
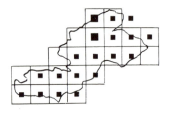

Golden Oriole *Oriolus oriolus*

Very scarce vagrant, has bred

The first proved breeding of this species in Scotland was in 1974, when a pair was seen feeding 2 fledged young on 17 July in East Fife. A male had been reported singing there in May 1973. There have been no more breeding records, but several sightings, though none in the 1980s. Baxter and Rintoul (1935) mentioned three old records for South Fife: one shot on the estate of Raith, near Kirkcaldy, on 22 April 1870; a female 'got' at Markinch about 10 May 1908; and a fine male found dead on 16 May 1910 at Inverkeithing (VFF:69).

There is a very nice story attached to this first breeding record. Apparently the pair was discovered by a European bird watcher, who remarked to a local fellow enthusiast that he was so glad to see the Golden Oriole so common in this country, as it was rather rare at home!

Red-backed Shrike *Lanius collurio*

Scarce passage migrant

The Red-backed Shrike visits Fife on passage in spring and autumn, usually in ones and twos, but in 1985, 6-7 individuals were about Fife Ness for a week, as well as a bird which was ringed at Kilrenny Common. They were nearly all males. There have been the following records:

Spring:	*Autumn:*
6-7 Fife Ness/Balcomie 15-21.5.1985	1 juv. Fife Ness 17.9.1984
1 Kilrenney, May 1984	1 St Andrews 16.9.1983
1-2 Balcomie 25-26.5.1984	1 juv. Fife Ness 31.8.1980
1 St Andrews 17.6.1980	1-2 Fife Ness 18.9-8.10.1976
1 Kingsbarns 12.5.1973	1 juv. Fife Ness 31.8.1974
1 Fife Ness 9-10.5.1970	2 adults Fife Ness 1.9.1974
1 near Falkland 4.6.1964	1 imm. Fife Ness 18.8.1969
1 Earlshall 21.5.1950	1 Fife Ness 22.9.1967
	1 juv. Fife Ness 23.9.1967
	1 juv. St Andrews 23.10.1966
	1 Fife Ness 6.9.1963
	2 Fife Ness 6.9.1958

(one reported at 'Gask Hill' in 1976 was not in fact in Fife SB10:114).

Baxter and Rintoul (1935) said that it occured not uncommonly on passage, and that it was mostly males (which still holds true), with records from Fife Ness, Crail and Pittenweem, but gave no dates. Harvie-Brown (1906) found it an apparently casual visitor, but had no records for North Fife. It therefore appears that the Red-backed Shrike has been seen more regularly on passage since the 1960s.

Lesser Grey Shrike   *Lanius minor*

Very rare vagrant

There has been only one record, of a bird at Wormiston on 8 June 1958 (EBB8:92).

Great Grey Shrike   *Lanius excubitor*

Scarce passage migrant and occasional winter visitor

There are more records of the Great Grey Shrike than of the other shrikes, but only a very few in recent years, the most recent being one at Elie on 10 October 1982, and one at Fife Ness 13-14 October the same year. Most records are of singles on autumn passage, and fall between 2 October and 20 November, whereas there are only three winter records, all in the 1960s: one at Peppermill on 16 January 1961; one at Thornton on 6 February 1969; and one at Kincardine on 5 March 1966. In spring nearly all records fall in April, when it has been recorded at Tentsmuir Point, Morton Lochs, Fife Ness and Kirkcaldy, with one later record from Cambo Ness on 10 May 1975. In autumn it has been recorded at a number of places all over Fife: Peppermill, Cleish Hills, East Lomond, Falkland, Balmakin (Colinsburgh), Elie, Anstruther, Fife Ness (more than fifteen times), Kingsbarns and Leuchars.

   The Great Butcher-Bird, as it was also called, was mentioned in the *New Statistical Account* as a very rare visitor to Carnock parish (1836), but Harvie-Brown (1906) had no records for North Fife; while Boase mentioned only one record of a bird in mid-November 1916 (BNF:118). In South Fife, Baxter and Rintoul (1935) said it occurred not uncommonly, but chiefly in winter, and they mentioned one record of a bird at Largo on 7 March 1917 (VFF:114), whereas further back

Dalgleish (1885) had records of 5 individuals shot since 1859: 3 at Tulliallan, 1 at West Grange and 1 at Brucefield.

The 1982 records were the first for five years, so it appears that this shrike is getting rarer again.

Woodchat Shrike *Lanius senator*

Very rare migrant

There are two records for the Fife mainland: one being a bird near Kinghorn on 21-22 May 1953 (EBB:669); the other one at Kilconquhar on 30 May 1965 (SB4:101).

Jay *Garrulus glandarius*

Local resident

The Jay favours woods and plantations, and it has recently been spreading in the area: since 1980 reports of its presence in the breeding season have come from Blairadam forest, Dean plantation (Dunfermline), Dunniker woods, Valleyfield, Wemyss wood and Lochmill Loch, with proved breeding at Drummie wood, Falkland, Pitcairn (East Lomond), Tentsmuir forest (where it is common), and Scotscraig.

In 1983 a great irruption took place in October, when thousands of Jays flooded into Britain. There were few signs of this in Fife, although there were increased numbers on Tentsmuir at the time, and one flying west at Randerston on 8 October was undoubtedly part of this influx. There were also 8 at Harran Hill wood on 23 December 1983.

The Jay has apparently always had a patchy and fluctuating distribution. It was mentioned in the *New Statistical Account* of Inverkeithing and Burntisland (1836); and Baxter and Rintoul (1935) said it had been reported earlier last century as 'not uncommon' in the west by Dunfermline and Blairadam, but by 1876 it nested here in only one wood, being much persecuted by 'Gamekeepers, gardeners and makers of flies for fishing'. They thought it had spread again slightly, and it had bred at Markinch since 1931 (VFF:62). In North Fife, Boase reported that some pairs nested near Cupar at the beginning of this century, and it had also nested once in Tentsmuir in 1924, but was not seen here again till after the Second World War, when Grierson found it quite numerous in the forest area; and there were also some around Ladybank in the 1950s (BNF:99).

The *Breeding Atlas* showed it only breeding in the Tentsmuir square (1968-72), so it has definitely been spreading the last fifteen years.

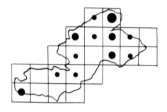 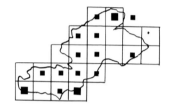

Magpie   *Pica pica*

Resident in West Fife

The Magpie was mentioned in the *Old Statistical Account* of Carnock (1794), and in the *New Statistical Account* of Inverkeithing (1836). This bird apparently used to be very common everywhere in the county, and its total disappearance from East Fife was, according to Baxter and Rintoul, entirely due to the success of gamekeepers in persecuting it to extinction. They mentioned eg. that Magpies at Lahill (Largo) were so numerous and fearless about 1900 that they used to come close to the windows and steal the chickens, and also that Magpies bred at Airdrie wood in 1921, in the same tree as a Heron, the nests being described as 'jostling each other'. By the time of writing (1935) it was, however, very scarce everywhere (VFF:60). The same kind of persecution took place in North Fife, where W. Berry said it was common all over in the 1870s, but by the 1940s it had become very scarce, and was shot on sight (BNF:99). In 1984 it was reported present at eight sites in West Fife and as far east as Kirkcaldy, where there were 10 in December, and there was also a bird about at Guardbridge from 9 November to 1 December that year. This is one of those very rare occasions when reports of the spread and increase of a species are not welcomed, as the Magpie is an enthusiastic murderer of all small birds.

 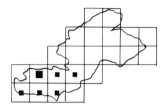

Chough   *Pyrrhocorax pyrrhocorax*

Formerly visitor, now extinct

Corvus graculus, which Baxter and Rintoul considered to be the Chough, was mentioned as an occasional visitor to Dunfermline in the *New Statistical Account* (1844). Baxter and Rintoul (1935) said that it used to breed across the Firth of Forth, at St Abb's Head, up to 1867, with a few sporadic records of the 'Red-legged Crow' there as late as 1903. However, it is unlikely that it ever bred in Fife.

Jackdaw   *Corvus monedula*

Common resident

The Jackdaw is usually seen in the vicinity of towers and old buildings, but also on grassfields, often in company with Rooks. It is found throughout Fife, but perhaps not in such great numbers as in many other parts of the country. Harvie-Brown (1906) said it was abundant and increasing, although he gave no specific numbers for North Fife; Boase (1964) had a record of 200 at old Forgan in late April 1918, but said it was generally scarce about Peat Inn and Dura Den (BNF:99). W. Berry, however, found it 'multitudinous' about Tayfield in the 1940s.

Occasionally, large flocks of Jackdaws are seen on migration, such as was noted on 8 January 1964, when 'a great procession of Rooks and Jackdaws was seen over Cupar, at dusk, passing for more than an hour, and it was reckoned that 20,000-30,000 birds had passed' (SB3:90).

Very large flocks were also mentioned by Baxter and Rintoul at Largo
Bay earlier this century (VFF:57).

There is no evidence of any change in status.

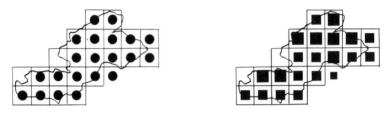

Rook   *Corvus frugilegus*

Common resident, but declining; also winter visitor

The Rook is extremely sociable, nesting in colonies in large trees. The
latest national Rookery Census in 1975 found 149 rookeries in Fife, with
a total of 7,400 nests, which indicated an average of nearly 50 nests per
rookery—well below the Scottish average of 78.9 (SB9:327-334). The
breeding total, however, represented a huge drop of more than two
thirds compared with the census in 1945, when 26,683 nests were
counted, and this fall was dramatically worse than the national average
decline for Scotland of one third (see also B of S:13). Grierson
mentioned that the main rookery at Earlshall in the 1950s contained
over 500 pairs with smaller rookeries elsewhere on Tentsmuir, but said
that a certain percentage of these birds were destroyed annually, the
average being about 1,500 for the area (SB2:153). Recent declines are
not, however, so much related to direct human persecution as to crop

spraying, felling of suitable trees, and all the modern methods of large-scale farming.

Great movements of Rooks take place in winter (see also Jackdaws), when birds are going to roost. In 1975, six active winter roosts were listed in Fife (SB8:309-314), two out of which had 3,000-5,000 birds: Raith Park (Kirkcaldy), and Montrave (both new roosts), with the other four attracting 1,500-2,000 Rooks: Craighall (Ceres); Kirktonbarns (Newport), Otterston and Ramornie (Ladybank). This last roost was apparently known to Baxter and Rintoul in 1949, when they recorded over 60,000 birds here; while 4-5 other unused roosts were also mentioned, some of which had been active in the preliminary survey in 1969-70 (SB6:166-170), which indicates that roosts change a good deal.

Rooks obviously fly quite a considerable way to and from their winter roosts, and they probably move about much more than is generally supposed. There is a very interesting ringing record of a bird ringed as a chick at Pori (Turin), Finland on 20 June 1976, which was shot for a Crow by a farmer near Cupar on 4 September 1977 (1531km).

It was undoubtedly the Rook which was meant in the *Old Statistical Account* of Carnbee, where the 'Crows' were blamed by the farmers for being very destructive to their newly sown corn. This led to the following incident: 'A servant of the Earl of Kelly, who had just finished the sowing a rich field with oats, was much vexed to see it in a little covered all over with crows; in various ways did he endeavour to drive them off, but all in vain, till at last he shot some of them, when to his great astonishment, upon opening up their stomachs, he found them quite full of cobworm, and not one grain of oats' (EP edition:p.111).

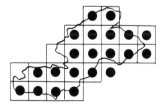 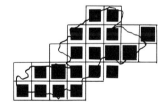

Carrion Crow   *Corvus corone*

Common resident

The Carrion Crow is widespread, numerous, and increasing. It is far less sociable than the Rook, and will drive away other Crows from its territory in the breeding season. After the breeding season, and in winter, sizeable flocks may occur such as 120 at Pittenweem dump on 8 December 1982; and Baxter and Rintoul also recalled seeing constant streams of Carrion Crows passing Largo on their way to roost, and they had even watched birds coming in over the sea from the east at Fife Ness, mostly in singles, but once as many as 20 together (VFF:52).

Many birdwatchers who have lived in Fife over the past two or three decades have noticed the increase of the Crow. The decline of Earlshall and other parts of the Tentsmuir area as a good breeding area for ducks and terns has been partly attributed to the end of careful keepering, which kept the number of crows and foxes within bounds.

Yearly one or two Hooded Crows, *C.c.cornix,* are usually reported in winter, and there are records, mostly in coastal areas, from Tayport to Peppermill. W. Berry as well as Baxter and Rintoul mentioned that it used to be much commoner in Fife; and the crows in Millais' drawing of the Eden estuary in *The Wildfowler of Scotland* (1901) are all hooded. It even bred in Fife at one time; eg. Dalgleish (1885) reported that a pair had bred at West Grange 'many years ago', but by 1917 it had practically ceased to even winter here (B of S:7). Hybrid Hooded-Carrion Crows are sometimes seen: one frequented the Pitcairn area for most of 1983.

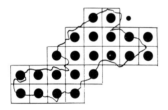 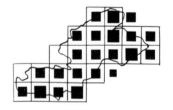

Raven						*Corvus corax*

Vagrant

There are no recent records of this species in Fife, but Baxter and Rintoul (1935) said it used to breed on the Lomond Hills, and speculated if the old Ravenscraig Castle near Kirkcaldy was so named, because Ravens once bred here. On 15 November 1925, however, a Raven and a Peregrine were seen passing over Largo, vigorously mobbing and bullying one another (VFF:50).

Starling   *Sturnus vulgaris*

Common resident

The Starling nests in holes in buildings or trees, in nesting boxes or thick ivy, and it may do so singly or in small colonies. It is abundant throughout Fife, and large flocks of juveniles are a common sight from about the beginning of July onwards, especially in coastal areas, Starlings also roost together, sometimes in vast numbers, and there were 6,000 in the reedbeds at Kilconquhar on 8 August 1960—a smallish flock by Starling standards.

In autumn a certain amount of migration takes place, when visitors arrive to spend the winter here, probably with our local Starlings staying on, for this species is even commoner in winter in the area. A large winter roost has for some years been located under the Forth road bridge, and when birds occasionally fly in front of drivers across the lanes it is like driving through a porridge of Starlings. Smaller roosts are found at a number of other places such as Guardbridge and Tayport, and birds ringed at a winter roost near Elie in 1968 were recovered the following summer in Norway, Sweden and Finland (SB5:352).

It now seems amazing that the Starling was not so very long ago a very rare bird: it was not mentioned in the *Old Statistical Account,* and only as 'rare' in the *New Statistical Account* of Dysart (1840), and it 'occurred' at Kilrenny (1843). Harvie-Brown drew up a map in *The Fauna of the Tay Basin and Strathmore* (1906), where he showed the spread of the Starling breeding in Scotland, and the first records for Fife were: 1840 in the South-west, 1844 in Central Fife, 1856 in the North-east (FT:138). Baxter and Rintoul (1935) mentioned the first Starling's nest to have been found at Lahill was in 1852 (VFF:65).

Absence of detailed records makes it difficult to say whether the Starling is still increasing as a breeding species in Fife. Certainly, it is extremely abundant in winter, as shown by the *Winter Atlas* below.

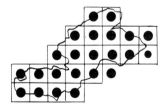 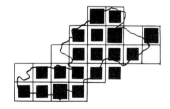

Rose-coloured Starling
Sturnus roseus

Scarce vagrant

The most recent record of this rather striking (when adult) mid-European species was a bird seen on several occasions by non-birdwatchers in St Andrews, in May and June 1983, who provided a convincing description. Before that, there is a record of one at Lundin Links on 6 September 1962, and another at Tayport on 31 March 1954 (EBB4:50). A much earlier record was one seen between Crail and Anstruther about 1896 (VFF:68); Harvie-Brown (1906) mentioned Mugdrum island as a good place in his introduction, but in the text he only had a vague record of a possible juvenile there seen by Drummond Hay sometime in the 1870s.

House Sparrow
Passer domesticus

Common resident

The House Sparrow is common near human habitation of any kind, but especially farm buildings, and in winter may be seen in sizeable flocks on cultivated land. There has been, in recent years, some evidence that the House Sparrow is less common than it used to be, and where it was once abundant, it is only present in small numbers, or even absent: Dr John Berry eg. says it is now (1985) absent from Tayfield, where formerly numbers of pairs bred yearly (pers.com.)

The Sparrow population, however, seems to fluctuate somewhat. Baxter and Rintoul, (1935) said that after the hard winters of the early 40s the Sparrow was extremely scarce in Fife, and only ten years later was it beginning to reach anything like its former abundance (B of S:95). It is, nevertheless, still a very common bird.

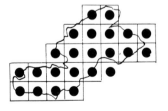
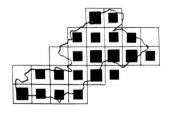

Tree Sparrow   *Passer montanus*

Local common resident

The Tree Sparrow often breeds under bridges and other tall structures
in small colonies, and it is far less common in the area than the House
Sparrow. On the continent it often feeds in gardens with the House
Sparrows, but I have never seen this habit in Fife, although Tree
Sparrows are occasionally mixed up in flocks of House Sparrows
around farms. In East Fife, they are frequently seen around Crail,
which is interesting, as there used to be a breeding colony here before
1928. A number of old-established colonies were mentioned by Baxter
and Rintoul as all died out by the end of the 1920s, such as at Leuchars,
Burntisland and North Queensferry, and they found nesting birds
gradually diminishing in numbers (VFF:77), but the Tree Sparrow has
obviously been recovering since: it started to nest again at Morton
Lochs in 1963, after being absent for about forty years (SB2:159), and 50
birds were counted there on 30 November 1970. At Newburgh, it
nested again in 1964 after thirty years' absence, and about 60 birds were
here in early October 1964. The *Breeding Atlas* showed it breeding in
practically every square (1968-72).

   Baxter and Rintoul also thought that Tree Sparrows migrated, and
they had noted flocks 'obviously of immigrants' at Fife Ness. How
many of the flocks we see in winter are immigrants is uncertain, but
there were about 200 at Kilconquhar in the winter of 1972, while
maximum counts in 1984 were 35 at Shanwell meteorological station
(Tayport) on 26 October, and 28 in the stretch from Buckhaven to East
Wemyss. Other places where good numbers have been recorded in
recent years are Caiplie, Parbroath and Elie estate.

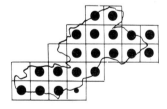
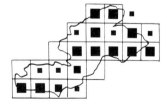

Chaffinch   *Fringilla coelebs*

Common resident

The Chaffinch breeds throughout the area wherever there are trees of any size: in woods, plantations, gardens and hedgerows, and it is one of our commonest nesting birds.

In the autumn there is evidence of passage; eg. at Fife Ness passage was noted from 18 September, with a maximum of 100 on 2 October 1976, and these birds were probably continental Chaffinches. Baxter and Rintoul were also of the opinion that our resident population was augmented in winter by migrants from overseas (VFF:78).

In winter, Chaffinches flock in large numbers: 1,000 at Lindores on 22 December 1979 is the maximum count in recent years, while there were 700+ at Morton Lochs on 11 February 1978, and 250 there on 24 February 1984.

The Chaffinch was mentioned in the *New Statistical Account* of Inverkeithing (1836), and it appears always to have been common in Fife.

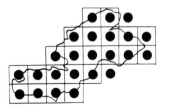

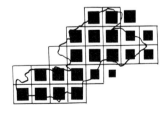

Brambling   *Fringilla montifringilla*

Winter visitor in varying numbers

The first Brambling appears usually in late September-early October, with the earliest date in the last twenty-five years being 22 September, when one was at Fife Ness in 1976, and another at Wormiston in 1985. In winter, however, the Brambling is generally found in flocks, and not infrequently in company with other finches, especially Chaffinches: 1,000 at Lindores on 22 December 1979, and 1,000 at Dunbog on 11 December 1966 are peak counts; 600 at Longannet on 20 January 1960 was regarded as exceptional, as was 500 at Anstruther in mid-February 1970. Places where smaller numbers have been reported in the last twenty years are Flisk, Tayport, Kinsbarns, Cambo, Fife Ness, Crail, Balcarres, Elie estate, Methil docks, Purin Den (Lomond Hills) and Burntisland.

Records suggest that the Brambling is getting scarcer as a winter visitor: the peak count in 1984 was 60 on the Lomond Hills on 31 March, and peaks have been falling since the early '70s. Baxter and Rintoul (1935) mentioned, however, that wintering numbers varied extraordinarily, and also that there were 'Brambling years', when great numbers would winter in South Fife (VFF:79). Harvie-Brown (1906) found it rare in North Fife, whereas Boase (1964) said Bramblings did visit the north in small numbers, the biggest flock being 20 at Morton Lochs in January 1952 (see also SB2:158).

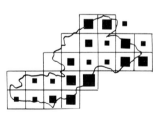

Greenfinch   *Carduelis chloris*

Common resident

The Greenfinch breeds commonly throughout the area, preferring hedges, bushes and shrubbery in gardens and the edges of woods.

In winter it flocks—often with other finches—and may be seen on stubble fields and other arable land. 250 at Morton Lochs on 26 February 1984 is the biggest count in recent years, but further back, on 30 November 1959, a vast flock of about 1,500 finches was reported near Carnbee on kale and newly cleared sugar beet, composed mostly of Chaffinches and Greenfinches, with some Bramblings and Goldfinches among them (SB1:213). Baxter and Rintoul thought it probable that some of these wintering flocks were immigrants, a theory also supported by Grierson (1962), who considered a flock of 500 seen with an equal number of Linnets on the Eden estuary on 8 November 1953 as undoubtedly on passage, whereas the regular wintering flocks in the Tentsmuir area of about 100 were probably resident (SB2:157).

Harvie-Brown (1906) found the Greenfinch very common, and there is no change in status this century.

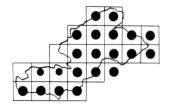 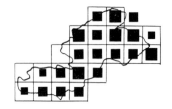

Goldfinch   *Carduelis carduelis*

Fairly common resident in varying numbers

The Goldfinch nests high up in trees in gardens, parks and avenues, but breeding numbers vary greatly, so that in some years it is positively scarce, whereas in others it is quite common, as eg. 1985. In North Fife it appears always to have been scarce—certainly this century—but also in South Fife Baxter and Rintoul (1935) felt it had greatly diminished in numbers since last century due, they thought, to the improvement in agriculture, and the disappearance of much uncultivated land where thistles and other weeds had provided food for the Goldfinches. They also considered another reason for decline to be their attractiveness as cagebirds, which had caused them to be much trapped (VFF:71). In the 1960s, however, breeding in Fife was reported as increasing, at High Valleyfield even 'tremendously' so (SB2:429), and the *Breeding Atlas* showed confirmed breeding in 12 squares. In the late 1970s, numbers were again greatly reduced, but have recently increased once more.

Post-breeding flocks are seen from August onwards (eg. 43 at Crail on 20 August 1983; 30 at Holl reservoir on 26 August 1984). The largest flock reported in recent years was 200+ in Largo Bay in December 1977. Autumn and winter parties of between 30 and 50 birds have also been reported at Sauchope Links (Crail), Fife Ness, Kingsbarns, Tentsmuir, Pitcairn and Lumrainans (70+ here on 1 October 1984). Baxter and Rintoul thought our resident population was joined by small numbers of winter visitors.

The Goldfinch was mentioned in the *New Statistical Account* of Burntisland (1836), where it was (even then) said to be less common 'since the great snowstorm of 1822', thus confirming that fluctuation in numbers is nothing new.

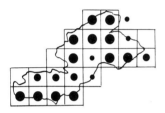 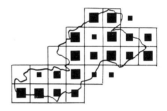

Siskin   *Carduelis spinus*

Winter visitor, may have bred

There are records of Siskin arriving at Fife Ness from 9 September onwards, with other September and early October records from Kellie Castle, Elie Ness, Earlshall, Tulliallan and Longannet. The Siskin is mostly seen in the tops of alder and birch, when it is not flying over, and flocks of up to 85 have been reported in recent years (eg. 85 at Lochore Meadows on 25 October 1984; with smaller numbers at Otterston reservoir, Glenrothes Park, Newport, Tentsmuir and Earlshall). There are a few ringing records, which give some indication of where our winter visitors come from, and where they go to: one ringed at Wormit on 2 April 1981 was caught a month later at Kiltarlity (Highland) on 11 May 1981 (142km), and another adult male ringed at Bridgewater, Somerset on 28 December 1980 was checked at Wormit on 31 March 1981 (587km).

Very few Sisken, if any, breed in Fife. Breeding has been suspected in the past at Tulliallan (1963), and at Tentsmuir, Scotscraig, St Fort and Devilla forest (1980s), but it remains unconfirmed so far.

Siskens were mentioned as 'occasional' in the *New Statistical Account* of Monimail (1836); and Harvie-Brown (1906) thought it was increasing and spreading south in the Tay and Strathmore area; but it was still regarded as scarce in North Fife by Boase (1964). It had, however, been suspected of breeding at Tentsmuir in 1923 (BNF:120). Baxter and Rintoul (1935) mentioned 'Siskin years', but gave no specific reference to South Fife. Records suggest that the Siskin has increased in the last thirty years, as in the 1950s even at Tentsmuir it was regarded only as 'occasional' by Grierson (SB2:158).

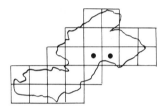
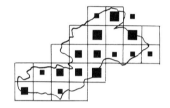

Linnet   *Carduelis cannabina*

Common resident

The Linnet nests in thickets of gorse, bramble and thorn, and is plentiful throughout the area both in the breeding season and to a lesser degree in winter. In winter many of the breeding sites are deserted as the Linnets gather in large flocks to feed on stubble and other arable land, and they are also frequently seen along the shores at this time. The largest flocks reported in recent years were 300 at Flisk on 26 November 1983, with 200 at Brunton on the same day. A certain amount of movement takes place in winter: thus much of the area was deserted in the January frosts in 1982. A considerable number of winter immigrants were also thought by Baxter and Rintoul to reach our area, which is confirmed by recent reports: eg. 50 Linnets were observed flying in off the sea at Fife Ness on 31 August 1984, while there were 150 birds near Crail the next day.

There is no apparent change in status this century.

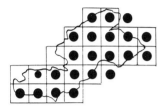 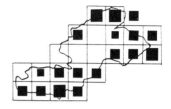

Twite   *Carduelis flavirostris*

Scarce winter visitor

The Twite arrives fairly late in the season, the earliest record in recent years being an exceptional flock of 38 at Fife Ness on 15 October 1982. The Twite frequents only open countryside with rough pastures and stubble fields, and also saltmarshes by the coast; and in recent years reports of flocks up to about 20 have come from Limekilns, Blairadam, the East Lomonds, Burntisland, East Wemyss, Kirkcaldy, Methil docks, Kilrenny, Anstruther, St Andrews, Tentsmuir Point, Tayport and Gauldry, while in the 1960s several records came from the Cult Ness-Longannet area.

The Twite has bred in Fife, but not within the last fifty years. Harvie-Brown (1906) mentioned that W. Evans had found several at Tentsmuir on 31 May 1885 (FT:122); and Grierson (1962) said Twite had nested there in 1923, and possibly in 1921, but all records since then were of wintering birds only (SB2:158). Baxter and Rintoul (1953) had no records of breeding in Fife, and added that 'Thirty or forty years ago we used to see large flocks every winter in the fields in Fife, but it is now

quite a long time since we have met with any of these large gatherings'
(B of S:61). So the Twite has definitely become scarcer this century.

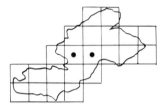 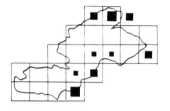

Redpoll   *Carduelis flammea*

Locally common resident

There are several sub-species of Redpoll, but the race commonly seen
in Fife is the Lesser Redpoll *C.f.cabaret*. It frequents woods, where it
favours birch and alder, as well as coniferous plantations. It is not
uncommon locally, and good places to see it are eg. Morton Lochs,
Magus Muir, Kippo plantation in East Fife, the plantations on the
Lomond Hills in central Fife, and Devilla forest in the west. In autumn,
migration has been noted at Fife Ness in late September and October,
and Fife-ringed birds have been recovered in Middlesex (J.Cobb).
In winter sizeable flocks may be seen: 70 at Lochore Meadows on
5 December 1984 was the biggest count in recent years.

In winter the Lesser Redpoll is occasionally joined by the Mealy
Redpoll *C.f.flammea,* and there are records of this Continental race
from eg. Morton Lochs (2 on 7 November 1981, 3 in December the
same year); Tentsmuir (a male on 8 May 1980; one at Raith in
December 1973; and Fife Ness (one on 22 October 1972). Baxter and
Rintoul (1953) mentioned vast flocks of the Mealy Redpoll, which
visited Scotland from time to time, the last being 1910-11, when there
were 'great numbers in East Fife, every time we went out to the east we
saw flocks of hundreds in the bushes and trees and along the walls of the
golf course at Balcomie' (B of S:54). Elsewhere they had records of
similar periodic irruptions since 1820 (VFF:83).

Such invasions of Mealy Redpolls have not been experienced in the last fifty years, but instead the Lesser Redpoll appears to have increased. It was regarded as rare in North Fife certainly till 1930, though a nest was found near Newport about 1915 (BNF:120). Grierson (1962) said it was seen regularly at Tentsmuir since 1930, but nesting had not been proved; for South Fife, Dalgleish (1885) regarded it as an uncommon winter visitor only in the west, though Baxter and Rintoul (1935) said it now bred commonly at Culross, and elsewhere here and there in dens, but nowhere in any numbers (VFF:84). Though numbers in the last few years seem to be below their peak around 1980, the Lesser Redpoll now breeds in a number of places throughout Fife.

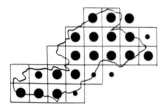 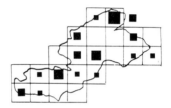

Common Crossbill *Loxia curvirostra*

Present in varying numbers

The Common Crossbill frequents coniferous woods and plantations, often in the vicinity of deciduous trees. It has bred in Tentsmuir forest in the 1980s, and pairs have also been reported recently at Milldeans wood, and in two or three localities on the Lomond Hills, but it remains very scarce as a breeding bird. The *Handbook of British Birds* (1943) suggests that nesting records usually follow irruptions, and an irruption did in fact take place at Tentsmuir in early March to April 1980, when many small parties of 6-20 birds were reported, with maximum numbers of 60 seen during this period. In 1982, the largest flock in Fife was 40 on 11 September in Tentsmuir forest, while other recent sightings have come from Morton Lochs, Guardbridge (4 flying south on 11 November 1984), Carriston reservoir and Barrington Muir. Further back there was a single at Fife Ness on 13 October 1966, and 3 in Devilla forest near Bogside on 11 April 1964. Ballantyne (1982) said it had occurred in Wemyss Wood, but gave no date.

The 'Grossbeak', which probably refers to the Crossbill, was mentioned at Monimail in the *New Statistical Account* (1836); and it was reported to Harvie-Brown by W. Berwick as an 'occasional visitor, not common' to North Fife at the end of last century. Berwick also said that a large flock visited Stravithie in 1856, when a large fir wood was cut down and the Crossbills fed on the fir tops (FT:128). Baxter and Rintoul (1935) said that the first reliable record for South Fife was a Crossbill shot near Colinsburgh on 16 May 1910, after which they saw the species on several occasions in July and August, but only on passage (VFF:88); and elsewhere they mentioned having seen 12 Crossbills among other migrants at Balcomie at 15 August 1952, all young birds, after easterly winds (EBB2:70).

Despite their varying numbers, it is probable that the Crossbill has increased this century, and breeding here is certain now.

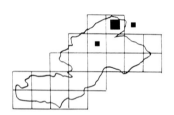

Scottish Crossbill   *Loxia scotica*

Very rare vagrant

It is mentioned in the *Birds of Scotland* (Baxter and Rintoul, 1953) that this crossbill has been recorded in winter in very small numbers in Fife, but no details are given.

Scarlet Rosefinch   *Carpodacus erythrinus*

Very rare visitor

The Scarlet Rosefinch, or 'Scarlet Grossbeak' as it used to be called, has only very recently been recorded for mainland Fife, when an immature was seen by R. W. Byrne at Fife Ness on 19 May 1985. This record is still to be considered by the Rarities Committee. The immature bird looks very similar to the House Sparrow, with which it often associates, so it needs an observant eye to spot it.

Bullfinch   *Pyrrhula pyrrhula*

Common resident

The Bullfinch is found in a variety of habitats from gardens to woods, where it nests in thickets of thorn, thick hedges and other places with plenty of tall, dense cover. It is not uncommon locally. In winter Bullfinches may flock: thus eg. there were 35 in the sea buckthorn at Kinshaldy on 16 January 1983; 26 on East Lomond on 24 December 1984, and 20 at Star Moss on 11 December that year. It is, however, surprisingly vulnerable in hard weather.

The Bullfinch was mentioned in the *New Statistical Account* of Burntisland (1836); but Baxter and Rintoul (1935) found it curiously uncommon in South Fife. They said it did not breed in East Fife, and even in the west it had become much scarcer (VFF:87). In North-east Fife it was said by W. Berwick to be far from common about the end of last century (FT:123); whereas Grierson said it occurred at Tentsmuir in the 1950s, but probably only on passage, 8 on 30 September 1952 being the largest count he had (SB2:158).

Records therefore indicate a slight increase in the last thirty years.

Occasionally birds of the Northern race *P.p.purrhula* are seen on passage, and Baxter and Rintoul mentioned several caught in the autumn of 1910 near Kirkcaldy, and also at Balcaskie in November 1921 (VFF:85). A female at Fife Ness on 6 October 1968 was thought to be of this race.

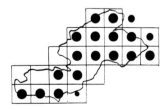

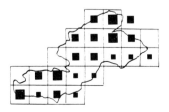

Hawfinch   *Coccothraustes coccothraustes*

Rare, status unclear

There are only two recent records of the Hawfinch: an immature at Morton Lochs on 1 December 1982; and a bird at Kippo plantation on 25 April 1981. Further back one was seen near Boarhills on 10 November 1951 (EBB2:19).

The first breeding record, not only for Fife, but for Scotland, came from near Newport in 1903, where a nest was found, close to Scotscraig House, in the beginning of August. The nestlings had flown when the nest was discovered, but one unhatched egg, as well as the nest itself, is now in the Royal Scottish Museum. The incident is well described by W. Berry in the *Scottish Naturalist* (1904:11-15). W. Berry also said he had once seen one in Tayfield park; and Boase (1964) mentioned a Hawfinch shot and another seen near Newport in 1905, and that there was a further report of breeding at Newport about 21 April 1908, while a dead juvenile was found at Lochmalony, north of Cupar, on 13 September 1928 (BNF:119). In South Fife early records have been: one picked up dead near Kirkcaldy on 25 May 1901, and another near Burntisland in 1905 (VFF:71). There have been none since.

The Hawfinch is extremely shy and secretive in its habits, and as it usually frequents high tree tops, such as may be found in old wooded parkland and well-grown deciduous or mixed woods, it may easily be overlooked and under-recorded.

Lapland Bunting   *Calcarius lapponicus*

Scarce migrant and winter visitor

The following records have occurred since 1970:

Autumn:	*Winter:*
4 Crail airfield 26.10.1985	1 Tayport 15+22.1.1984
1 Crail airfield 12.11.1983	1 Crail airfield 23.1+13.2.1983
1 Fife Ness 7+21.11.1981	2 Methil docks 8,1.1982
1 Fife Ness 23.10.1980	1 Eden estuary 17.1.1970
1 Fife Ness 3.10.1979	
1-6 Fife Ness 21-28.9.1976	*Spring:*
1-3 Fife Ness 1-2.11.1975	1 East Shore (St Andrews) 14.5 1977
1 Fife Ness 1.10.1973	1 Tentsmuir 4.4.1976
	1 Ardross, Elie 24.4.1973

In addition Ballantyne (1982) recorded 'a small party' at Wemyss estate in January 1973. The Lapland Bunting was not mentioned by Harvie-Brown, and neither Grierson nor Boase had any records of it for North Fife; whereas Baxter and Rintoul said it had occurred at the Isle of May, but had no records for mainland Fife. As far as can be traced, there were no records submitted in the 1950s or 1960s.

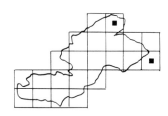

Snow Bunting   *Plectrophenax nivalis*

Winter visitor in varying numbers

The earliest date of arrival in the last twenty-five years is 9 September
1969, when 2 Snow Buntings were at Fife Ness for nearly a week, but
arrival is often not till October (eg. a vast flock of 600 were reported at
Tentsmuir Point in October 1951 (SB2:159)). From then on, flocks of
varying sizes may be seen, especially along the shore in East Fife but
also on the Lomond Hills where 50-100 were reported in November
1985. Following a few years when Snow Buntings were positively
scarce, numbers were somewhat up again in 1984 with flocks of around
50 birds reported from Burntisland, Kirkcaldy, Largo Bay and Coble
Shore (Eden), all between 20 and 28 January. Other places where the
Snow Bunting has been seen in recent years are Methil docks (65 on 12
January 1982), Stenhouse, Crail, Fife Ness, Kingsbarns, West Sands (St
Andrews), Kinshaldy and Tentsmuir. In 1977, on 28 November, 300
were found at Crail, an area where in the '60s and '70s many such huge
flocks were recorded, and during these years other flocks of over 100
were seen at Pittenweem, Largoward and Longannet.

Birds are usually away by the end of March, but a few may still be
around in April, such as one at Methil docks on 11 April 1982. One was
inland on West Lomond on 19 April 1983, and in 1985 one flew over
East Lomond on 12 May.

The Snow Bunting was mentioned in the *New Statistical Account* of
Inverkeithing and Kinglassie (1836). It was apparently never common
in North Fife apart from at Tentsmuir, where W. Berry said large flocks
used to feed on the adjacent stubble fields (unpublished notes); and
Grierson found flocks of 45-60 in the early 1950s. For South Fife, Baxter
and Rintoul (1953) observed that it was extraordinarily faithful to old
winter quarters, and they knew the exact spot on the shore at St
Andrews where flocks had been for the last forty years at least (B of
S:91). Elsewhere, they talked of 'Snow Bunting years', when huge

immigrations took place, such as in December 1874. In October-November 1911 they saw a very large flock at St Monance, and another at Balcomie Farm, where 'the newly acquired bit of the Golf Course was covered with them; there must have been thousands' (VFF:94).

Such flocks are never seen now, and records suggest that the Snow Bunting, in spite of some recent recovery, has become much scarcer in the second half of this century.

Yellowhammer *Emberiza citrinella*

Common resident

The Yellowhammer, or 'Yellow Bunting' as it used to be called, is common in most parts of the area throughout the year. It nests in hedges, gorse bushes and young trees, often by the roadside, and after the breeding season and in winter it flocks on stubble fields and other arable land when more than 100 together are not uncommon: eg. 130 were seen at Ladybank on 8 January 1984, and 120 at Clayton (between St Andrews and Cupar) on 18 January 1983. All the older reports found it common, and there seems to have been no change in status this century.

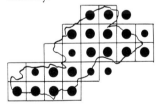
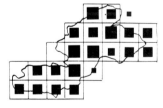

Ortolan Bunting *Emberiza hortulana*

Very rare migrant

Only two records of this Mediterranean species, both of immatures at Fife Ness: one on 14 October 1966, and another on 19 May 1985.

Little Bunting   *Emberiza pusilla*

Rare passage migrant

The most recent records of this rare Eastern bunting are single birds at
Fife Ness on 19 September and 14 October 1984. The previous records
were much further back: one was seen near Boarhills on 17 November
1947, and there was one on the railway bank near Lower Largo on 12
April 1934 'after a prolonged period of easterly gales' (B of S:84 and
VFF:92).

Yellow-breasted Bunting   *Emberiza aureola*

Very rare migrant

Only one record of this Eastern species, which was a single at Fife Ness
on 29 August 1979.

Reed Bunting   *Emberiza schoeniclus*

Common resident and passage migrant

This bunting breeds commonly throughout the area where there is a
suitable habitat of reed-beds and reedy vegetation alongside standing
or slow-running water. In autumn and winter it may roost in numbers
in similar sorts of habitat: 500 at Guardbridge in October 1970 was
exceptional, but many of these may have been migrants; 25 at Tayport
on 23 January 1984, and similar kinds of numbers at Drumrack on 30
January 1983, are more like the usual numbers seen then. Baxter and
Rintoul (1935) considered it to some extent only a summer visitor to
South Fife, leaving the area when cold weather set in, although some
stayed, chiefly in the coastal districts, which is still the case. In autumn
and spring a certain amount of migration takes place, when there are
several records from Fife Ness, eg. of 30 Reed Buntings there on 29
September 1972, and 15 on 25 October 1981; while there were 15 also at
Fife Ness on 6 May 1983.

The 'Reed Sparrow', which no doubt refers to this species, was mentioned in the *New Statistical Account* of Inverkeithing (1836). There is no apparent change in status this century.

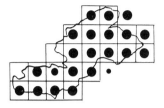 

Black-headed Bunting   *Emberiza melanocephala*

Very rare vagrant

There is only one—very old—record of this species, of a male, in winter plumage, caught near Dunfermline on 5 November 1886 (VFF:91). This bunting is normally found in South-west Europe and Asia.

Corn Bunting   *Miliaria calandra*

Locally common resident

The Corn Bunting breeds in grassland by stone walls and bushy edges, or on rough pasture, especially near the coast. It is a common bird in the East Neuk, where the local BTO breeding survey in 1985 showed the stretch from Fife Ness to St Monance in May to hold at least 12 singing males, with more pairs inland; but also that the Corn Bunting is less common in North Fife, while only a few pairs were reported in the central area, and none west of Lochore. The Corn Bunting has got much scarcer in recent years. Baxter and Rintoul (1935) said that it bred along the south coast of Fife in small numbers, especially in the east, although they had also seen it about Cullaloe (VFF:90). There were none here in 1985. In North Fife, Boase mentioned that 12 pairs had nested at Freuchie, increasing to 18 in 1948 (again none were reported in 1985). It had, however, apparently already then (1964) started to decline, for Boase went on to name about ten localities in the north where it had of late stopped breeding (BNF:123).

In winter, Corn Buntings flock near the coast: 75 at Fife Ness on 10 January 1982 is the largest party in recent years, whereas as many as 200 roosted at Kilconquhar in 1969 and 1972. Baxter and Rintoul thought the Corn Bunting was also a winter visitor to South Fife, while Boase found much of North Fife deserted in autumn and winter, so a fair amount of local movement probably takes place.

The decline in numbers since the middle of the century seems sadly to continue, though less so in the east of Fife.

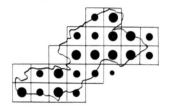
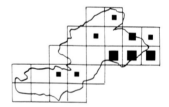

Bibliography

In the text, where no other reference has been given, the records referred to have been published in *Scottish Birds*, or since 1980 in the *Fife and Kinross Bird Report*. References are given in brackets in abbreviated form (see below).

Annals of Scottish Natural History, 1892-1911.

Atkinson-Willis, *Wildfowl in Great Britain*, London, 1963 (WGB).

Ballantyne, G. H., *The Wildlife and Antiquities of Kirkcaldy District*, Kirkcaldy, 1982.

Baxter, Evelyn V. and Rintoul, Leonora Jeffrey, *Geograhical Distribution and Status of Birds in Scotland*, Edinburgh, 1928; *A Vertebrate Fauna of Forth*, Edinburgh, 1935 (VFF); *The Birds of Scotland*, vols 1-2, Edinburgh, 1953 (B of S).

Berry, John, *The Status and Distribution of Wild Geese and Wild Duck in Scotland*, Cambridge, 1939 (WG+WDS).

Berry, W. (Unpublished notes on the History of Birds at Tayfield, Tentsmuir and Neighbourhood, 1872-47).

Boase, Henry, *Birds of North Fife*, unpublished typescript, 1964 (BNF). Accessible in the Waterston Library, Scottish Ornithologists' Club, 21 Regent Terrace, Edinburgh EH7 5BT.

British Birds, 1907- (BB).

Bruce, George, *The Land Birds in and around St Andrews*, Dundee, 1895 (LStA).

Cramp, Stanley (ed.), *The Birds of the Western Palearctic*, vols 1-4. Royal Society for the Protection of Birds and Oxford University Press, 1977-1985 (BWP).

Dalgleish, John J., 'List of the Birds of Culross and Tulliallan', in Beveridge, D., *Culross and Tulliallan*, Edinburgh, 1885. Vol. 2, appendix.

Edinburgh Bird Bulletin, 1950-1958 (EBB).

Excerpta E Libris Domicilii Domini Jaboci Quinti Regis Scotorum 1525-1533, (King James V's Household Books), Edinburgh, 1834 (ExDJV).

Estuary Enquiry: *Winter Shore Bird Counts* (1984-85), Section No. 22: St Andrews to Kincraig Head, organiser M. Moser; British Trust for Ornithology. Interim report only; all data on Birds of the Estuaries

Enquiry are held by the BTO, Beech Grove, Tring, Hertfordshire HP23 5NR.

Ferguson-Lees, James, Willis, Ian and Sharrock, J. T. R., *The Shell Guide to the Birds of Britain and Ireland,* London, 1983.

Fife and Kinross Bird Report, 1980- (F&K). Available from Chris Smout, Chesterhill, Shore Road, Anstruther, Fife.

Fife Ranger Service, *Bird Reports* (FRS): on Lochore Meadows (1981-)—available from Lochore Meadows Country Park, Crosshill, Lochgelly, Fife KY5 8BA; and on the Lomond Hills (1983-)—available from the Pitcairn Centre, Coul, Collydean, Glenrothes, Fife KY7 6NX.

Grant, P. J., *Gulls: a guide to identification* T. & D. A. Poyser, 1982.

Gray, Robert, *The Birds of the West of Scotland,* Glasgow, 1871.

Harvie-Brown, J. A., *A Fauna of the Tay Basin and Strathmore,* Edinburgh 1906 (FT).

Innes, J. L. *Morton Lochs and Tentsmuir Point Reserves (Fife), Bird Reports 1976.* Nature Conservancy Council South East (Scotland) Region. Copy available for consultation at the Nature Conservancy Council's local office, Rathcluan House, Cupar, Fife.

Kirke, D. J. Balfour, 'The Ornithology of Burntisland', in *Folkarde's Guide to Burntisland,* Burntisland, 1911.

Millais, J. G., *The Wildfowler in Scotland,* London, 1901; *British Surface Feeding Ducks,* 1902, *British Diving Ducks,* 1913.

Moser, M., *An Assessment of the Importance of the Eden Estuary and the First of Tay for non-breeding Population of Waders,* British Trust for Ornithology Report to the Nature Conservancy Council, July 1983 (BTO:Eden). Copy available for consultation at the NCC Office, Rathcluan House, Cupar, Fife.

New Statistical Account 1834-1845.

Pemberton, John E. (Ed.), *The Birdwatcher's Yearbook and Diary,* 1986, Buckingham Press.

Report on Bird Migration, 1970-1975, British Trust for Ornithology (RBM).

Ringing and Migration, 1975- , British Trust for Ornithology (R+M).

Scottish Birds, 1958- Scottish Ornithologists' Club (SB).

Scottish Naturalist, 1871-1964 (incorporating the *Annals of Scottish Natural History*). (Scot. Nat.)

Sharrock, J. T. R. (Ed.), *The Atlas of Breeding Birds in Britain and Ireland,* British Trust for Ornithology, 1976 (ABB); *Frontiers of Bird Identification,* Macmillan Journals Ltd, 1980.

Sinclair, Sir John, *The Statistical Account of Scotland: Fife,* 1791-1799; new edition edited by Withrington and Grant, EP Publishing, 1978.

Tay Ringing Group Report, 1980- (TRG). Also available from the Scottish Ornithologists' Club Bookshop, 21 Regent Terrace, Edinburgh EH7 5BT.

Valentine, Easton S., *Fifeshire,* Cambridge, 1910.

Wildfowl and Wader Counts, 1979- (WWC). Available from the Wildfowl Trust, Slimbridge, Gloucester GL2 7BT.

Wildfowl Trust Counts (WT counts). All the data (1960-) are accessible at the Waterston Library, Scottish Ornithologists' Club, 21 Regent Terrace, Edinburgh EH7 5BT.

Gazetteer

Abdie (parish of), NO 2617
Aberdour, NT 1985
*Abertay Sands, NO 5228
Airdrie estate, NO 5608
*Anstruther, NO 5603
Ardross, NO 5100
Auchterderran, NO 2195
*Auchtermuchty, NO 2311
Auchtertool, NO 2290
Ayton (parish of), NO 2919

Balcarres estate, NO 4804
Balcaskie estate, NO 5203
Balcomie (golf course), NO 6210
Balhousie, NO 4306
*Ballo Loch, NO 2205
Balmakin, NO 4805
*Balmerino, NO 3625
Barnyard marsh, NO 4802
*Bass Rock, NT 6087
*Benarty, NT 1598
Billow Ness, NO 5602
Birkhill, NO 3323
Black Devon (drains Castlehill reservoir in
    the Ochils), NS 9693
Black Loch, NO 2615
Blairadam forest, NT 8195
*Bluther Burn (Torry Bay), NT 0186
Boarhills, NO 5714
Bogside (Devilla forest), NS 9690
Buckhaven, NT 3598
*Burntisland, NT 2386

Caiplie, NO 5805
Cambo, NO 6011
*Cameron reservoir, NO 4710
Camilla Loch, NT 2291
Carlhurlie reservoir, NO 3905
Carnbee reservoir, NO 5206
Carnock (parish), NT 0489
Carr Rock, NO 6411
*Carriston reservoir, NO 3203
Castle Cliff (*St Andrews), NO 5117

Cellardyke, NO 5704
*Ceres, NO 4011
Chance Inn, NO 3710
Charlestown, NT 0683
*Clatto reservoir, NO 3607
Clayton, NO 4318
*Cleish Hills, NT 0696
Clune, NT 1794
*Cocklemill Burn (Largo Bay), NO 4601
Colinsburgh, NO 4703
Craighall estate, NO 4010
*Craigluscar reservoirs, NT 0690
Craigmead car park, NO 2206
Craigrothie, NO 3710
*Crail, NO 6107
Crombie Point, NT 0384
Crossgates, NT 1488
*Cullaloe, NT 1887
Culross, NS 9885
Cult Ness, NT 1281
*Cupar, NO 3714

Dairsie, NO 4117
*Dalgety, NT 1683
Dean plantation, NT 0587
Denburn wood, NO 6108
Deveron, NO 3405
Devilla forest, NS 9688
Donald Rose reservoir, NO 3303
*Dreel Burn (Anstruther), NO 5403
Drumcarrow, NO 4513
Drummie, NO 3205
Drumrack, NO 5408
Dumbarnie Links, NO 4402
Dunbog, NO 2818
Dunearn Hill (Burntisland), NT 2385
*Dunfermline, NT 0987
Dunino, NO 5310
Dunniker wood, NT 2894
Dunshelt, NO 2510
Dura Den, NO 4114
Dysart, NT 3193

Earlsferry, NT 4899
Earlshall estate, NO 4620
Earlshall (southern part of Tentsmuir),
    NO 4922
East Grange (Dunfermline), NT 0088
East Lomond, NO 2406

East Neuk, NO 50 (what Baxter and Rintoul
 referred to as the East Neuk we would
 now call 'Fife Ness')
East Shore, NO 4921
East Wemyss, NT 3496
Edenmouth, NO 4920
*Elie, NO 4900

*Falkland, NO 2507
Fetterdale, NO 4725
Fiddinch, NO 4813
*Fife Ness, NO 6309
Fife Ness Muir, NO 6508
*Flisk, NO 3122
Forgan, NO 4425
Forth Road Bridge, NO 1280
Freuchie, NO 2806

Gateside, NO 2803
Gauldry, NO 9823
Gillingshill reservoir, NO 5206
Gilston, NO 4407
Glenrothes, NO 2601
Glenvale, NO 1705
*Guardbridge, NO 5518

*Harperleas reservoir, NO 2105
High Valleyfield, NT 0087
Hill of Tarvit, NO 3811
*Holl reservoir, NO 2203

*Inverkeithing, NT 1382
*Isle of May, NT 6599

Keavil, NT 0686
Kellie Castle, NO 5205
Kelly Law, NO 5106
*Kelty, NT 4215
Kemback wood, NO 4215
*Kenly Burn (Boarhills), NO 5613
Kettlebridge, NO 3007
*Kilconquhar Loch, NO 4801
Kilmany, NO 3821
Kilmaron Castle, NO 3516
Kilminning, NO 6308
Kilrenny, NO 5705
Kinaldy, NO 5110
*Kincardine (-on-Forth), NS 9387
*Kincraig, NT 4699
*Kinghorn Loch, NT 2587
Kinglassie, NT 2398
Kingskettle, NO 3008
Kingsmuir, NO 5408
Kinkell Braes, NO 5215
Kinneddar, NT 0392

Kinshaldy (middle part of Tenstmuir),
 NO 5022
*Kirkcaldy, NT 2791
Kippo, NO 5610
Kirkforthar, NO 2904
Kirktonbarns, NO 4426
Kittock Den, NO 5610

*Ladybank, NO 3009
Lahill, NO 4403
*Largo Bay, NO 4002
Largo Law, NO 4205
Largoward, NO 4607
Lathocar, NO 4910
Leslie, NO 2410
*Leuchars, NO 4521
*Leven, NO 3800
Limekilns, NT 0883
*Lindores Loch, NO 2616
*Loch Fitty, NT 1191
*Loch Gelly, NT 1992
*Loch Glow, NT 0895
Lochmalomy, NO 3620
Lochmill Loch, NO 2216
*Lochore Meadows, NT 1695
Lochshaw Moss, NS 9890
Lomond Hills reservoirs, NO 2204
Longannet, NS 9485
Low Valleyfield, NS 9086
Lower Largo, NO 4102
Lucklaw, NO 4122
Lumphinnans, NT 1792
Lundin Links, NO 4121
Luthrie, NO 3319

MacDuff's Castle, NT 3497
Magus Muir, NO 4515
Markinch, NO 2901
*May Island, NT 6599
Melville, NO 2912
*Methil, NO 3699
Milldean's wood, NO 3205
Milnathort, NO 1204
Monimail, NO 2914
Montrave, NO 3706
Moonzie Burn (Guardbridge), NO 4319
*Moorloch, NS 9488
Morton, NO 4626
*Morton Lochs, NO 4626
Mossgreen (Gateside), NT 1488
Mossmorran, NT 3497
Mount (Melville?) Hill, NO 3316
*Mugdrum Island, NO 2219
Myres Castle, NO 2411

Index of Bird Names